The Marketisation of Higher Education and the Student as Consumer

Until recently government policy in the UK has encouraged an expansion of higher education to increase participation and with an express aim of creating a more educated workforce. This expansion has led to competition between higher education institutions, with students increasingly positioned as consumers and institutions working to improve the extent to which they meet 'consumer demands'.

Especially given recent government funding cuts, the most prevalent outlook in higher education today is one of business, forcing institutions to reassess the way they are managed and promoted to ensure maximum efficiency, sales and 'profits'. Students view the opportunity to gain a degree as a right, and a service which they have paid for, demanding a greater choice and a return on their investment. Changes in higher education have been rapid, and there has been little critical research into the implications. This volume brings together internationally comparative academic perspectives, critical accounts and empirical research to explore fully the issues and experiences of education as a commodity, examining:

- the international and financial context of marketisation
- the new purposes of universities
- the implications of university branding and promotion
- league tables and student surveys vs. quality of education
- the higher education market and distance learning
- students as 'active consumers' in the co-creation of value
- changing student experiences, demands and focus.

With contributions from many of the leading names involved in higher education including Ronald Barnett, Frank Furedi, Lewis Elton, Roger Brown and also Laurie Taylor in his journalistic guise as an academic at the University of Poppleton, this book will be essential reading for many. *The Marketisation of Higher Education and the Student as Consumer* offers a groundbreaking insight into the effects of government policy on the structure and operation of universities.

Mike Molesworth is Senior Lecturer in Online Marketing and Consumer Behaviour at the Media School, Bournemouth University, UK.

Richard Scullion is Senior Lecturer in Marketing Communications and Political Communications at the Media School, Bournemouth University, UK.

Elizabeth Nixon is Lecturer in Marketing Communications at the Media School, Bournemouth University, UK.

The Marketisation of Higher Education and the Student as Consumer

Edited by Mike Molesworth,
Richard Scullion and
Elizabeth Nixon

Routledge
Taylor & Francis Group

LONDON AND NEW YORK

First edition published 2011
by Routledge
2 Park Square, Milton Park, Abingdon, Oxon, OX14 4RN

Simultaneously published in the USA and Canada
by Routledge
270 Madison Avenue, New York, NY 10016

Routledge is an imprint of the Taylor & Francis Group, an informa business

© 2011 Mike Molesworth, Richard Scullion and Elizabeth Nixon
for selection and editorial material and in the name of the
contributors for individual chapters.

Typeset in Galliard by
Florence Production Ltd. Stoodleigh, Devon
Printed and bound in Great Britain by
TJ International Ltd, Padstow, Cornwall

British Library Cataloguing in Publication Data
A catalogue record for this book is available
from the British Library

Library of Congress Cataloging-in-Publication Data
  The marketisation of higher education : the student as consumer / edited
  by Mike Molesworth, Elizabeth Nixon and Richard Scullion.
       p. cm.
    Includes bibliographical references.
  1. Education, Higher—Great Britain—Marketing.   2. College students as
  consumers—Great Britain.   I. Molesworth, Mike.   II. Nixon, Elizabeth,
  1982–   III. Scullion, Richard.
  LB2342.82.M373 2011
  371.2'42--dc22   2010011637

ISBN13: 978–0–415–58445–6 (hbk)
ISBN13: 978–0–415–58447–0 (pbk)
ISBN13: 978–0–203–84282–9 (ebk)

Contents

Illustrations

Notes on contributors

Ronald Barnett is Emeritus Professor of Higher Education at the Institute of Education, London. His work concerns the conceptual understanding of the university and higher education. His books include *Realizing the University in an Age of Supercomplexity*, and *A Will to Learn: Being a Student in an Age of Uncertainty*. In 2009, he was Special Adviser to the UK's Select Committee Inquiry into Universities and Students and is currently Senior Research Consultant at the University of Surrey. He is a past-Chair of the Society for Research into Higher Education and has been an invited speaker in 30 countries.

Roger Brown is Professor of Higher Education Policy at Liverpool Hope University. He was previously Vice Chancellor of Southampton Solent University and Chief Executive of the Higher Education Quality Council, and before that a senior civil servant. He was elected as Vice President of the Society for Research in Higher Education in 2007. His third book *Higher Education and the Market* is due to be published by Routledge in summer 2010.

Chris Chapleo is Senior Lecturer in Marketing at the University of Portsmouth. His research interests are in marketing and branding in the non-profit sector, particularly education. He has published and spoken widely on aspects of higher education branding, and is involved in ongoing consultancy projects in the sector. Prior to academia he held senior marketing roles in the publishing and leisure sectors, as well as higher education, where his interest in the topic first began.

Lewis Elton started academic life as a mathematical physicist in 1947, before becoming Head of Physics at Battersea College of Technology – now Surrey University – in 1957. He left physics and the headship in 1972, and since then has developed a research-oriented approach to university teaching and learning, supported more recently by the concept of the Scholarship of Teaching and Learning, which stresses the primacy of learning.

Nick Foskett is Vice Chancellor of the University of Keele. His academic background is as Professor of Education (at the University of Southampton), with a research and teaching specialism in policy and leadership in higher education and further education. His particular interest has been in the impact and operation of educational markets, where he has published extensively and provided consultancy to institutions and government both in the UK and internationally.

Frank Furedi has been exploring the different manifestations of the way that contemporary Western culture attempts to give meaning to social experience since 1995 when he published a study on the international contraceptive pill panic of 1995. The varied response to this panic in different societies led him to ask questions about why some cultures have a more developed consciousness of risk than others. In recent years Frank has devoted himself to researching and developing a sociology of fear and the construction of contemporary risk consciousness.

Paul Gibbs is Professor of Education in the Institute of Work Based Learning at Middlesex University and Academic Director of the Cyprus Office. His main research interests concern the nature of being as shown through work, marketing and learning.

Andy Hagyard joined the University of Lincoln in 1995 as a specialist in modern languages. His main role now is Learning and Teaching Co-ordinator in the Centre for Educational Research and Development. As part of this role he has supported moves to strengthen links between teaching and research, with a particular interest in the learning development needs of students engaging in research.

Helen Haywood is Senior Lecturer in Marketing. Her expertise is in international marketing management and much of her research to date has been investigating the choice-making process amongst international students studying in the UK. Helen is currently studying for her Doctorate in Education at Southampton University.

Rebecca Jenkins is Postgraduate Researcher, three years into her PhD on the consumer imagination. In particular, she is interested in how people think and feel about goods and experience, specifically in relation to significant life events (such as moving house, having a baby, retiring, graduating and so on).

Stella Jones-Devitt is Employer Partnerships Quality Manager at Teesside University. This chapter was written when Stella was joint co-ordinator of a cross-disciplinary Critical Thinking Research Cluster Group at York St John University considering how academic engagement in critical thinking can assist effective learning organisation development.

Felix Maringe is Senior Lecturer in Education at the University of Southampton with a specific research interest in the area of education markets, higher education marketing, choice and decision making in HE, and the internationalisation of HE.

Colin McCaig is a Senior Research Fellow at the Centre for Education and Inclusion Research, Sheffield Hallam University. He completed a doctorate in educational policymaking in the Labour Party, 1994–1999, at the University of Sheffield. His research interests include access and admissions issues and institutional policymaking, directing the Review of the Impact of the Schwartz Report Fair Admissions to higher education in 2008. He has published on Labour education policy, the impact of widening participation and student finance issues both in the UK and Europe.

Mike Molesworth is a Senior Lecturer in consumer behaviour and interactive media at Bournemouth University. His research interests are in emerging consumer cultures including online consumer behaviour, digital virtual consumption and the consumer imagination, and the consumer-like experiences of higher education students.

Liz Morrish is Principal Lecturer in Linguistics at Nottingham Trent University. She has previously studied experimental phonetics and disordered speech, and has a PhD from Leeds University. Her current research and teaching interests are language and sexual identity, and language and gender. She is the author (with Helen Sauntson) of *New Perspectives on Language and Sexual Identity*. Liz is on the organising committee of the Lavender Languages and Linguistics conferences held annually in Washington DC and the Queering Paradigms II conference to be held in Brisbane, Australia in 2010.

Mike Neary is the Dean of Teaching and Learning at the University of Lincoln and the Director of the Lincoln's Centre for Educational Research and Development. Before taking up this post in 2007, Mike was a Reader in the sociology department at the University of Warwick where he taught political sociology. During this time, Mike was the Director of the Reinvention Centre for Undergraduate Research, a collaborative CETL between Sociology at Warwick and the School for the Built Environment at Oxford Brookes University. He is co-editor of *The Future of Higher Education: Policy, Pedagogy and the Student Experience* and has recently completed a research project, Learning Landscapes in Higher Education, funded by HEFCE, SFC and the HEFCW.

Katherine Nielsen is an Associate Tutor of Anthropology at the University of Sussex. Her doctoral research is supervised within the Centre for Higher Education and Equity Research (CHEER) and examines the learning outcomes of international students in Ireland, student-driven learning, the creation of independent education opportunities outside of the formal university setting, personal and geographic exploration through international mobility, and the impact of such experiences on the construction of identity and self-confidence.

Elizabeth Nixon is Lecturer in the Media School at Bournemouth University, where she teaches social and marketing research methods and consumer behaviour. Previously, she worked as a researcher in Bournemouth University's CETL, before becoming embroiled in the study of consumer culture. Her PhD studies explore the everyday practices of people who seek to resist or live alternatives to consumerist notions that the essence of the 'good life' can be found within the market.

Johan Nordensvärd is Fellow in Social Policy and Development. His research interests are global citizenship, corporate citizenship and human rights. He specialises in education and how education policies are used in discourses around development, economic growth and social exclusion. From a theoretical perspective, he has an interest in narrative theory and how these construct and constrain agency within public policy. His PhD was an empirical study of the relationship between public and ontological narratives of citizenship among young people in northern Germany.

Catherine Samiei is Lecturer in Academic Development at York St John University. This chapter was written when Catherine was a joint co-ordinator of a cross-disciplinary Critical Thinking Research Cluster Group at York St John University considering how academic engagement in critical thinking can assist effective learning organisation development.

Helen Sauntson is Lecturer in English Language and Linguistics at the University of Birmingham, UK. She holds a PhD from the University of Birmingham. Her main research areas are classroom discourse analysis and language, gender and sexuality. She is the author (with Liz Morrish) of *New Perspectives on Language and Sexual Identity*. She is the editor (with Sakis Kyratzis) of *Language, Sexualities and Desires: Cross-Cultural Perspectives* and *Gender and Language Research Methodologies* (co-edited with Kate Harrington, Lia Litosseliti and Jane Sunderland).

Richard Scullion is Senior Lecturer in marketing communications and political communications. His research focuses on political advertising, civic culture and consumer choice. He is Secretary of the Political Marketing special interest group of the Academy of Marketing. He has also written about pedagogic issues – specifically on the implications of growing marketisation of the higher education sector in the UK. He holds a PhD from the London School of Economics.

Laurie Taylor is Visiting Professor in the Department of Politics and Sociology at Birkbeck College, University of London and a Fellow of Birkbeck College. He also holds visiting professorships at the London Institute and Westminster University and has been awarded honorary doctorates by the Universities of Leicester, Nottingham and Central England. His contributions to social science were recognised in 2003 by his election to the Academy of Learned Societies for the Social Sciences. His contribution to business development was recognised last year by his appointment as an ambassador for Investors in People.

Joanna Williams is Lecturer in Higher Education and Academic Practice at the University of Kent. Prior to this, she taught in the further education sector and in secondary schools. Joanna has recently undertaken research into the impact of the politics of social inclusion upon post-compulsory education and her latest publications are on this topic.

Acknowledgements

The editors would like to acknowledge the work of contributors who helped to review and comment on individual chapters and the overall structure of the book. In particular we would like to thank Professor Roger Brown for his helpful comments on the conclusion and for his ongoing support. We would also like to thank those academics who have shown an interest in this project, but whose chapters we did not have room to include. Clearly there is plenty to be written about the marketisation of higher education and students as consumers beyond the content of this edited collection. We would also like to thank The Centre For Excellence in Media Practice CETL at Bournemouth University who funded the research in Chapters 15 and 16.

Chapter 1

Introduction to the marketisation of higher education and the student as consumer

Frank Furedi

Since the late 1970s the culture of academic life has been transformed by the institutionalisation of the policies of marketisation. At least outwardly universities increasingly ape the managerial models of private and especially public sector corporations. Quaint academic rituals and practices have been gradually displaced by management techniques as departments mutate into cost centres often run by administrators recruited from the private and public sector. Whatever one thinks about the costs and benefits of these changes, marketisation is a reality that academics have to live with. This collection of articles addresses this reality and offers a variety of perspectives on the not-so-quiet managerial revolution in the university.

Advocates of marketisation argue that this process will turn higher education into a more flexible and efficient institution. They claim that the expansion of the market into the lecture hall will provide better value for money and ensure that the university sector will become more efficient and more responsive to the needs of society, the economy, students and parents. The policy-driven term 'marketisation' is fundamentally an ideological one and as this collection of articles indicates, its meaning is far from self-evident. As the chapters by Roger Brown and Nick Foskett suggest, marketisation does not necessarily mean or lead to the creation of a market in the sale and purchase of academic education. Indeed it is not always clear what is being bought and sold. So is the student purchasing instruction in an academic discipline or buying a credential necessary for the pursuit of a profession? Or is he or she doing both? It appears that what we have is a highly controlled quasi-market that forces institutions to compete against one another for resources and funding.

In one sense there is very little that is unique about the embrace of competition by higher education. Academia has always been a highly competitive enterprise and since medieval times universities often possessed a profound sense of institutional self-interest and regarded one another with a degree of suspicion. Universities have always competed for resources, and in modern times for research funding. These forms of rivalries have existed in an uneasy relationship with the imperative of academic collaboration. Academics are members of an intellectual community who need to collaborate with another. Yet they are also individuals who are concerned with cultivating their own reputation and are sometimes fiercely aggressive towards each other. However, this form of competition has little to do with the late-twentieth-century market-driven ideology that prevails in higher education. What is new and potentially disturbing about the market-isation of education is the attempt to recast the relationship between academics and students along the model of a service provider and customer.

It is important to understand that marketisation is as much a political/ ideological process as an economic phenomenon. So for example, through the medium of marketisation governments often promote clearly defined political policies. As the chapter by Colin McCaig suggests, marketing has become a vehicle for the promotion of widening participation. It is difficult to avoid the conclusion that marketisation is as much about social engineering as economic concerns. In practice, a quasi-market in higher education propped up by state subsidies and micro-managed through government intervention co-exists with genuine market-driven activities. There are of course dimensions of university life that are relatively open to the imperative of the market. The influence of the market mechanism is fairly apparent in the international student bazaar. In this domain there is fierce competition between universities, who with the help of their governments seek to position themselves as global players in a lucrative sphere of economic activity. Universities, particularly those who possess an international reputation for research, also sell patents, provide consultancy and services and launch private companies. Higher education has also become involved with the provision of leisure and conference services and operates in this sphere according to the norms that prevail amongst private sector service providers.

In principle there need not be any objections to universities competing for funds and selling the fruits of their research. It is not this relatively distinct and contained form of economic activity that has led to academic disquiet about the marketisation of education. Often it is the cultural, intellectual and pedagogic consequences of marketisation that represent a cause for concern. From a cultural perspective the project of marketisation represents the attempt to commodify academic education. Specifically it is oriented towards the transformation of what is an abstract, intangible, non-material and relational experience into a visible, quantifiable and instrumentally driven process. The various rituals of commodifica-tion, such as quality control, auditing and ranking performance, quantifying the experience of students and constructing league tables, are essentially performative accomplishments. Attempts to endow these rituals with symbolic significance are promoted through the act of branding, mission statements or student surveys. The chapters by Liz Morrish and Helen Sauntson, Chris Chapleo and Stella Jones-Devitt and Catherine Samiei offer compelling evidence of these rituals of commodification.

The tendency to commodify higher education does not represent a triumph of free-market economics. Indeed it can be argued that the marketisation of education has been paralleled not by a decrease but an increase in state intervention and the micro-management of university life. The very attempt to regulate economically the provision of academic education is itself a highly politicised activity. Governments are desperately mobilising students and their parents to place universities under market pressure. As the article by Joanna Williams shows, newspapers in England are literally inciting students and their parents to complain and force universities on the defensive. The promotion of student consumer consciousness is not simply motivated by the idealisation of the customer-service-provider model. As customer, the student is expected to serve as the personification of market pressures on an otherwise archaic and unresponsive university. Since according to the logic of marketisation, the customer is always right, the university had better listen to the student. Appeals to the identity of student-as-customer are underpinned by an agenda that seeks to discipline academic life through consumer pressure on higher education. From this perspective the complaining pushy-parent is likely to emerge as the hero in the drama of marketisation.

The culture of complaint has encouraged the emergence of a form of 'defensive education' that is devoted to minimising sources of disputes that have the potential to lead to complaint and litigation. Defensive university education encourages a climate where academics are discouraged from exercising their professional judgment when offering feedback or responding to disputed marks. Courses, especially ones that do not rate highly in student surveys, are modified and made customer friendly. Academics have become more defensive and circumspect about expressing their views with clarity. They write formulaic letters of reference and refrain from stating opinions that could provoke complaints from their customers. One of the most obvious strategies for avoiding complaints is to flatter students. Feedback is often used as a vehicle for validating the efforts of a student instead of pointing out weaknesses in presentation and argument.

Sadly many universities have embraced the student-as-customer model. For example the 1994 Group of UK-based universities has adopted the idea that the customer is always right and that flattering them is the way forward. In its statement 'Enhancing the Student Experience', the 1994 Group notes that students 'play an important role as "change agents", challenging the established modes of learning, and contributing to making it more exciting and relevant' (2007: 16). The conceptualisation of students as change agents may represent a form of unwitting manipulation of students to act in accordance with the logic of marketisation. However, it is likely that sections of the leadership of higher education have come to internalise the ideology of marketisation to the point where they find it difficult to distinguish between an academic relationship and a commercial transaction. Consequently there is a growing tendency to represent students acting in their role as customers as providing a positive contribution to academic pedagogy.

'Students know how they want to be taught and have ideas about how techniques can be improved' is the conclusion drawn by the 1994 Group (2007: 6). Aside from a disturbing tendency to equate academic teaching with a technique, the assimilation of the idea that the customer 'knows how they want to be taught' reduces academics to a service provider. As always the commercialisation of education encourages institutions to provide what customers want rather than what they need to become truly educated. This is a problem that philosophers have wrestled with since the beginning of human civilisation.

Socrates revisited

Criticism of the practice of treating students as customers was forcefully pursued by Socrates and Plato in ancient Greece. The principal reason why Socrates was critical of Sophist philosopher teachers was because they charged money for their services. Socrates took the view that payment for teaching compromised the relationship between teacher and student. According to Xenophon, Socrates compared those who peddle their wisdom to those who sell their caresses. Today, such an anti-mercenary stand is likely to strike one as unnecessarily purist and unrealistic. However as J. S. Mill wrote back in 1866, even in an age where the language of cash dominates everyday life there is a lot of sense in Socrates' concern with the commercialisation of education and relating to students as customers. Mill echoed Socrates' concern and noted that paid teachers 'attain their purposes' not 'by making people wiser or better, but by conforming to their opinions, pandering to their existing desires, and making them better pleased with themselves and with their errors and vices than they were before' (Mill 1978: 401).

Mill was writing almost a century and half before the celebration of 'student satisfaction' and the 'student experience' was integrated into the culture of higher education. But it is unlikely that he could have imagined just how uninhibited the universities' 'pandering' of 'existing desires' has become. The current worship of student satisfaction has fostered a climate in which institutions are obsessed with pleasing students and avoiding complaints and fear that disputes with fee-paying customers could lead to litigation. In some cases institutions have adopted practices that border on bribery to get their undergraduates to give the right answers to student satisfaction surveys. There is considerable pressure on academics to put on their customer services hat and do their best not to put students off. Neither Socrates not Mill would have been surprised by the current massaging of examination conventions that aim to avoid customers becoming disappointed by poor results.

From a Socratic perspective the very term 'student satisfaction' is an irrational one. Why? Because students need to be placed under intellectual pressure, challenged to experience the intensity of problem solving. Such an engagement does not always promote customer satisfaction. Not a few individuals at the receiving end of a Socratic dialogue felt provoked and angry. Today, this old philosopher would not rank very high in a student satisfaction survey. So the question worth asking is 'ought the satisfaction of the student customer be one of the central objectives of the university?' From the perspective of the development of a stimulating and creative academic life, the answer must be a resounding NO! The moment that students begin to regard themselves as customers of academic education, their intellectual development is likely to be compromised. Degrees can be bought; an understanding of a discipline cannot.

Mill took the view that the commercialisation of education threatens the integrity and independence of teachers and academics. In particular he feared that commercial pressures would drive educationalists to accommodate prevailing prejudice and encourage them to subordinate the educational needs of students to the project of attracting potential customers. At one point in his writing, Mill paused and asks what Plato would make of the situation in nineteenth-century England. He imagines Plato saying 'schoolmasters, and the teachers and governors of universities, must, on every subject on which opinions differ provide the teaching which will be acceptable to those who can give them pupils, not that which is really the best' (Mill 1978: 402). What Plato is really saying is that once teaching becomes subordinate to an agenda that is external to itself it will become distracted from maintaining its integrity. The pressure to accommodate and compromise will prevail. Today such trends express themselves through grade and degree inflation and the adoption of conservative and instrumentalist skills-based pedagogy. As Socrates and Plato anticipated, the commercialisation of education is driving universities to adopt pedagogic techniques that have little intellectual value. Even the Sophists would be disturbed by an academic culture that is so whole-heartedly devoted to the flattering of students.

In comparison to Athens in the fourth century BC and Victorian England we live in a world where the transformation of the student into a customer has become an accomplished fact. Moreover the tendency to recast an academic relationship into a commercial transaction is no longer represented as the unintended consequence of powerful economic forces but as the explicit objective of higher education entrepreneurs and policy makers. Indeed instead of being embarrassed about treating the academy as a credentials bazaar many universities celebrate their new-found role. On open days, after boasting about their department's incredibly high RAE ratings, academics compete with one another to assure potential customers that their courses are less demanding than those of rival establishments. In this consumerist climate, no lecturer wants to gain a reputation for being 'awkward', 'demanding' or a 'hard marker'. Consequently the culture of positive marking and grade inflation has become a fact of campus life.

Many of the ideas of Socrates and Mill may well be outdated. But tragically their fear that students do not get what is 'really the best' when their teachers become peddlers of ideas has proved to be all too true. The idealisation of the role of customer of academic learning conveys the promise of student choice. As Richard Scullion, Mike Molesworth and Elizabeth Nixon indicate in their chapter on this subject the promise of student choice is rarely realised. In the abstract every student can choose to purchase seminar tickets from Trinity College, Cambridge. In reality the exercise of choice is constrained by access to cultural capital and socio-economic realities. Nevertheless the ideology of choice has a powerful influence on shaping students' identities and works to distract them from realising the potential of their intellectual engagement.

Experience shows that the provision of academic teaching does not fit easily into the paradigm of consumption. It becomes something else if it becomes commodified and bought and sold. Commodification inexorably leads to standardisation, calculation and formulaic teaching. It reduces quality into quantity and transforms an academic relationship between teacher and student into a transaction dominated by concerns that have little to do with education. Thankfully academic and research-based knowledge cannot be standardised and pre-packaged consumer goods, which is why the tension between academic life and marketisation is ultimately irreconcilable. Either academics mutate into the trainers of customers or marketisation works as essentially an ideological or public relations accomplishment. Although the marketisation of education has acquired a formidable influence in Anglo-American universities, its future trajectory is far from clear. This collection of articles provides a unique opportunity to reflect and debate a phenomenon that is likely to exercise a powerful influence on the academy.

Although written from different perspectives this collection of articles shares a common interest in demystifying the workings of the marketisation of higher education. Through their analysis it becomes evident that there is little about this process that we should take as self-evident. Concepts like marketisation, the higher education market, student choice, the branding of universities or the meaning of consumption need to be unpacked and carefully analysed. After reading this collection it is likely that academics will have to start rethinking many of their assumptions about the institutions they inhabit.

Roger Brown's and Nick Foskett's chapters on government policy provide excellent overviews of the workings of what is a highly politicised quasi-market in higher education. In different ways the contributions of Ronald Barnett, Paul Gibbs and Lewis Elton are devoted towards an exploration of the potential for a constructive form of accommodation to the marketisation of universities. Barnett is relatively upbeat about this development and takes the view that 'the presence of the market may lead to a student taking a heightened interest in his or her learning'. The chapters by Morrish and Sauntson, Chapleo and Jones-Devitt and Samiei provide important insights into the workings of the new rituals associated with the market in higher education. McCaig's analysis of the marketing of wider participation raises questions about its relation to student choice. Through an analysis of the conceptual distinction between consumer, customer and client, Felix Maringe offers a compelling critique of the consumer metaphor. Katherine Nielsen engages with a problem rarely discussed, the tensions raised by the attempt to sell education as a form of authentic (tourist) experience.

The focus of section 3 is the student. Johan Nordensvärd outlines and advocates a citizenship perspective on the status of students and counterposes it to the consumer model. Mike Neary and Andy Hagyard advocate a more radical approach – what they call the pedagogy of excess – towards the transformation of student life. In an important phenomenological study of the management of student desires, Helen Haywood, Rebecca Jenkins and Mike Molesworth look at the way that higher education fuels consumer fantasy. Williams offers a disturbing analysis of the way in which the media associates education with an instrumentalist ethos. The media self-consciously mobilises students and parents to adopt the role of the complaining consumer focusing their anger at the university. The question of student choice is forcefully addressed by Nixon, Scullion and Molesworth. Their study calls into question the numerous pedagogic claims made on behalf of student choice. They suggest that the pursuit of student choice tends to avoid experimentation and encourages conservative attitudes towards learning. Socrates would have agreed and perhaps it would help if higher education policy makers acquainted themselves with his dialogues.

References

1994 Group (2007) *Enhancing the Student Experience*. Available from http://www. 1994group.ac.uk/documents/public/SEPolicyStatement.pdf (accessed 28 May 2010).

Mill. J. S. (1978) 'Grote's Plato', in J. M. Robson (ed.) *Collected Works of John Stuart Mill*, vol.11. Toronto: University of Toronto Press.

Marketisation of higher education in context

Chapter 2

The march of the market

Roger Brown

It appears that everywhere there is a trend towards 'marketisation' (Williams 1995). Higher education systems are being liberalised, with private 'for profit' providers entering and competing with publicly funded and private 'not for profit' ones. Tuition fees are being introduced or raised so that students and their families are bearing an increasing share of the costs of teaching. Maintenance grants are being supplemented with, or replaced by, loans. Institutional rankings and other aids to consumer choice are proliferating whilst universities and colleges devote increasing resources and energy to marketing and branding. In short, the market is coming to dominate what Burton Clark many years ago called the 'triangle of coordination' (Clark 1983), at the expense of the academy and the state.

This chapter discusses, on the basis of existing scholarship, what is meant by marketisation; distinguishes marketisation from 'privatisation'; describes the principal features of a higher education market; and considers how far a number of developed higher education systems have moved down the market route. For this purpose, the chapter distinguishes between systems that already incorporate some market features, and those still in the process of acquiring them. It should be noted that it does not discuss the implications or make recommendations: the aim is rather to indicate some of the general issues with marketisation as a backdrop for the rest of the book (for such a discussion, see Brown 2010).

The meaning of marketisation

In economic theory, a market is a means of social coordination whereby the supply and demand for a good or service are balanced through the price mechanism. Consumers choose between the alternatives on offer on the basis of perceived suitability for them (price, quality, availability). It is often held that organising economic relations on these lines represents the best use of society's resources. Markets provide both greater 'static efficiency' (the ratio of outputs to inputs at any point in time) and greater 'dynamic efficiency' (sustaining a higher rate of growth over time through product and process innovation and better management of resources) than any alternative. In particular, markets are often contrasted favourably with 'command economies', where both prices and quantities are controlled by the state.

In relation to student education, a 'pure' market would have the following main features:

1   legally autonomous institutions
2   little or no regulation of market entry (hence plenty of market competition including from private and 'for profit' providers)
3   no regulatory limits on the prices charged (fees) or the numbers enrolled
4   the cost of teaching met entirely through fees which would approximate to average costs
5   the cost of fees met from users' (students and their families) own resources: there would be no subsidies from the taxpayer
6   users would decide what, where and how to study on the basis of effective (valid, reliable and accessible) information about the price, quality and availability of relevant subjects, programmes and providers.

The fact that no developed system has all of these characteristics suggests that there may be limitations on the theory of markets as applied to higher education. The main ones include:

1   the fact that higher education confers both collective (public) and individual (private) benefits. Because of the risk of under-supply, the provision of first cycle education (including student living costs) and academic research are subsidised in most systems
2   because of the key role which higher education plays as an accreditor of knowledge, especially the knowledge required for the practice of the professions, market entry and competition are also regulated in most systems
3   because of the difficulties of obtaining and disseminating proper information about quality, there is a case for a mixed system of regulation, with important roles for the state and the academy, as indeed is the case in most systems
4   further problems arise with the amount of product differentiation and the difficulty which institutions face, by virtue of the length of the product life cycle, in moving rapidly in response to market signals.

Marketisation and privatisation

Before looking more closely at the main features of marketisation as it applies to higher education, it may be worth distinguishing marketisation from 'privatisation', the penetration of private capital, ownership and influence into what may previously have been publicly owned and funded entities and activities. Conceptually, the two are distinct, and indeed the term 'quasi-markets' has been coined (Le Grand and Bartlett 1993) to describe the organisation of the supply of services on market lines where very little or no private capital is involved, the public funding of academic research being a case in point. In practice, however, marketisation will usually involve some degree of privatisation. This reflects the fact that marketisation and privatisation have common origins, the underlying beliefs of which were usefully summarised by the late Peter Self:

> The 'free market' and market-led growth are the principal and over-whelmingly the most important sources of wealth; large incentives are necessary to market efficiency; the wealth created by a free market will trickle down from the successful to benefit all members of society; the market is intrinsically more efficient than government; to gain greater 'efficiency', government should be redesigned according to market methods and incentives.
>
> (Self, 1999: 26–28)[1]

Characteristics of higher education markets

How then should we recognise the marketisation of higher education? The following key indicators are suggested:

1   institutional autonomy
2   institutional competition
3   price
4   information.

Institutional autonomy

The issue here is the freedom that institutions have to determine their mission, subjects, programmes, awards, fees (if any), admissions, student numbers, staff numbers, terms and conditions etc. In other words, the freedom to specify the product and to procure and deploy the resources to deliver it.

In the more marketised systems, institutions enjoy a considerable degree of autonomy in most or all of these respects. In others, they may either not be legally autonomous or they may be autonomous but still be subject to all sorts of controls, for example over the introduction of new subjects or programmes. In some Continental European systems staff remain civil servants employed by the education ministry. Restraints also continue over such matters as carrying over unspent moneys from one financial year to the next.

Institutional competition

The issue here is the amount of competition between institutions for students, revenue and status. This in turn points to a number of market requirements:

1   relative ease of market entry, with regulation being used to facilitate competition and provide basic consumer safeguards rather than to constrain competition that could threaten standards

2   genuine possibilities of student choice: students have a real choice of what, where and how to study. This is not only a function of overall system policy. It can also be a matter of geography (in larger countries, students may have greater difficulty in travelling to study) and funding (if there is limited public support for the costs of courses and living costs, many students will be constrained to attend a local institution)
3   institutional funding should be linked to numbers of enrolments, providing institutions with incentives to recruit
4   an absence of externally imposed limits on the numbers or categories of students that individual institutions can enrol.

Together, these requirements create conditions for genuine competition between institutions, which is reinforced by competition on price (see below).

Public and private institutions

Competition can of course include competition from private, including 'for profit', institutions. In principle, there are two distinctions that can be made:

1   between 'public' and 'private' institutions
2   between 'not for profit' and 'for profit' institutions.

Unfortunately, both distinctions turn out to be rather less helpful when closely analysed.

The usual basis for the first distinction is the source of ownership and control. But even where this is clear, there is also the question of funding. In the more marketised systems both public and private institutions receive both public and private funding. This then leads to the broader issue of accountability because funding implies some degree of accountability even if the mechanisms for this are not always clear. Large and prestigious institutions like the Ivy League universities and colleges in the US are effectively public institutions, even if they sometimes behave more like multinational corporations.

The 'for profit'/'not for profit' distinction also turns out to be less helpful than it appears. Certainly in theory there is a clear distinction between an organisation, the first claim on whose trading surplus lies with its owners (the proprietor and/or shareholders), and one that is under no such constraint. But in practice 'not for profit' universities and colleges in marketised systems often behave in ways indistinguishable from 'for profit' ones, cutting out less sustainable programmes or subjects, investing in various non-core operations and engaging in all sorts of revenue-raising activities (Weisbrod 1988). This growing commercialisation is indeed one of the challenges that marketisation and privatisation together offer to the long-term autonomy and health of higher education.

Price

There are several variables here, namely:

1   whether there is a tuition fee
2   whether the fee covers a significant proportion of the costs of provision
3   whether institutions are able to charge what they like and/or whether there are either controls or associated conditions (or both) (in the UK institutions wishing to charge the full permitted fee must offer bursaries and submit a widening participation plan to a special regulator)
4   whether and to what extent the fee is subsidised, for example through the availability of an income contingent loan
5   whether students' living costs are subsidised in any way.

Information

The issue here is whether students have access to information that assists them in their choice of programmes and/or institutions (and whether they use it). This leads on to the more general question of how, in a marketised system, quality can be protected.

According to market theory, quality is protected automatically as consumers use the available information to select the product that is most suitable for them: suppliers that do not provide goods that are suitable go out of business. In higher education the difficulty is that the product is not visible and the opportunities for repeat purchases are limited (Cave *et al.* 1992).

This does not of course stop either commercial publishers or government agencies from producing information to guide students and funders in the form of institutional rankings and 'league tables'. There is a vast literature on this subject, so vast indeed that (at least without going mad) no one can possibly have read everything that has been written (for useful recent summaries, see Dill and Soo 2005; Van Dyke 2005; Yorke and Longden 2005; Usher and Savino 2006; Marginson 2007; Salmi and Saroyan 2007; Centre for Research and Information in Higher Education *et al.* 2008; Fidler and Parsons 2008; Hazelkorn 2008; Kivisto and Holtta 2008; Kehm and Stensaker 2009). From these and other writings it seems clear that the main limitations on rankings and league tables as guides to quality include:

1   lack of transparency especially in how indicators/scores are weighted
2   a focus on input indicators (staff and student qualifications, resourcing) when it is what institutions do with those inputs that matters
3   a tendency to focus on full-time, undergraduate provision and institutions at the expense of specialist, postgraduate, small and predominantly part-time providers
4   the ranking of institutions as if they all had the same student intakes, resources, etc. More generally, the creation of the impression that some

institutions are better than others when in a diverse, mass system there can be no one 'best university' or single view of quality. League tables indeed strengthen the market position of institutions that are already prestigious and well funded, at the expense of those that may be seeking to build reputation by attending to the needs of students and employers

5   league tables also reinforce the tendency to see higher education as a product to be consumed rather than an opportunity to be experienced

6   by encouraging institutions to game play, they reinforce another market tendency, that of using their resources to improve their attractiveness instead of using them to improve quality. Volkwein and Sweitzer (2006: 145) add that since institutions only change slowly, annual surveys should be discouraged.

In short, rankings misrepresent the work of universities and colleges in the interest of selling newspapers (Brown 2006).[2]

A marketised system

This discussion suggests that a fully marketised system of student education would be one where:

1   there is a significant amount of competition between institutions for students, reflecting the requirements listed earlier, including a significant amount of choice for students and other funders about where to put their 'vote'

2   tuition fees exist and represent a significant share of the cost of teaching

3   private support for those costs represents a significant share of institutional funding.

As we have already seen, research funding is more often a quasi-market where the state uses its monopsonistic position to increase the proportion of funds that are the subject of competition between institutions (for a useful recent summary, see Salmi 2009).

Survey of systems

Against this background, it is suggested that developed higher education systems can be broadly divided into two groups:

1   those that already incorporate a significant degree of marketisation ('marketised systems')

2   those where marketisation has still to develop ('marketising systems').

The remainder of this chapter discusses the evolution of markets in the first group and the pressures for marketisation in the second.

Marketised systems

The United States is often seen as the closest there is to a marketised system, given that no major system is fully marketised. US institutions have a high degree of autonomy. There is a considerable amount of competition amongst a diverse range of institutions. This reflects a liberal entry regime and means that, except in remote locations, students have a wide range of choices. There is a substantial and significant private sector consisting of both 'not for profit' and 'for profit' universities and colleges. Institutions compete on tuition which typically represents about half of the cost of teaching: the balance is made up of institutions' own funds together with state appropriations (for public institutions) and donations (for private ones). There are state and institutional subsidies for both tuition and living costs. Institutions spend a considerable amount of effort on marketing and branding, the US being the home of institutional rankings and league tables. There is also strong competition for federal research funds and donations. The proportion of private revenue to institutions is very high as is the level of expenditure per student.

The United Kingdom has moved down the American path. Again, there is considerable competition for both students and research funds amongst a wide range of autonomous institutions. Market entry has been liberalised so that a small number of private providers now have powers to award their own taught degrees (Bachelor's and Master's) and there is one private university. Tuition fees were first introduced in 1998 and now represent nearly 40 per cent of institutions' income for teaching, the rest being from state grants. There are state and institutional subsidies for students. Private fundraising for institutional development is still in its infancy but the proportion of private income has been increasing and in 2005 stood at 33 per cent (the US figure is 65 per cent; the OECD average is 27 per cent – OECD 2008: 253).

Australia is in a broadly similar position to the UK though competition for research funding is more recent. Other countries with a significant degree of marketisation include Canada and New Zealand. Amongst the Continental European systems, the Netherlands has a significant degree of competition for both students and research funds. In 2007, tuition fees represented 6 per cent of university income in the research universities and 18 per cent in the Universities of Applied Science (UAS); the share of third party (non-governmental) revenue reached 28 per cent in the universities and 14 per cent in the UAS (Jongbloed 2010).

Japan (and Korea) stand somewhat apart from this. Japan has a substantial private sector (78 per cent of institutions and 76 per cent of students) (Huang 2010) and a high level of private expenditure on both teaching and student support. Both private and public institutions charge fees: traditionally, the private sector has charged more but some convergence is now taking place. However this marketisation has only been gradual, as a number of recent reforms attest. These include the incorporation of national and public universities (including a Global Centres of Excellence Programme launched in 2007), the incorporation of national and public universities, the ending of civil servant status for staff in the national and public sectors, the introduction of company or corporation universities, and evaluation of teaching quality. There have also been reforms to university governance to strengthen governing bodies and weaken faculty meetings. There are some parallels here with the situation in Continental Europe which we shall look at shortly.

Before doing so, it may be worth emphasising that even in the marketised systems state funding and regulation play a crucial role in determining the scale, character and direction of the provision. Even in the US, public sources represent a third of expenditure on institutions (this is an average figure so many institutions rely much more heavily on the state). The state's role in research funding is even greater. The state determines and implements the criteria for market entry and underpins the academic regulatory framework by virtue of the fact that only students attending institutions accredited by one of the regional accrediting commissions can receive federal financial support.

Marketising systems

Before considering a number of systems that are introducing some degree of marketisation, it may be worth reflecting on the causes. As with the more marketised systems, these are a mixture of ideology and pragmatics.

Gareth Williams's 1995 summary of the beliefs that underlie the introduction of market approaches has not yet been bettered:

> that efficiency is increased when governments buy academic services from producers, or subsidise students to buy them, rather than supplying them directly, or indirectly through subsidy of institutions;
>   that as enrolments rise, the private sector must relieve governments of some of the cost burden if acceptable quality is to be obtained;
>   that many of the benefits of higher education accrue to private individuals, so criteria of both efficiency and equity are served as students or their families make some contribution towards the costs of obtaining the benefits
> (Williams 1995: 179; cf. Goedegebuure et al. 1994: 323–4)

Ideologically, there is a strong belief on the part of many governments and policy makers that market competition makes institutions more efficient and responsive to stakeholders. Pragmatically, marketisation (and privatisation) may be the only way, given the difficulties of cutting costs, of sustaining an expanded higher education if quality is to be protected.[3] The issue is the balance between market and 'non-market' (Wolf 1993) coordination and how society can gain the benefits of competition without the detriments.[4]

A further, more recent factor has been the desire on the part of the European Union to 'modernise' European higher education systems to enable them to make the maximum contribution to the development of their societies (and compete with the most prestigious systems worldwide), a process encapsulated in the Lisbon Declaration but also one of the drivers behind the Bologna Process.[5] As a result, most of the Continental European countries are introducing some elements of marketisation into their higher education systems.

Germany is a good example. Over the past decade, German universities have gradually gained more autonomy in financial, organisational and staffing matters. They are able to select their students and some Länder (in Germany, higher education is basically a Land responsibility) have introduced tuition fees. Another important development is the Excellence Initiative. This promotes outstanding science and research in Germany in order to raise its visibility in the international scientific community. Organised by the German Research Council and the German Council of Science and Humanities, through a peer review process with international experts, the Excellence Competition in 2006/7 selected excellent projects in three areas: 39 Graduate Schools, 37 Clusters of Excellence and nine Institutional Strategies. The Federal Government and the Länder will provide 1.9bn Euros from 2007–2011 and a further 2.7bn Euros thereafter (Hartwig 2010).

In some other European countries the move towards the market has been more limited. The Nordic countries are distinguished by their strong public (and limited private) support for higher education, both institutions and students. Finland is a good case study (Holtta *et al.* 2010). The right of institutions to charge fees has recently been accepted but only for students from outside the European Economic Area (established between the member states of the European Free Trade Association, the European Community and the European Union). There is limited competition for students. There is practically no freedom of entry for new suppliers. There is some competition for research funding. There has been some move towards granting institutions greater autonomy and finance. But, as in many Continental European countries, ministry approval is needed for the introduction of new subjects or courses, reflecting the important role of central forecasts of labour market needs that provide the context for individually negotiated performance agreements between institutions and the government (in other words, resource allocation is driven not by student demand but by labour market forecasts). Similarly, and again as in many other Continental European countries as well as Japan, academic staff are civil servants though new legislation will change this and give institutions some discretion in determining salaries and terms and conditions. The role of the state in regulating higher education in Finland is thus strong and likely to remain so.

Elsewhere in Europe, marketisation is proceeding in the form of two steps in a market direction, one step back. Italy and Portugal are good examples. In Italy greater autonomy has been given to institutions and there has been greater pressure on them to increase non-state funding and compete for students, research funds and scholars. However, so far the effects have been limited, partly owing to the absence of sufficient state financial support (so that reforms have been implemented without extra financial resources) and partly because of academic resistance (Rostan and Viara 2009). In Portugal there has been an increase in competition between institutions but also a strengthening of regulation, for example in how the Bologna Process has been implemented and in quality evaluation. Even where new legal possibilities were created for institutions, such as public foundation status, constraints were also introduced (Teixeira and Amaral 2010).[6]

It would be good to think that this somewhat crabwise approach reflects the overall ambivalence of the literature on the impact of marketisation to date (Brown 2010). It is more likely to be a product of three factors:

1   a strong belief in equity and an avoidance of inequalities between different categories of institutions and students, except where these can be justified as, for example, through the creation of separate sectors of higher education with separate and distinctive missions
2   an inability to see how the various aspects of marketisation are linked, and the need for an integrated, coherent and consistent strategy which is pursued with tenacity over time if the benefits are to be secured
3   the strength of academic resistance, especially at professor/head of department level, and the relative weakness of university heads and governing bodies.

It is also the case, at least for the Nordic countries, that there are good grounds for caution.

As we have seen, one of the drivers of marketisation in Europe has been the desire to 'catch up' with the American and British systems, by making universities more autonomous and less reliant on state funding. One of the measures is the 'performance' of the various systems in the international university rankings, where the top positions in the Shanghai Jiao Tong (SJT) University and Times Higher QS university rankings are dominated by the American and British institutions. However, as John Gerritsen (2008) has pointed out, if you take the number of Top 500 (SJT) universities relative to population size, four of the top ten systems are Nordic: Sweden (1st), Finland (3rd), Norway (5th) and Denmark (8th). Whilst the US produces one top university for every 1.9 million people, Sweden does so for every 822,000.[7]

Conclusion

The marketisation of higher education is a complex process, with every major system falling somewhere between the market and non-market extremes. Nevertheless there is a clear international trend towards introducing greater competition, including price competition, into the provision of student education and, as a quasi-market, into the supply of academic research. Even the Nordic countries, bastions of public support for a non-market system, are beginning to introduce some market features. Whether the recent events in the financial markets, and the clear evidence of market failure even in the supply of conventional services to which the theory of markets is best suited, will slow or reverse this trend, can only be a matter of conjecture.

Two concluding comments can be offered.

First, whilst the main drivers of marketisation include the need to accommodate larger numbers of students without compromising on quality, we should not underestimate the influence of the various rankings and league tables and the way in which these reinforce the pressures for the pursuit of prestige within the academy (Brewer *et al.* 2002; Calhoun 2006; Brown submitted for review). Deem *et al.* (2008) draw attention to the way in which these are driving national strategies for higher education in Europe and Asia as they have long driven institutional strategies in the US.

Second, we should not overlook the key role of the state in determining the extent and the pace of marketisation. Roger Geiger recently pointed out that federal student aid is now the largest source of revenue for US higher education (Geiger 2009). This trend to fund institutions via the student began with the Reagan reforms of funding in the 1980s which reflected neo-liberal beliefs in the power of the market and the inutility of state intervention. It seems unlikely that there will be any serious reversal of the 'march of the market' until these beliefs have given way to a more socially responsible perspective. This takes us not only beyond the scope of this chapter but even beyond the scope of this book.[8]

Notes

1   Belfield and Levin (2002) distinguish between 'external' and 'internal' privatisation, where external privatisation refers to the market entry of privately owned providers whilst internal privatisation refers to the increased contribution of private forces to institutional revenues.

2   It is becoming increasingly clear that one of the main impacts of rankings is upon institutional managers, and especially institutional heads (see Hazelkorn 2008; Volkwein and Grunig 2005) even though, as Marginson (2007: 5–6) and others have pointed out, rankings also take judgements of quality out of the hands of the academy.

3   There is an extensive debate in the literature about whether universities can reduce costs without damaging quality. On the one hand, it is said that cost reduction is difficult because of the customised nature of the 'product' (Baumol *et al.* 1989; cf. Archibald and Feldman 2008). On the other hand, it is argued that institutions could make better use of modern communications technology to educate as well or better whilst containing or reducing costs (see, for example, Vedder 2004). In a recent issue of *The Chronicle of Higher Education* Vedder is quoted as saying: 'With the exception of – *possible* exception of – prostitution, I don't know any other profession that's had no productivity advance in 2,500 years' (Parry 2009: speaker's emphasis). Vedder goes on to advocate online education as the application of technology to lower rather than add to costs.

4   In a review of the literature, Brown (2010) finds that marketisation is generally held to increase institutional efficiency and responsiveness, increasing user satisfaction and making the resources allocated to higher education go further. The main detriments are seen to be increased stratification (both of institutions and of the social groups served), reduced diversity at institutional level, reduced quality and value for money,

and increased intra-institutional differentiation (activities, structures, personnel). Marketisation also poses a threat to the implicit 'contract' between higher education and society whereby institutions enjoy certain privileges (such as academic freedom) in return for producing valued public goods.

5   The Director-General for Education and Culture at the European Commission was quoted in *The Chronicle of Higher Education* recently to the effect that she would like to see European universities securing more private financing, including increased tuition, and become less reliant on government support: 'we still have countries where universities are strongly controlled and regulated by the state, which doesn't necessarily help competitiveness' (McMurtrie 2009).

6   This ambivalence towards liberalisation is not however confined to Europe or Asia: 'public universities hear time and time again from both elected public officials and governing board members that they desire a more market-focused, cost-effective, and competitive paradigm for the university. Yet these are the first people to hold up their hand to halt the changes necessary to respond to the marketplace' (Duderstadt *et al.* 2003: 98).

7   It is interesting to note that six of Gerritsen's ten countries – Sweden, New Zealand, Switzerland, Norway, Austria and Australia – were also in the top ten for levels of spending on educational core services per tertiary student in 2005 (OECD 2008: table B1.1b). New Zealand, Switzerland, Austria and Australia were also amongst the seven OECD countries, for which we have data, that spent above the country mean on educational institutions per student for all services relative to GDP per capita. In other words, their propensity to spend on teaching is relatively high.

8   Arthur Hauptman (2001: 93, 97) refers to Nicholas Lemann's (1998) description of the 'new American consensus', a consensus focused on the primacy of suburban, middle class interests, 'government of, by and for the comfortable'.

References

Archibald, R. B. and Feldman, D. H. (2008) 'Why do higher education costs rise more rapidly than prices in general?', *Change* (May/June): 25–31.

Baumol, W. J., Batey Blackman, S. A. and Wolff, E. N. (1989) *Productivity and American Leadership: The Long View*. Cambridge, MA: MIT Press.

Belfield, C. R. and Levin, H. M. (2002) *Education Privatization: Causes, Consequences and Planning Implications*. Paris: UNESCO International Institute for Educational Planning.

Brewer, D. J., Gates, S. M. and Goldman, C. A. (2002) *In Pursuit of Prestige: Strategy and Competition in US Higher Education*. Somerset, New Jersey: Transaction Publishers.

Brown, R. (2006) 'League tables – do we have to live with them?', *Perspectives*, 10(2): 33–8.

Brown, R. (ed.) (2010) *Higher Education and the Market*. New York and London: Routledge.

Brown, R. (Submitted for review) 'A balanced higher education system', *Higher Education Policy*.

Calhoun, C. (2006) 'The university and the public good', *Thesis Eleven*, 84 (February): 7–43.

Cave, M., Dodsworth, R. and Thompson, D. (1992) 'Regulatory reform in higher education in the UK: incentives for efficiency and product quality', *Oxford Review of Economic Policy*, 8(2): 79–102.

Centre for Higher Education Research and Information, The Open University and Hobson's Research (2008) *Counting What is Measured or Measuring What Counts?*

Report to the Higher Education Funding Council for England (HEFCE). Bristol: HEFCE.

Clark, B. R. (1983) *The Higher Education System*. Berkeley and Los Angeles: University of California Press.

Deem, R., Mok, K. H. and Lucas, L. (2008) 'Transforming higher education in whose image? Exploring the concept of the "world-class" university in Europe and Asia', *Higher Education Policy*, 21: 83–97.

Dill, D. D. and Soo, M. (2005) 'Academic quality, league tables and public policy: a cross-national analysis of university ranking systems', *Higher Education*, 49(4): 495–533.

Duderstadt, J. J. and Womack, F.W. (2003) *Beyond the Crossroads: the Future of the Public University in America*. Baltimore MD: The Johns Hopkins University Press.

Fidler, B. and Parsons, C. (2008) 'World university ranking methodologies: stability and variability', *Higher Education Review*, 40(3): 5–34.

Geiger, R. L. (2009) 'Markets and the end of the current era in US higher education', paper presented to the *22nd CHER Annual Conference*, Porto 10–12 September.

Gerritsen, J. (2008) 'The real Shanghai Jiao Tong winners', *University World News* (31 August). Available from http://www.universityworldnews.com/article.php?story= 20080828150333316 (accessed 25 March 2009).

Goedegebuure, L., Kaiser, F., Maassen, P. and Meek, L. (1994) in F. van Vught and E. de Weert (eds) *Higher Education Policy: An International Perspective*. Oxford: Pergamon Press.

Hartwig, L. (2010) 'Diversification and competition in the German higher education system', in R. Brown (ed.) *Higher Education and the Market*. New York and London: Routledge.

Hauptman, A. M. (2001) 'Reforming the ways in which states finance higher education' in D. Heller (ed.) *The States and Public Higher Education Policy: Affordability, Access and Accountability*. Baltimore and London: The Johns Hopkins University Press.

Hazelkorn, E. (2008) 'Learning to live with league tables and ranking: the experience of institutional leaders', *Higher Education Policy*, 21(2): 193–216.

Holtta, S., Jansson, T. and Kivisto, J. (2010) 'Taming the beast: Finnish system', in R. Brown (ed.) *Higher Education and the Market*. New York and London: Routledge.

Huang, F. (2010) 'The case study of Japan', in R. Brown (ed.) *Higher Education and the Market*. New York and London, Routledge.

Jongbloed, B. (2010) 'Markets in Dutch higher education: improving performance and quality in a hands off governance setting', in R. Brown (ed.) *Higher Education and the Market*. New York and London: Routledge.

Kehm, B. and Stensaker, B. (eds) (2009) *University Rankings, Diversity and the New Landscape of Higher Education*. Rotterdam and Taipei: Sense Publishers.

Kivisto, J. and Holtta, S. (2008) 'Information as a regulative element in higher education systems', *Tertiary Education and Management*, 14(4): 331–44.

Le Grand, J. and Bartlett, W. (1993) *Quasi-Markets and Social Policy*. Basingstoke: Macmillan.

Lemann, N. (1998) 'The new American consensus', *New York Times Magazine* (1 November): 37–43.

Marginson, S. (2007) 'Global university rankings', in S. Marginson (ed.) *Prospects of Higher Education – Globalisation, Market Competition, Public Goods and the Future of the University*. Rotterdam and Taipei: Sense Publishers.

McMurtrie, B. (2009) 'European official speaks frankly about collaboration, quality and costs', *The Chronicle of Higher Education* (30 October).

Organisation for Economic Cooperation and Development (OECD) (2008) *Education at a Glance 2008: OECD Indicators.* Paris: OECD. Available from http://www.oecd.org/document/9/0,3343,en_2649_39263238_41266761_1_1_1_1,00.html (accessed 25 May 2010).

Parry, M. (2009) 'Obama's great course giveaway', *The Chronicle of Higher Education* (7 August).

Rostan, M. and Vaira, M. (2009) 'Faltering effects of market-oriented reforms in higher education. Some evidences from the Italian case', paper presented to the *22nd CHER Conference*, Porto 10–12 September.

Salmi, J. (2009) *The Challenge of Establishing World-Class Universities.* Washington, DC: The World Bank.

Salmi, J. and Saroyan, A. (2007) 'League tables as policy instruments: uses and misuses', *Higher Education Management and Policy*, 19(2): 31–61.

Self, P. (1999) *Rolling Back the Market: Economic Dogma and Political Choice.* New York: St Martin's Press.

Teixeira, P. and Amaral, A. (2010) 'Portuguese higher education: more competition with less market regulation?', in R. Brown (ed.) *Higher Education and the Market.* New York and London: Routledge.

Usher, A. and Savino, M. (2006) *A World of Difference: A Global Survey of University League Tables.* Toronto: Educational Policy Institute, Canadian Education Report Series (January).

Van Dyke, N. (2005) 'Twenty years of university report cards', *Higher Education in Europe*, 30(2): 103–25.

Vedder, R. (2004) *Going Broke by Degree: Why College Costs Too Much.* Washington, DC: AEI Press.

Volkwein, J. F. and Grunig, S. D. (2005) 'Resources and reputation in higher education: double, double, toil and trouble', in J. Burke (ed.) *Achieving Accountability in Higher Education: Balancing Public, Academic, and Market Demands.* San Francisco: Jossey-Bass.

Volkwein, J. F. and Sweitzer, K. (2006) 'Institutional prestige and reputation among research universities and liberal arts colleges', *Research in Higher Education*, 47(2): 129–48.

Weisbrod, B. A. (1988) *The Non-Profit Economy*, Cambridge, MA and London: Harvard University Press.

Williams, G. (1995) 'The "marketisation" of higher education: reforms and potential reforms in higher education finance', in D. D Dill and B. Sporn (eds) *Patterns of Social Demand and University Reform: Through a Glass Darkly.* Oxford: Pergamon Press.

Wolf, C. (1993) *Markets or Governments: Choosing Between Imperfect Alternatives.* Cambridge, MA: MIT Press.

Yorke, M. and Longden, B. (2005) *Significant Figures: Performance Indicators and 'League Tables'.* London: Standing Conference of Principals.

Chapter 3

Markets, government, funding and the marketisation of UK higher education

Nick Foskett

Markets and the changing face of higher education

Higher education in the UK has been characterised in the last two decades by significant and rapid change. Despite the expansion of higher education (HE) that had taken place in the wake of the Robbins Report (1963), by the mid 1980s there were less than 60 universities, and participation rates were approximately 6 per cent – only six in every hundred 18-year-olds progressed to take an undergraduate degree. Twenty years later the landscape of higher education has been transformed, with some 140 universities and university colleges providing undergraduate programmes for 42 per cent (and rising) of all 18-year-olds. In addition to the growth of British undergraduates, universities have seen significant expansion of 'overseas' student numbers. In the mid 1980s students from outside the UK numbered approximately 20,000, while by 2008 this had grown to 350,000. And it has not only been in student numbers where expansion has been witnessed. Universities are all, to varying degrees, engaged in other academic and scholarly activities, ranging from provision for Continuing Professional Development (CPD), to research activity funded by government, charities or the private sector, to enterprise ranging from direct consultancy services to the generation of spin-out companies to the commercialisation of research products and all have shown significant growth since 1980 (HEFCE 2007). In the space of these two decades the British university system may be characterised as changing from a small collegium of medium-sized, research- and education-focused organisations to a knowledge-based service industry of medium and large enterprises with diverse missions, profiles and character – as Teixeira *et al.* have indicated, 'all across the world, higher education has become a large enterprise' (2004: 1). Universities have become a key element of the economic profile of the UK, just as they have become a key component of the global service sector (Bretton 2003).

The giant has awoken in response to the direct intentions of government. Based on a discourse of the role of HE in national economic success and as a key catalyst to fundamental social change (e.g. Dearing 1997; Leitch 2006; Stephens 2009), governments have cajoled, incentivised and directed the expansion of the sector. At the heart of this has been a perspective that the key route to expanding higher education effectively and efficiently is the use of market mechanisms, and the watchword of 'marketisation' has become a central concept in the sector. Scan the literature and the discourse of higher education since 1980 and it is as if competition and market forces have arrived, through government edict, into a world where they had no presence before. The exposure of universities to the marketplace has grown significantly over that time, in a way which has changed many fundamental tenets of HE management and leadership. But it is certainly not true that markets are new to universities, for markets have always been a familiar part of higher education, and what has changed has been their character, modus operandi and impact. What we are seeing is not a process of marketisation, but a process of enhanced marketisation, with markets driving the world of universities in a way unprecedented in their history.

Universities operate in the world of post-compulsory education. While educating young people has never been their only function it has, for almost every university, been the most significant of their activities, providing progression from schools to, for most students, their final stage of formal education. But while school education is compulsory to some level in every country of the world, progression to university has never been compulsory. The first university was established in Fez, Morocco in the ninth century AD, and the oldest university in the UK is the University of Oxford whose origins can be traced back to 1167. But as post-compulsory institutions, from their earliest foundation universities have operated in the marketplace. They have sought to persuade young people (or their families or sponsors) to choose to attend, they have sought sponsors to provide the funding to support scholarly activities and they have sought the brightest and best as their academic staff. In each arena the presence of 'choice' has obliged universities to compete with alternatives to their services and, from the moment the second university was established, to compete with other universities. Higher education markets, therefore, are at least eleven centuries old.

Universities and markets – the first 750 years

Within the United Kingdom there are two groups of the world's oldest universities. First there are the ancient foundations, those universities established at some time between 1250 and 1850 and with a long history of scholarship and teaching – these are the universities of Oxford and Cambridge in England, and the universities of St Andrews, Glasgow, Aberdeen and Edinburgh in Scotland. Their establishment and continuance has been based on endowment by the Crown, by the state, by local communities and by patronage by the wealthy and influential in society. For much of their history they have been the educational institutions of the social elite and have provided the educated individuals to lead society, government and commerce. While exposed to the market in the sense that competition for that patronage and influence clearly existed, these universities have been protected from the negative impact of competition by their oligopolistic position, their rich endowments and, ultimately, their place in the British 'establishment' through the position and influence of their alumni.

The second group are the civic universities established from 1825 onwards. The University of London, and the universities of the industrial cities of Britain (for example, the universities of Leeds and Manchester), were built on industrial and commercial wealth, the demands of a rapidly growing economy and the commitment to culture, science, the arts and philanthropy of the elite social and business communities in those cities. Their establishment, while facilitated by government, was underwritten by endowment and patronage, and their survival was ensured even in competitive markets in the same ways as the 'ancient' universities.

Such organisations have been described by Carlson (1975) as occupying a 'domesticated' market environment. In such an environment, institutions, while competing in a nominal way, are in fact assured of long-term survival, in that financial losses are underwritten by endowments or by government or some other key supporter simply writing them off or ignoring traditional market failures. Universities were able to make operational decisions by giving primacy to non-financial priorities – academic objectives, and cultural and social requirements were more important than balancing the books.

The period through to 1980 saw a continuation of the domesticated environment for UK higher education, even though the university scene changed in many distinctive ways over that time. The sector grew in the number of universities, and in the number of students obtaining degrees. Underpinning this growth was the recognition by government of the economic and social importance of universities. With this came the need to ensure their survival through funding and to invest in both a steady growth in the numbers of graduates being produced and in the knowledge generation of the sector through its research. Four key elements of this underwriting by government can be identified:

1   the establishment of the Universities' Grants Committee (UGC) in 1917, which ensured that government funding was provided for universities
2   the establishment of the dual funding model by the UGC in which universities received funding not only for teaching but for undertaking research
3   the growth in the number of universities, through the creation of the redbrick institutions of the inter-war and post-war period and the further wave of 'plateglass' institutions following the Robbins Report (1963)
4   the provision of student funding through a non-repayable grants system, which enabled students to attend university in effect at no personal financial cost.

This expansion of the system, however, did not expose the sector to major challenges from market forces. By 1970 student demand for places still significantly exceeded supply. Recruitment of academic staff remained buoyant on the basis of good salary benefits, high social status, attractive lifestyle and contracts guaranteeing lifetime tenure. The research environment was supported through guaranteed UGC funding, in a period when the cost of even intensive 'big science and engineering' was comparatively modest. While the markets operated in these environments, therefore, the higher education sector was secure in both its present and its future.

So what was the nature of 'higher education marketing' in such a domesticated operational environment? The first observation must be that it was not called 'marketing', for the term had an association with the competitive commercial environment that would have been quite unacceptable culturally within higher education (Kotler and Fox 1995). Despite this, however, every university was still of necessity engaged in marketing activities – but in the context of very limited competition this was essentially transactional in nature. Universities produced prospectuses to enable prospective students to choose from the programmes they offered and to give some insights into the life, environment and culture of the institution. They produced occasional press releases to inform the media of significant research developments, the opening of new buildings or the conduct of the great occasions of university life such as graduation. However, external relations remained a low key issue, with little resource, limited expertise (most marketing was undertaken by non-specialists within the academic administration) and low profile within the institution (Keen and Greenall 1987; Smith *et al.* 1995). Indeed, part of the character of universities was to retain the mystery and mystique of elite institutions to whom only small proportions of the community could aspire to enter and who managed their own affairs detached from the world of markets and business.

Markets, marketisation and the modern British university

Turning to the market

The 1970s and 1980s brought the domesticated environment for universities to an end. The key driver in this stepwise change was the global economic challenge brought about, *inter alia*, by rising world oil prices and the decline of traditional industries in 'the North' in competition from emerging economies in 'the South'. In the UK we can trace the transition point quite precisely to the Ruskin College speech by Prime Minister James Callaghan (1976), in which he started a national debate about the nature, purpose and success of the education system in Britain. The economic challenges of the 1970s had caused government to look at the reasons for and solutions to the negative impacts of a changing world order, and the questions posed to education at all levels were pointed. The economic malaise was blamed squarely on the failure of the education system to generate an educated society in which young people had the skills and knowledge to enable them to contribute positively to economic success. The 'post-war settlement'

(Salter and Tapper 1981) in which professionals in the public sector were trusted by government to design and operate an effective education system was deemed to have failed, with the conclusion that government intervention would be essential to turn the system round. And not only would government need to engage more directly, it would need to explore ways of growing the education system to produce larger numbers of better educated graduates to ensure the UK economy would be highly competitive in global markets. Hence the scene was set for an interventionist engagement with higher education.

The pursuit of markets as the main driver of public sector provision is traditionally attributed to the Conservative government of Margaret Thatcher in the UK, elected in 1979. The concept of the market as an effective mechanism for the 'management' of the education sector, however, dates back to the ideas of Milton Friedman (1962) and Friedrich von Hayek (1976). The essential principles are straightforward. Markets are driven by consumer choice, and choice means competition between providers. Competition means that the supply side must continuously seek to gain advantage in the market in terms of price, quality of service or the development of innovative products or services. This will serve to stimulate innovation and promote efficiency and lower costs. Hence in the context of a moribund education sector it would stimulate change and the raising of standards. Market mechanisms, therefore, were seen to stimulate quality improvements, raise standards of achievement and also enhance the libertarian values of 'choice'. And in addition, competition should drive down unit costs, which should enable governments to grow the education sector without a proportional increase in public expenditure. The key question, therefore, was how markets in education, and specifically in higher education, should be promoted.

Quasi-markets in higher education

Through the 1980s and 1990s enhanced marketisation emerged through a number of policy and statutory changes, and despite changes in government has continued through to the present (Foskett 1996; Williams 2004). This commitment to the competition for resources between universities, to the sharing of the cost of higher education between government and students, and to the concept of customer-provider relationships in HE between students and institutions is enshrined, for example, in the 2009 policy document *Higher Ambitions; The Future of Universities in a Knowledge Economy* (DBIS 2009) and in the Lord Browne review of student fees commissioned in December 2009.

Although the UK was amongst the first of the OECD countries to adopt such 'new public management policies' (Deem 2001), such a pattern of enhanced marketisation has been a global phenomenon, and the transitions and interventions we shall describe below can be found in most parts of the globe – see, for example, Kirp's description of HE markets in the USA (2003), Teixeira *et al.*'s international review of higher education markets (2004), Weber and Duderstadt's summary of the current environment of higher education internationally (2008) and Roger Brown's chapter in this book.

This commitment to markets as the strategic way forward for higher education is fundamentally challenging for governments. As Kirp (2003: 2) has indicated, 'the notion that higher education is a "market" needs to be unpacked, because the system doesn't look like the market portrayed in any Economics 101 textbook'. While governments seek some of the benefits of the market (efficiency, choice, etc.) there are too many aspects of education where government is directly involved or where the downside risks of markets may be too damaging to mean that simply leaving things to classical 'free markets' is possible. In the UK, government is, for example, the direct source of funding for most education and research, and seeks to ensure that higher education delivers against a whole set of social and economic objectives. Hence the market has to be constructed to be what has been termed a 'quasi-market' (Le Grand 1990), in which the hand of government provides significant guidance and influence on how the market operates. For the key markets in higher education, that is the markets for undergraduate 'home' students, and the markets for research funding, it is a highly structured quasi-market that has been in operation.

What are the key elements of these quasi-markets? Teixeira *et al.* (2004: 4–5) indicate that:

> The introduction of quasi markets in higher education is a combination of three main vectors. The first is the promotion of competition between higher education providers. The second is the privatisation of higher education – either by the emergence of a private higher education sector or by means of privatisation of certain aspects of public institutions. And the third is the promotion of economic autonomy of higher education institutions, enhancing their responsiveness and articulation to the supply and demand of factors and products.

Within the UK a wide range of approaches, strategies and implements have been used to shape and drive quasi-markets, each of which reflects one or more of Teixeira *et al.*'s 'vectors' (although privatisation is as yet of limited development), and it is important for those operating in HE markets, whether at operational or strategic level, to understand this 'market architecture'.

Marketising the universities

To increase the number of students in HE, it has been necessary to extend the capacity of the system. This has been achieved by increasing the number of student places funded by government, and enabling growth both in the number of providers and the capacity of those already in existence. The number of universities has grown, principally through:

1   the transfer of the former polytechnic sector from local authority control to a position as independent corporations with university 'title'

2   the development of a range of other institutions (for example, teacher train-
    ing colleges) into, first, university colleges awarding the degrees of other
    institutions and then into independent universities.

With increasing numbers have come two important elements of the quasi-
market – increasing supplier diversity to facilitate consumer choice and the
imposition of managerial approaches which give institutions substantial autonomy
but combined with market accountability. In other words, universities as
independent corporations must decide their mission and strategy to ensure
survival in the marketplace.

How has supplier diversity emerged in what was traditionally a highly
homogeneous sector? Size, location, history and range of academic disciplines
on offer are obvious differentiators, but a key distinctor has been between those
universities with a primarily teaching mission and those with a mission which
emphasises research as either the driver of education or as the institutional key
raison d'être. Perhaps most important, though, has been differentiation by
perceived status and quality, indicated typically by the surrogate measures of
entry/admissions grades and research reputation. Hence the perceived highest
status universities are those demanding high A level grades for admissions and
achieving high ratings in periodic reviews of research quality (the Research
Assessment Exercises, or RAEs), but with admissions grades themselves simply
serving as a price mechanism for high-demand institutions. While the Russell
Group of 19 elite research-led universities, therefore, would see themselves as
having market primacy by these indicators, and teaching-led former university
colleges with a regionally based mission might generally be seen as having least
market presence at a national level, the diversity of institutions has meant that
there is strong evidence of local, regional and national competition across the
wide diversity of students now entering higher education.

Growing demand and promoting choice

With diversity, autonomy and market accountability in place on the supply side
of the market, how has the demand side been developed? The student body has
become much more diverse as their numbers have grown. Government policy,
drawing strongly on a commitment to inclusion and equity, has sought to
increase diversity in social class, gender, ethnicity and age profile in higher
education, but in reality the principal diversity achieved has been in relation to
the prior achievement of students entering HE. Most are still from the same
social classes as entered university in the 1970s, although some progress on
improving participation across ethnic groups has been achieved (Reay *et al.*
2005). With a diverse 'customer base' therefore, it has become possible for
institutions to differentiate by target groups, and this is reflected in their missions.
Those unable to, or choosing not to, compete for the highest achieving entrants,
however, find themselves in competitive arenas in which they have to actively

seek applicants and students rather than simply being able to choose from a large pool of applicants – hence the distinction between 'recruiting' and 'selecting' universities is well established in the HE market.

An important dimension of the architecture of UK HE markets is the centrality of the choice process for potential students and its link to financial flows in the system. Choice has always existed for potential students in the HE system, but the policy trend of the last quarter century has been towards 'enhanced choice'. Enhanced choice is characterised by an explicit emphasis on choice through the provision of public domain comparator information provided by both the government and the media.

Students choosing to take up a place at a university bring with them three direct sources of funding:

1   the funding provided by government to the university, through the Higher Education Funding Council, for the provision of a place
2   in England, Wales and Northern Ireland, the course fee paid by the student direct to the university, now usually in the form of a loan from the Student Loan Company
3   the student's expenditure on university services such as accommodation etc.

In detail the first of these (Funding Council funding) is extremely complex, and links student numbers *directly* to funding only in part, as most funding comes through formula-driven block grants. However, it is a mechanism used strongly by government to shape the detail of the market by providing additional or less funding for particular types of programme or discipline, for example in its prioritisation of funding for foundation degrees in inviting bids for additional student places by universities from 2003 onwards.

The second element of financial flow (student fees) has been a market mechanism introduced in the UK since 2000. Student fees, whatever their level, provide a simple market mechanism which means that 'more students = more income'. Although the Higher Education Act of 2003 introduced the idea of variable fees as a market mechanism, the imposition of a fee cap maximum has meant that for almost all universities, they have not yet become a price differentiation mechanism in the market. However, the prospect of raising the cap from its current level of around £3,000 to a higher figure, or of removing it altogether, has emerged as a likely political decision beyond 2010 – and in either situation it will result in greater fee differentiation becoming a real part of the HE market.

The third element is an important yet less considered part of the financial architecture of the HE market. In a strict sense such student expenditure is simply their activity in non-HE markets, and is subject to market conditions much more based on free market principles – students can choose where to live, where to shop and where to buy books, for example. However, the typical cost of living and the operation of local markets in these fields are an important element of the decision about which university to choose – hence they act as influencers on where the other two financial elements flow to, as well as bringing income to universities directly in proportion to student numbers.

Satisfying demand for higher education

But what is it that universities are 'selling' in these quasi-markets? Universities differentiate themselves in many ways in terms of the programmes and research that they offer. However, government intervention in the market is still strong through their influence on the nature, scale and quality of the 'product'. In relation to research, government shapes the market by being the principal provider of research funds (directly, or via the UK Research Councils, or through the so called 'QR' (Quality Research) strand of Funding Council funding), and which therefore shapes the research themes and priorities for universities to focus on. In addition they act as the main arbiters of research quality through the use of periodic research assessment processes (RAEs) which identify who the strongest research providers are in each field. This data then drives funding decisions by the UK government and, importantly, funding decisions on research and research students by other organisations within and beyond the UK.

In relation to teaching programmes, government, through the Funding Councils and other quangos such as the Quality Assurance Agency, shapes the curriculum by providing benchmarks for curriculum coverage in each discipline and through its monitoring of educational standards through institutional audit. It also delimits the size of the market for most disciplines by dictating the number of funded places it will provide. Indeed, in some professional training fields, such as medicine, nursing or teacher training, government dictates precisely the number of training places and can change these numbers in short timescales.

The processes of audit and inspection are an important quasi-market mechanism used by government. While primarily concerned with ensuring quality and value for money, the data from inspection and audit enables comparative judgements to be made about institutions and programmes. Information is key within markets in enabling choosers to make informed choices, and the culture of students (and parents) accessing and using such comparative data is actively promoted by government. Some of this is government provided (for example the results of National Student Surveys (NSS) of student satisfaction with programmes and institutions), but some is provided through private commercial organisations (for example, the league tables of institutions produced by national newspapers such as *The Guardian, The Independent, The Times* and *The Sunday Times* available in the public domain). The impact of such market elements is important, for not only does it provide an important source of information to assist with choice but it also drives the priorities that institutions have in directing their time and effort. Activities that will produce positive league table effects (for example data on 'library spend per student') are often prioritised for the use of resources, while practice in some areas may be shaped by league table priorities

– for example, average A level grades of new entrants are an important league table measure, so universities may choose to prioritise entrants with good A levels over those from alternative widening participation pathways. The hand of government, therefore, is heavy in shaping the market.

International markets and higher education

An important dimension of HE markets in recent years has been the growth of international markets (Maringe and Foskett 2010). From a very low base in the 1970s and 1980s, the growth of international markets has been rapid: by 2007–2008 UK universities had 235,000 students enrolled from outside the European Union, and a further 115,000 EU students, which represents 13 per cent of the total student body. There have been two key drivers of this growth. First, the push of universities into the market by government has forced all to consider alternative sources of income, and income from international activities provides an attractive option to many. Such markets are principally about international students on teaching programmes, but also include collaboration on research bids and the development of enterprise opportunities abroad. At its extreme it has included the construction of campuses overseas, such as the University of Nottingham's campus at Ningbo in China.

The second driver, though, has been the processes of globalisation (Scott 1998; Neubauer and Ordoñez 2008). The growth of global trade, communications and interconnectedness has stimulated a global view of higher education (Deem 2001) and the World Trade Organisation recognises higher education as a large globally traded service worth some $200 billion per annum (Bretton 2003). Slaughter and Leslie (1997) have stressed that these processes have put significant pressure on both national HE policy makers and individual universities to change the way they operate. Universities have been drawn into the global HE business through rising demand for international education and transnational education provision, and also through a view that all their students (home or overseas) should be exposed to an education that equips them as global citizens. Research increasingly addresses global issues (climate change, energy supply, international business) or seeks to develop technologies or products that impact on international markets, and universities actively seek international partners to prosecute these agendas. These dimensions of change have pushed universities towards a more entrepreneurial perspective in their operations, and have challenged the existing suite of skills of university leaders (Clark 1998; Fielden 2008; Foskett 2010)

International education markets are even more diverse and volatile than home markets. Understanding and engaging with them requires the same basic set of operational and strategic skills as home markets but with a level of sophistication and complexity that is hugely challenging. Unlike home markets, they are much closer to operating as 'normal' classical markets rather than quasi-markets, as there are fewer direct constraints on how universities operate within them. Indeed, universities are supported in their engagement with international markets by organisations such as The British Council and UKTI (UK Trade and Industry) in recognition that they are a straightforward service industry operating in an international arena.

The rise of competition and marketing in higher education

The market architecture that we have considered above has clearly stimulated the enhanced marketisation of UK higher education. Universities are faced with competition and market forces driven by the quasi-market imposed by government, and find themselves in strongly competitive environments for many of their activities, both at home and abroad. They compete with other universities at local, regional and national level and with alternative options such as direct employment. Scott (1996) has indicated that in reality this scene represents a number of separate markets which overlap but have distinctive characteristics. For example, a university may offer programmes at Foundation, Bachelor's, Master's or Doctoral levels in a huge range of academic and professional fields, by different delivery modes (full-time, part-time, distance learning), and with different precise content and coverage. Each of these will be offered within a specific marketplace, where providers are differentiated *inter alia* by detailed product, reputation, quality indicators and admissions criteria. This in turn is set within a national HE market framework where groups of similar institutions serve different sorts of markets. Research on higher education choice (e.g. Foskett and Hemsley-Brown 2001; Reay *et al.* 2005) shows how students choose within limited market arenas that are sometimes geographically specific but more often are determined by perceived status and market value. Some students, for example, will be choosing from teaching-led institutions offering low entry grades, while others will be choosing from research-led, high entry standards universities, but these groups of choosers are largely confined to their chosen market or 'circuit of universities'. As Scott (1996: 22) has indicated

> In . . . higher education there is a diversity of providers . . . [but] the marketplace is highly segmented with the result that effective competition between them is much reduced. The universities of Oxford and Derby are not trading in the same 'markets'.

The picture that emerges from this description of UK higher education is of the importance of markets to the operation and existence of every university. In contrast to the 'domesticated' environment of earlier years, enhanced marketisation has moved universities into, what Carlson (1975) has termed, a 'wild environment'. A wild environment is one in which each institution must design and implement its own strategy, make its own judgements about its business organisation, aims and values, and compete with other institutions in the sector – and, most importantly, its very survival depends upon a market accountability with limited or no government protection in the event of miscalculations in the market. The key feature of such a wild environment is the requirement to move from a transactional approach to marketing, in which marketing is simply an operational tool of the organisation, to a strategic approach to marketing in which the very existence and future of the organisation is shaped at a strategic level by decisions which are market driven.

In such a context the growth of marketing functions is inevitable and essential, and at the same time the adoption of a market-focused perspective by those providing strategic leadership is critical. The last decade has, in particular, seen a strong momentum in this direction. A study of marketing activity in universities in the early 1990s (Smith *et al.* 1995) showed that although all were engaged in marketing, comparatively few were organised in a strongly professional way, using professionally qualified marketing staff, and operating at the strategic core of the university. Today's pattern is very different. All universities have expanded their operational marketing functions, and few are worried about using the 'M' word in the everyday language of the institution. And at strategic level, marketing has a key place in the management and leadership of the UK's universities. Most now have a specific appointment at second tier level (Pro Vice Chancellor) to lead marketing and/or external relations activities, and heads of institutions increasingly focus on the role of surveying, shaping and responding to the external environment and markets. Most recent advertisements stress the 'external focus' required of new Vice Chancellors, while development programmes such as the Leadership Foundation's Top Management Programme (TMP) major on strategic leadership, market engagement and internationalisation (Shiel and McKenzie 2008; Foskett 2010).

This all reflects the exposure of universities in the marketised worlds they inhabit, where understanding 'risk' is now a key leadership skill. Market risk is still cushioned to some extent in that small number of old-established universities whose wealth of endowment leads to financial security and whose market primacy makes them also resilient to market changes – they are the last to feel any 'winds of change'. But for most, the marketisation of the higher education arena in the UK has so changed the context of universities that to mitigate the risks they face all have had to review fundamentally what it means to be a university and what sort of university they might wish to be. The strategy for the university must be a strategy for their marketplaces.

References

Bretton, G. (2003) *Universities and Globalisation: Private Linkages and Public Trust.* Geneva: UNESCO.

Callaghan, J. (1976) 'The Ruskin College Speech, 18 October 1976', in J. Ahler, B. Cosin and M. Hales (eds) *Diversity and Change: Education Policy and Selection.* London: Routledge.

Carlson, R. (1975) 'Environmental constraints and organisational consequences: the public school and its clients', in J. Baldridge and T. Deal (eds) *Managing Change in Educational Organisations.* Berkeley, CA: McCutchan.

Clark, B. R. (1998) *Creative Entrepreneurial Universities: Organisational Pathways of Transformation*. New York: Elsevier.

DBIS (2009) *Higher Ambitions; the future of universities in a knowledge economy*. London: Department of Business, Industry and Skills.

Dearing, R. (1997) *Report of The National Committee of Inquiry into Higher Education* (The Dearing Report). London: HMSO.

Deem, R. (2001) 'Globalisaton, new managerialism, academic capitalism and entrepreneurialism in universities. Is the local dimension still important?', *Comparative Education*, 37(1): 7–20.

Fielden, J. (2008) *The Practice of Internationalisation: Managing International Activities in UK Universities*. London: UK Higher Education International Unit.

Foskett, N. H. (ed.) (1996) *Markets in Education: Policy and Practice – Volume 2: Markets in Post-Compulsory Education*. Southampton: Centre for Research in Education Marketing, University of Southampton.

Foskett, N. H. (2010) 'Global markets, national challenges, local strategies; the strategic challenge of internationalisation', in F. Maringe and N. H. Foskett (eds) *Globalisation and Internationalisation in Higher Education: Theoretical, Strategic and Management Perspectives*. London: Continuum Press.

Foskett, N. H. and Hemsley-Brown, J. V. (2001) *Choosing Futures: Young People's Decision-making in Education, Training and Careers Markets*. London: RoutledgeFalmer.

Friedman, M. (1962) *Capitalism and Freedom*. Chicago: University of Chicago Press.

HEFCE (Higher Education Funding Council for England) (2007) *HEFCE Strategic Plan 2006–11 Updated April 2007*. Bristol: HEFCE.

Keen, C. and Greenall, J. (1987) *Public Relations Management in Colleges, Polytechnics and Universities*. Banbury: Heist Publications.

Kirp, D. L. (2003) *Shakespeare, Einstein and the Bottom Line – The Marketing of Higher Education*. Cambridge, MA: Harvard University Press.

Kotler, P. and Fox, K. (1995) *Strategic Marketing for Educational Institutions* (2nd edn). Englewood Cliffs: Prentice Hall.

Le Grand, J. (1990) *Quasi Markets and Social Policy*. Bristol: University of Bristol School for Advanced Urban Studies.

Leitch Report, The (2006) *Prosperity for all in the Global Economy: World Class Skills*. London: TSO.

Maringe, F. and Foskett, N. H. (2010) *Globalisation and Internationalisation in Higher Education: Theoretical, Strategic and Management Perspectives*. London: Continuum Press.

Neubauer, D. and Ordoñez, V. (2008) 'The new role of globalized education in a globalized world', in P. Taylor (ed.) (on behalf of GUNI – The Global University Network for Innovation) *Higher Education in the World 3: Higher Education: New Challenges and Emerging Roles for Human and Social Development*. London: Palgrave Macmillan.

Reay, D., David, M. E. and Ball, S. (2005) *Degrees of Choice: Social Class, Race and Gender in Higher Education*. Stoke-on-Trent: Trentham Books.

Robbins Report, The (1963) *Higher Education* (Cm 2154). London: HMSO.

Salter, B. and Tapper, T. (eds) (1981) *Education, Politics and the State: The Theory and Practice of Educational Change*. London: Grant McIntyre.

Scott, P. (1996) 'Markets in post-compulsory education – rhetoric, policy and structure', in N. H. Foskett (ed.) *Markets in Education: Policy and Practice – Volume 2: Markets in Post-Compulsory Education*. Southampton: Centre for Research in Education Marketing, University of Southampton.

Scott, P. (ed.) (1998) *The Globalisation of Higher Education*. Buckingham: Open University Press.

Shiel, C. and McKenzie, A. (eds) (2008) *The Global University: The Role of Senior Managers*. London: Development Education Association.

Slaughter, S. and Leslie, L. (1997) *Academic Capitalism*. Baltimore, MD: Johns Hopkins University Press.

Smith, D., Scott, P. and Lynch, J. (1995) *Marketing in Further and Higher Education*. Leeds: Centre for Policy Studies in Education, University of Leeds.

Stephens, D. (ed.) (2009) *Higher Education and International Capacity Building; Twenty-five years of Higher Education Links*. London: Symposium Books.

Teixeira, P., Jongbloed, B., Dill, D. and Amaral, A. (eds) (2004) *Markets in Higher Education – Rhetoric or Reality?* Dordrecht: Kluwer Academic.

von Hayek, F. (1976) *Law, Legislation and Liberty: Vol. 2 Rules and Order*. London: Routledge and Kegan Paul.

Weber, L. E. and Duderstadt, J. J. (2008) *The Globalization of Higher Education*. London: Economica.

Williams, G. (2004) 'The higher education market in the United Kingdom', in P. Teixeira, B. Jongbloed, D. Dill and A. Amaral (eds) *Markets in Higher Education – Rhetoric or Reality?* Dordrecht: Kluwer Academic.

Chapter 4

The marketised university: defending the indefensible

Ronald Barnett

Introduction

The marketised university polarises opinion. There are those who consider that the contemporary university should recognise that it is placed in a competitive marketplace and that it should compete by marketing itself and its products and its activities (for example, Hills 1999). For those universities that are mainly state funded, state funding is bound to fall short of a university's legitimate wants and so marketing is necessary for additional income generation. This pro-market camp has its own nuances as between those who believe in the virtues of the market as a rational device for determining the allocation of scarce resources and for securing 'efficiency' on the one hand and those who consider that, contingently, for its own effectiveness (for 'quality management' or even for its own 'freedom'), the university should understand itself as a provider of services in a competitive marketplace. Either way, market disciplines are urged on the university.

In the other camp, there are those who consider that the shift towards the marketised university is having a deleterious impact on the university (for example, Reid 1996). There are nuances in this position, too. There are those who are prompted by a concern with the student experience and the claimed effect on the pedagogical relationship wrought by the student market, as students become 'customers'. There are also those who are concerned about the university as a social institution and who believe that marketisation is corrupting the university as an embodiment of public goods.

Noticeable in this polarisation of views – between the pro-marketers and the anti-marketers – are two similarities. Both would claim to ground their positions on empirical evidence *but* also both are imbued with a value position focused on the market as such. That is to say, the empirical evidence that each side would point to serves as a rationalisation of a prior position taken up either in favour of or against the market. The issue of the market in higher education, therefore, is an ideological site (cf. Barnett 2003). The positive *and* the hostile positions are taken up first and the evidence is found to support the position taken. It appears as if there is a debate, since evidence is brought to bear by the opposing parties but for the most part it amounts to a trading of fixed value-laden positions.

Is there, then, a way through that will allow a less value-driven view to be developed? Is the market – which for many is indefensible – defensible? Is there something intrinsically or logically problematic with the marketisation of higher education? Alternatively, are there features of markets that might turn out to be beneficial for the development of higher education and the university? Might there just be available a position that offers a reconciliation of the polarised positions?

Context: market plurality and market fuzziness

Worldwide, universities experience the presence of the market to some extent. 'Partial marketisation is a feature of many if not most national systems' (Marginson 2007: 42; also see Brown in this book). In most higher education systems, universities have some freedom to generate income for themselves and are not totally dependent on state finance. To a greater or lesser extent, universities tend to be operating in the public sector *and* be placed in markets. Perhaps the presence of the market is visible most prominently in the USA and the UK but Continental Europe is moving with some pace in that direction and across the world, features of markets are apparent. China is permitting some of its universities to generate income for themselves.

Universities are increasingly complex organisations and are therefore capable, in principle, of being active in several markets. So-called third stream activities ('knowledge transfer', patents, establishing of private companies, consultancy activities) are developing apace. Universities are also finding that they have other capabilities that offer them a market position, in hotel and leisure services (with conference suites and sports and health facilities) as well as opening their lecture halls and classrooms for the conference trade. But research and teaching are themselves complexes of activities, some of which are characteristically market settings (securing funds for research projects from non-government providers and putting on postgraduate and short courses).

At this point, though, the picture becomes fuzzy. For many of the activities which are income generating have features both of the public sector *and* of the market sector. The boundary between the two is increasingly fluid (see Enders and Jongbloed 2007). Biomedical research may be competitively funded, or part-funded, by charities and lead to findings published in (publicly available) academic journals. Students on postgraduate courses will characteristically secure their funding from several sources, even on a single course, including scholarships, private finance and employer support. Consultancy activity may lead to publications in the form of reports that are made freely available on the internet. So higher education markets are multiple, fuzzy and reflective of different interests and values: the private and the public; competitiveness and universality are all evident at once even in a single activity. Higher education markets constitute a nice example of 'liquid modernity' (Bauman 2000).

We should further acknowledge that universities evince differing postures towards market activities and that disciplines vary even within a single institution. Value positions towards markets differ across both universities and disciplines independently of each other. Consequently, there is both responsiveness and resistance towards markets, even within the one university. Occasionally, such oppositions will appear in vivid form: Senate may debate whether it should accept a 'donation' from a particular private source (say, to establish a new business school) but for the most part, this value diversity remains relatively subdued. It becomes more evident over matters of resource ownership. Whether departments should be 'cost centres' can give rise to difficulties, for some departments may be better placed to generate income (and be 'successful' in markets) more than other departments.

Markets in academic life

So far, I have made two points. First, a quasi-conceptual point: the matter of markets in higher education constitutes an ideological landscape, replete with interests. Crudely, on one side are the apologists for the so-called 'neo-liberal' repositioning of universities and endorsers of 'academic capitalism' (Slaughter and Leslie 1997); on the other side are those who hold to the idea of universities as sites of public and personal goods, independent of market constraints. Second, this ideological terrain is overlaid with empirical complexity, in which universities and – differentially – disciplines take up market challenges and opportunities with some alacrity. The empirical story is one of fuzziness and fluidity: fuzziness over what is to count as a market; and fluidity over the way in which markets and other influences spill over each other. This empirical story – I shall contend – both makes more difficult a resolution of the ideological debate and opens up spaces for such a resolution.

A market is said to constitute a means of allocating scarce resources in an economic way. Connected with this idea are further ideas: for example, that there are suppliers (plural) to meet wants and that those with wants have the ready resources in turn to pay for the service sought. Placed in the context of a higher education market, a number of issues then arise. For example, what is the likelihood that resources will always be available to those who wish to gain access to higher education? In short, who pays? Second, are there always suppliers available to meet legitimate needs? Does the local university actually offer the part-time courses that its putative students might want? Third, what is meant by 'economic' here? Is it implied that there might be courses in a single subject that are offered at different standards and so warrant different fee levels?

Here, I want to turn our attention to the pedagogical relationship. The key problem can be stated simply. It is the claim that the introduction of a market dimension harms the pedagogical relationship. The logic here is clear enough. The encounter between student and teacher should be a direct relationship in which there is a concern on the one side to teach and a concern on the other side to learn. Further, in higher education especially, learning requires that a student give of themselves, give themselves up to the material and experiences before them such that they can form their own authentic responses and interventions. It is in the context of such a view of the pedagogical relationship that the worldwide thirty-year-long research into 'deep learning' has had its point; and it is in this context, too, that the contemporary concern about plagiarism also has its point. The learning, characteristic of higher education, is one in which students go deeply into matters, with their offerings emerging as a result. All this, it is alleged, is prejudiced by the marketisation of the pedagogical relationship.

These concerns are pertinent and have plausibility on their side. The question I wish to raise here, however, is whether such an impairment of the pedagogical relationship is necessary or is contingent. If the relationship is a necessary (that is, inevitable) conjunction, then we are right to be concerned about marketisation *tout court*. If, on the other hand, such an impairment is merely contingent, then we need to inquire further into the conditions under which the pedagogical relationship is impaired. What factors in addition to marketisation are likely to produce such an impairment?

Let us address the second possibility first, that the introduction of the market dimension into the pedagogical relationship will not have an inevitably damaging effect but may do so only where other conditions are present. It is surely clear from the context that we observed in the first pages of this chapter that there are very many factors at work that might bear on the character of the pedagogical relationship. To summarise crudely, the institution, the discipline, the presence of research and scholarly opportunities, the relationship between a research strategy and the institution's parallel learning and teaching strategy, the degree and intensity of administrative requirements, the accountability and quality regime, the presence of the corporate sector, the student:staff ratios, and the institution's ethos and its care for its students are just some of the background factors that we noted earlier.

It is surely immediately apparent, from this listing, that the introduction of a market situation is but one factor among many that bears upon the pedagogical relationship. We may judge that there is no reason to believe that the presence of a market dimension into the pedagogical relationship will have a significance that overrides all those other factors. I conclude, therefore, that the proposition that there is only a contingent connection between the presence of a market situation and an impaired pedagogical relationship has at least *prima facie* validity. And it may be a weak connection at that.

Still, the more concerning situation remains. Could it be the case that the presence of a market situation *necessarily* induces an impairment of the pedagogical relationship?

The argument might run this way. In a market situation, students will be finding a significant level of resources to pay for their education. Any such student will expect a good return for that investment. They will expect both a high quality experience and a good degree. Such expectations will *necessarily* impair the pedagogic relationship, and on three grounds. First, the presence of such expectations will weigh such that the teacher will be focused on those expectations rather than on the matters in hand. Second, the expectation on the part of the student that his or her investment should in itself result in a return will diminish the readiness of the student to invest him or herself. The educational market economy is a 'closed' economy (Standish 2005). Higher education here becomes 'commodified'. Third, that particular expectation may generate a nervousness on the part of the institution to award a 'poor' degree (or, even worse, to judge any such student to have failed) and so standards will fall.

The argument in front of us is a logical argument. It is that the presence of a market dimension *necessarily* causes an impaired pedagogical relationship. But it is by no means clear that there is a necessary conjunction between a market situation and an impoverished pedagogical relationship. It is neither certain that teachers will necessarily focus on the students' expectations, nor that the student's finding the resources to meet the cost of his or her course will necessarily diminish his or her readiness to invest themselves in their experience, nor that the institution's standards and quality procedures will weaken. All of these are real possibilities – and there is probably sufficient evidence (if only anecdotal) to suggest that they all occur in practice. But the argument here is about a *necessary* conjunction between a market presence and a poorer student experience and that argument must fall. The possibilities in question are empirical and the extent of their occurring has to be a subject for empirical research.

We can conclude then that there is no reason (yet) to believe that the student becoming a customer will *necessarily* impair his or her experience as a student.

Consumer or customer?

In my introduction, I set up an opposition between two ideologies, on the one hand pro-market and on the other hand anti-market. I also intimated that I wanted to see if a third way, less value driven, was available. Let us, therefore, tackle those matters now.

We may begin by distinguishing the concepts of 'consumer' and 'customer'. A failure to make this distinction, and a consequent over-focus on the idea of 'consumer' as against 'customer', leads to some over-easy blows in the literature against the market (for example, Jonathan 1997).

A consumer is one who consumes the service extended to him or her. A customer, on the other hand, extends his or her custom to the provider. Characteristically, too, customers are deploying their own resources to make their purchases (of goods or services). In other words, the customer has a greater influence in a market relationship than the consumer. The provider of services or a product takes account of the customer, knowing that the *customers* can take their custom elsewhere. For the provider whose services or products are simply consumed, there is much less need to take account of its *consumers*. This is characteristically the case in situations where providers wield monopoly power (or influence such a proportion of the market as to be assured of there being users of the service or product in question). And this used to be – particularly in the UK – especially the case in public services. In such a situation, power lies with the provider much more than in the former situation.

It will be felt by many that, still, the language of either 'consumer' or 'customer' is in difficulty in the field of higher education. So far as the student qua consumer is concerned, the student is not simply a consumer of a monopoly service: there is competition between universities and the student can 'shop around'. Further, the student has to be intimately involved in his or her own higher education. Ultimately, the student has to educate herself. Her learning has to be her learning. It is not only that no one can effect the learning for the student. It is the more positive point that any learning of the first-hand kind implied by the idea of 'university' will be particular to the individual student. The connections, the insight, the meaning, the understanding involved, the potential that it opens, the imaginative world that it leads to: all these will be unique to a student as a person. So the idea of student-as-consumer of a standard product runs headlong into difficulty.

But here we have to return to the empirical story. Some universities are in effect in a monopoly situation. A student wanting to attend a local university may have no choice: there may be only one local university (and certainly only one offering, say, part-time courses). At the same time, so-called elite universities can be said to be in a corresponding situation in that the social positioning that they open out (in social, economic *and* cultural capital) exerts a hugely powerful attraction such that they have few rivals; and, for some would-be students, may have no rivals. Students attending either kind of university in those sets of circumstances may well be in effect 'consumers' of their higher education. Far from being engaged participants in their student experience, they may be willing to accept (to 'consume') the fare put before them for the economic and social (and even cultural) goods that they judge may accrue in the process, even if they harbour dissatisfaction about aspects of their experience.

What then of the idea of student-as-customer? As key elements in state policy over the past two decades or so, universities have been enjoined both to develop their specificity and exhibit greater diversity (cf. Huisman 1995), with bold 'mission statements' of their own. In the process, they have come to compete with each other for resources and for students (with students being the bearers of resources for the institution). Students, accordingly, have been constructed – it might be said – precisely as customers. With the introduction – in the UK and elsewhere – of fees borne directly by students, the identity of student-as-customer has been heightened. Students are the bearers of considerable resources and are being encouraged to think carefully about the university which they might attend.

At the same time, national course and institutional quality evaluations are in the public domain as are the outcomes of the annual student satisfaction survey. Data on which students can base their choices have expanded rapidly. Students are being all the time invited to frame themselves as customers making rational choices between competing providers. It is surely no coincidence that this heightening of students-as-customers has been accompanied by a shift on the part of the UK's national quality agency – the Quality Assurance Agency – from an overbearing and intrusive quality regime to a so-called 'light touch' regime (Williams 2009). That students are being invited to take on the burden of making considered choices becomes itself a powerful lever for quality improvement. Under those circumstances, a detailed, costly and heavy-handed state-controlled quality regime can be scaled down. Now, institutions can be relied upon to effect their own quality improvements in the wake of the arrival of a genuine student market.

An intermediate assessment of this situation is as follows. Students may be taking on the roles either of consumer or customer; and they may do so even willingly. The student-as-consumer is otiose to the proper meaning and value of higher education for higher education calls for an engagement on the part of the student that the role of consumer denies. The student-as-customer, however, is different. For precisely as customer, the student is engaged. The student has a stake in his or her experience. What is open is the character of the stake that the student as customer has in his or her experience.

Defending the indefensible

We now have the conceptual resources, I think, to defend the indefensible. The indefensible position is that markets and higher education can happily co-exist. The anti-marketers vehemently deny this. For them, the conjunction of higher education and markets are anathema on two grounds, pedagogical and social. Pedagogically, as we noted, the concept of higher education came to stand for a personal encounter with knowledge; one's learning has to be one's learning. Socially, higher education is held by the anti-marketers to stand also for public goods. My learning does not – or should not – deprive you of your learning. There is no zero-sum game here. Further, a genuinely higher learning, as well as being of personal value, should be of social value. And there is evidence, both in the USA and in the UK, that higher education confers substantial social benefits (HEFCE 2001). Graduates are more likely to be 'citizens', being involved in the working of democratic society, being socially responsible and living a more healthy lifestyle.

These two levels of arguments (personal and social), denying that markets and higher education can happily coexist, are inter-related. For connected with a conception of higher education as a personal good lie concepts of freedom, autonomy, authenticity, democracy and criticality. So the personal account of higher education has wide societal connotations. Recently, those connotations have been extended through the idea of student-as-global-citizen. Higher learning, in this concept, may have global benefits. It just may help to bring about a better world.

It is lines of reasoning such as this that lead to pleas for student fees to play no part in the funding of higher education. More generally, such lines of reasoning, it is held, run counter to the presence of markets per se. The personal conception of higher education is run aground by markets, in despoiling the student's untrammelled encounter with knowledge. Higher education is parochialised: the potential connection between a student's experience and infinity is broken (Standish 2005). The more social conception of higher education as a public good founders in the presence of markets because it hinders individuals' life chances in gaining access to higher education. Markets are characteristically unfair in their working for they seldom work on a 'level playing field'. In an unequal society, individuals' capacity to participate in higher education will be lessened by the development of a market situation. In turn, society becomes even more fragmented.

There is much in all of these arguments. The idea, therefore, that markets and higher education make uneasy bedfellows has right on its side. How, then, might the indefensible be defended? What defence in favour of markets might be adduced?

A first move lies in our earlier distinction between student-as-consumer and student-as-customer. To the extent that markets induce passivity on the part of the student and encourage a consumer-like stance, to that extent markets are to be regretted – and even resisted. However, it is far from clear that this is the typical mode of student being in the face of a market. On the contrary, it is plausible to argue that a consumer-like stance is likely to be engendered in a situation where higher education is *freely* available. There is no necessary association between markets and students-as-consumers.

Much more to the point is the suggestion that markets lead to students becoming customers. But there is again, I contend, no necessary conjunction here. That the student may take on some of the characteristics of a customer is not in itself problematic. The point turns on what it means for the student to become a customer. It means in the first place, as we saw earlier, that the student has a real stake in their own learning. But what might that mean? If it means that the student adopts a 'commodified' view of his or her learning with an eye to the short term (Gibbs 2008), then there is a problem. But this latter situation casts us back again to the problematic aspects of student-as-consumer. Here, the student comes to the view that his or her higher education can be bought much like any other product or service and absolves him or herself from much, if any, involvement in the character of the experience. The so-called commodification of higher education leads to a denial of responsibility on the part of the student.

I am not persuaded that this is a necessary concomitant of a market in higher education. To the contrary, the presence of a market may lead to a student taking a heightened interest in his or her learning, and that is all to the good. For such a heightened interest on the part of the student might lead to his or her *greater* efforts towards and energies in the learning required. Further, such a market situation might also lead, as the rhetoric in favour of markets urges, to a *heightened* attention to the teaching function on the part of the student's lecturers and tutors. We have here the makings of a virtuous circle in which the market may lead to *a mutually reinforcing attention to the pedagogical relationship for both student and teacher.*

Here lie inescapably, indeed, value judgements as to the very idea of higher education: just what is to count as a *higher* education?

Caring for the pedagogical relationship

I would contend the following. That there be a care (to use a Heideggerian term), a concern on the part of the teacher for the student; a care that runs parallel with the teacher's interests in his or her discipline or professional field. The care is twofold, therefore: a care for the discipline or professional field *and* a care towards the student. This latter care overlaps with the former care but is also beyond it. For in the pedagogical relationship in higher education, the teacher has an eye to the personally edifying properties of an authentic learning experience on the part of the student. Authentic encounters with a disciplinary or professional field can yield a transformation in the student (such that students on graduation day may be heard to say that 'this course has changed my life'). Higher education is able to elicit such transformations through the student being encouraged to 'leap forth' (Heiddeger 1998: 159) into strange, open-ended and challenging situations. In so doing, worthwhile dispositions and qualities are brought forward within the student. A higher education elicits 'epistemic virtues' (Brady and Pritchard 2003). (This is *not* to pretend that this always happens; there is much evidence to indicate that, in practice, higher education sometimes falls short of such a conception.)

As well as there being a care towards the student as a knower (an epistemological subject) and as an acquirer of skills (a practical subject), the teacher has also a care towards the student as a person. This ontological care trumps the other two forms of care, for it is through the student coming to have a larger sense of him or herself – aided by the formation of appropriate dispositions and qualities – that the student has the wherewithal to tackle challenging epistemological and practical tasks. The student is not going to put themselves out to advance their learning – practical or conceptual – unless they have a will to do so. While there lies a heavy responsibility on the teacher to help to nurture this unfolding, the student him or herself also bears responsibilities in helping him or herself to develop the relevant dispositions and qualities.

'Responsibility', 'authenticity', 'engagement': it is concepts such as these that help to fill out the character of the pedagogical relationship for both teacher *and* student. The question arises, therefore, as to the implications for such a conception of the pedagogical relationship of a heightened presence of the market relationship in it.

I have already suggested that a market relationship could help to *intensify* the level of engagement that both teacher and student have in the pedagogical relationship. But the issue presents itself as to the *kind* of engagement that a market relationship might induce.

The pedagogical relationship requires, we have just seen, a *putting-in* on the part of both the teacher and the student. The putting-in, however, differs between the two parties. The putting-in on the part of the students is towards the curriculum experiences in which they are involved – working on their essays, contributing to seminars, thinking through their contributions, taking care in the laboratory, trying out new skills, imagining themselves afresh in virtual life and engaging with other students. There is here an 'existential responsibility' on the part of the student (Gibbs 2004: 107). The putting-in on the part of the teacher is more complex. It is that of framing the curricular experiences *and* it is that of engaging the student. The teacher engages *with* the student in order to engage the student *on* his or her experiences. It is this asymmetry, this limited mutuality, that allows Buber to say of 'the relation of education' that it 'is based on a concrete but one-sided experience of inclusion' (2002: 118).

A worry is that a market presence may cause the pedagogical relationship to dissolve precisely at this point. Far from putting-in, a market presence may cause both student and teacher to adopt an extractive stance. The student's attention may be focused on the economic return that may accrue from gaining a degree (at this university); the teacher's attention may be focused on securing high satisfaction ratings in the course evaluations, so demonstrating the level of 'satisfaction' on the part of the students-as-customers. The 'other' in the pedagogical relationship becomes a means to an end quite outside the pedagogical relationship.

To the extent that such exteriorising is a function of a market presence in the pedagogical relationship, to that extent we must have misgivings about the 'marketisation of higher education'. But it cannot, I assert, be a necessary conjunction. It cannot *necessarily* be the case that a market presence causes this impairment of the pedagogical relationship. It may have precisely the effect of heightening the pedagogical relationship for there is now more at stake. Both teacher and taught may be stimulated to put more into the pedagogical relationship. Their in-putting may rise, not diminish.

Living with the marketised university

The marketised university is an intense university. Everything about it is intense. All its activities and its inner and external relationships become more intense. They take on extra dimensions, considerations and nuances. Partly, this comes about because the marketised university is a networked university, with multiple markets (audiences and stakeholders) as its context. Partly, this comes about because the marketised university is a layered university. Both its inner life and its exterior life are layered. Characteristically, within an institution, accompanying the pedagogical relationship, are both an institutional level of felt-life (its ethos) and a bureaucratic or organisational level of its life. In its external relationships, the university characteristically is engaged in primary and secondary relationships. Its primary relationships are those organisations with which it is engaged directly;

these include organisations and individuals with which either as purchaser or supplier it is in a direct market relationship. Its secondary relationships are engaged indirectly, such as with potential students. In both its inner and exterior life, market – or quasi-market – relationships can be found.

As we observed, worldwide, universities are moving into markets and it is doubtful that this particular genie can be put back into the bottle. Universities enjoy the economic freedom that markets open. The matter before us, then, becomes one of living in and with the marketised university: in what way(s) might this be possible? More particularly here, what might be a proper stance towards the market so far as students are concerned?

Markets as ideologies

Ideologies have *both* pernicious and virtuous aspects. They can be overbearing, brook no dissent, have only a partial reading of situations and claim to know persons' interests better than those persons themselves. At the same time, they can be energising, engendering greater collective spirit, and offer putatively rational bases for action. So too with the university 'in the marketplace' (Bok 2003). The presence of a student market can plausibly be promoted as a means of securing a higher quality experience, greater variety of provision and a surer determination of student wants. It can also be said to engender a heightened attention to the teaching function and a greater concern for the student. This is the account of marketisation in its virtuous form. But the market presence can be read in a more pernicious way, as we have seen. It can distort the pedagogical relationship, it can herald a shift from social knowledge to market knowledge (Buchbinder 1993), and it can exacerbate inequalities of access to higher education. It can, thereby, reduce both the potential personal and public benefits of higher education.

We have then this ideological contest, in which the marketisation of higher education is seen alternatively as having either virtuous or pernicious qualities. How, then, move forward? The implications of the explorations in this chapter (as well as other chapters in this volume) are surely twofold. First, the market is here to stay in higher education; there can be no ratcheting back in any substantial way. Second, ways need to be found such not merely that (a) the pernicious effects of the market presence are ameliorated but also that (b) the virtuous aspects are heightened. *Both* (a) and (b) are crucial.

Characteristically, the contending adherents in this dispute favour either (a) *or* (b). The anti-marketers put their faith in ameliorating the corrupting effects of marketisation. They call for fees to be abolished or reduced and for a good provision of bursaries (and even call in the UK for a national bursary scheme). The marketers, on the other hand, look to a heightening of the virtuous aspects, to greater responsibility being placed at the local level, and for more information to be made available to students (both prior to admission and during their studies). Largely missing in the debate are considerations as to how the pernicious effects of marketisation on the pedagogical relationship might be mitigated and how the virtuous effects of marketisation might be enhanced. Love (2008) is a welcome exception to this state of affairs.

Conclusion

We cannot escape the presence of ideology in higher education and so have to find ways of living effectively with it. Marketisation is one such ideology. As with all ideologies, it has both its virtuous and its pernicious elements. Unfortunately, the devil tends to have the best tunes: it will be the pernicious elements of marketisation that come to dominate proceedings unless countervailing measures are taken. At the heart of the emergence of the student-as-customer lies the pedagogical relationship. It is possible not just that the pernicious aspects of marketisation can be ameliorated but also that its virtuous aspects can be heightened. That is perhaps the crucial pedagogical challenge of our times.

References

Barnett, R. (2003) *Beyond All Reason: Living with Ideology in the University*. Buckingham: Open University Press.
Bauman, Z. (2000) *Liquid Modernity*. Cambridge: Polity.
Bok, D. (2003) *Universities in the Marketplace: The Commercialization of Higher Education*. Princeton: Princeton University.
Brady, M. and Pritchard, D. (eds) (2003) *Moral and Epistemic Virtues*. Oxford: Blackwell.
Buber, M. (2002) *Between Man and Man* (2nd edn). London: Routledge.
Buchbinder, H. (1993) 'The market oriented university and the changing role of knowledge', *Higher Education*, 26: 331–47.
Enders, J. and Jongbloed B. (eds) (2007) *Public-Private Dynamics in Higher Education: Expectations, Developments and Outcomes*. Bielefeld: transcript Verlag.
Gibbs, P. T. (2004) *Trusting in the University*. Dordrecht: Kluwer.
Gibbs, P. T. (2008) 'Marketeers and educationalists – two communities divided by time?', *International Journal of Educational Management*, 22(3): 269–78.
Heidegger, M. (1998) *Being and Time* (3rd edn). Oxford: Blackwell.
Higher Education Funding Council for England (HEFCE) (2001) *The Wider Benefits of Higher Education*. (Report, July, 01/46, by J. Bynner and M. Egerton). Bristol: HEFCE.
Hills, G. (1999) *From Beggars to Choosers: University Funding for the Future*. London: Politeia.
Huisman, J. (1995) *Differentiation, Diversity and Dependency in Higher Education*. Twente: Lemma/CHEPS.
Jonathan, R. (1997) 'Illusory freedoms: liberalism, education and the market', *special issue of Journal of Philosophy of Education*, 31(1).
Love, K. (2008) 'Higher education, pedagogy and the "customerisation" of teaching and learning', *Journal of Philosophy of Education*, 42(1): 15–34.
Marginson, S. (2007) 'The new higher education landscape', in S. Marginson (ed.) *Prospects of Higher Education: Globalization, Market Competition, Public Goods and the Future of the University*. Rotterdam: Sense.

Reid, I. (1996) *Higher Education or Education for Hire? Language and Values in Australian Universities.* Rockhampton: Central Queensland University.

Slaughter, S. and Leslie, L. L. (1997) *Academic Capitalism: Politics, Policies and the Entrepreneurial University.* Baltimore: Johns Hopkins University.

Standish, P. (2005) 'Towards an economy of higher education', *Critical Quarterly*, 47(1–2): 53–71.

Williams, P. (2009) *The Result of Intelligent Effort: Two Decades in the Quality Assurance of Higher Education.* London: Institute of Education.

Chapter 5

Adopting consumer time and the marketing of higher education

Paul Gibbs

> If there is a degree of passivity then, I hope, that without rejoining our student population to take to the barricades, that they become pickier, choosier and more demanding consumers of the higher education experience.
>
> (Lord Mandelson 2009)

Introduction

Time and temporality have received little attention in consumer, marketing or, until recently, higher education literature. This chapter attempts to compare the notions of timing implicit in education as *paideia* (transitional personal growth) with that implicit in consumerism and the marketing practices which foster it. This investigation uses Heidegger's three notions of being and their corresponding concepts of time to understand the phenomena of education and consumers. It suggests that the consumerist notion of time embedded in marketing tools changes what higher education might be through how individuals understand their being.

In my conceptual discussion I challenge higher education to resist the mission's being temporalised by consumerism.

Adopting consumer time: the dangers for higher education

My discussion is set against increasing corporate and government inroads into the realm of education, taking power from the academics and demanding that 'education serve the dictates of the marketplace and its demand for economic growth, [and] through the inroads of advertising and marketing' (Norris 2006: 459). This creates what Young (2002) considers to be the bureaucratic and machine-like modern university in which it is no longer customary to find teachers and students but 'suppliers' and 'consumers', with all that this entails. As a result academics may experience anxiety and alienation over what they take students to be and what they take themselves to be. In this crowding of activities in time, what is lost is the time to think.

These changes are having an impact on the very nature of education through changes in students' and academics' pace of work and their time perspectives of the form of education that institutions deliver. For example, Guthrie and Neuman (2007) suggest that traditional collegiate, academic decision-making methods are being threatened as the university becomes more responsive to the needs of the market. Moreover, Ylijoki and Mäntylä (2003) propose that there is a reduction of 'timeless time' (time not controlled by external constraints; time for reflective thought) and an increase in 'scheduled time' with its external imposition and accelerating pace. Clegg (2003), Ylijoki and Mäntylä (2003) and Ylijoki (2004) claim it affects research by accelerating the pace of work; decreasing autonomy over time management; causing a higher proportion of work on short-term projects; and increasing time pressures. Barnett (2007) has discussed that for students and academics alike there has been a transition from a time when both past and future were experiences within the being of the present, to one where temporality has become disintegrated and a linear sense of time predominates. To help understand the challenges faced by higher education communities and how they question their seemingly irresolute adoption of the tempo and rhythm of the world of the consumer I call upon a Heideggerian perspective on time. I first discuss Heidegger's complex ideas on time and then compare them to the characteristics of education, consumerism and marketing. Finally, I ask questions concerning the effect of marketing on the promotion of higher education's own temporality.

The temporality of Heidegger and time

Heidegger's approach to time is complex and as in all his work he tends to invent his own vocabulary. For our purposes this means three different categories of time and being. At the centre of Heidegger's understanding of being is the rejection of a singular idea of being, and the suggestion that it can take one of three forms. Each has associated with it a specific notion of time.

The first and most primordial form of being is 'Dasein', and its temporality in making sense of itself is called originary temporality.[1] Originary temporality is not the sequentialism that we commonly associate with temporality, where the future succeeds the present, which in turn succeeds the past. It is, as Blattner explains, 'a temporal manifold that can be present in any given moment of sequential time' (1999: 92). Originary temporality thus contains notions of the past and future integrated within the present. They are made known through horizons and are never brought actually into the present. This is because the future is not a latter-day now and the past is not an 'earlier than' now; they are not of our common understanding where the future is attained and recedes into the past. Moreover, the originary past is that which is already there; our social history. It is what we are attuned to, not a personal past which has been but one present that shapes our own present and that of others.

For instance, I can take on the role of a professor but the existential becoming of a professor is always futural; something to become. I can act in ways that are 'for-the sake-of' becoming a professor and be called a professor, but I can never reach what it is like to become a professor. This is a strange notion, but one we recognise in our everyday dealings with people. For example, people sometimes obviously overstate what they are in place of what they want to be. They may disguise their true identity, but are often 'out-ed' as frauds as their actions show them not to have the skills required of such a position. This is the existential notion of being that I propose ought to be fostered by higher educational institutions. It will not require the denial of other forms of being and times but will seek to use them purposefully as Dasein takes a stand on what it might be. I have called this Mode 1 time.

The second form of being is that of equipment, which gains its meaning from its cultural significance. The basis of its being is in its 'in-order-to' use in our practices; they are a means to an end. They form referential totalities such as an office, bedroom, lecture theatre or sports stadium which help us define ourselves within those worlds. The absence or malfunction of this equipment may cause us anxiety about our location or skills. For instance, with no whiteboard, chairs, PowerPoint or students, the room barely signifies to us that we are lecturers, in a lecture theatre, ready to start lecturing. Equipment is 'ready-to-hand' and its mode of time is world-time; a world that is signified by equipment. It is the equipmental structure of our environment that bestows its familiarity and allows us to understand what practices are appropriate and acceptable in this world. I have called this Mode 2 time.

Our everyday practices are performed and are deemed appropriate in worlds, for example the world of work or the world of the family. For here we tend not to take a stand on what we might be (that is Heidegger's notion of authenticity) but allow ourselves to be carried along with what others may want us to be; we fit in, we are accepted and find comfort in being just one of the crowd. Heidegger calls these worlds 'worldhoods' to distinguish them from the universe, and through them we begin to realise what we might be. These worlds' significance and meaning is derived from our practices and the use of equipment. The time that structures these worlds is a time that enables us to understand ourselves within that world and go about our social lives. Heidegger refers to it as 'datable time' in which entities have duration – a time span – and their temporal relationship defines the temporal structure of world time:

> The 'now', the 'then', and the 'on that former occasion' thus have a seemingly obvious relational structure which we call 'datability' [Dateierbarkeit]. Whether this dating is factually done with respect to a 'date' on the calendar must still be completely disregarded. Even without 'dates' of this sort, the 'now', the 'then' and the 'on the former occasion' have been dated more or less definitively.

(Heidegger 1962: 459)

The infrastructure of datable time is populated by the times to do something; to work, to play, to lecture and to have lunch. It is experienced differently depending on the circumstances of their occurrence; they are experienced and remembered in Mode 2 time. We temporalise ourselves by giving time for what the situation demands, whereas in what I will refer to as Mode 3 time, everything has a time when it happens.

The significances of these times are understood through their publicness. This aspect of our being is manifest in social acts of being with others, through which others can understand the same significances as ourselves. The temporal present – the now – provides the context in which this time is located and allows a succession of presents which is our common understanding of temporality: a past, a future and a present. For Heidegger, it is the time which turns out to be the kind of time in which the ready-at-hand (equipment identified as ready to use in order to do something) and the present-to-hand (objects whose function is not relevant to the way in which-the-world is encountered) are revealed. This 'requires that these entities which are not of the character of Dasein shall be called entities *within-time*' (Heidegger 1962: 465). Blattner summarises well this everyday experience of time as:

> the Now that spans from the formerly (the Earlier) to the then (Later on), which is dated by some event or activity in the world, which is significant in that it is appropriate or inappropriate for action, and which is public, accessible to all.
>
> (Blattner 1999: 134)

The third form of being is that of independent objects with characteristics which distinguish them and remain with them such as stones, trees or stars. They are present-at-hand and understood through inspection, for instance scientific inquiry. They have a mode of time that is called 'ordinary time'. The time of the universe is appropriated by Heidegger to give a social dimension to the durability and datability of world time, described above. This ordinary time is derived from ordinary notion of time. It is manifest within 'the horizon of concern with time which we know as astronomical and calendrical *time-reckoning*' (Heidegger 1962: 455). This is what I refer to as Mode 3 time.

We use it to reckon how we can describe the world of entities; it is abstract and successive; it is clock and calendar time. It is time in which the equipment and entities are encountered within time. Yet, as Heidegger describes, this temporal notion of time is not our ordinary understanding of time. This time levels off and covers up the temporality and shows itself as a sequences of 'nows' which are constantly 'present-at-hand',[2] simultaneously passing away and coming along. Time is understood as a succession, as a 'flowing stream' of 'nows', as the course of time (Heidegger 1962: 474).

In this sense, our everyday existence as 'Dasein' is determined by our realisation of our originary temporality (Mode 1 time) as presented through our everyday practices. If we hide our own temporality and live in the present, we become 'averaged'. That is, we accept the tranquillity of others as our norm. Such tranquillity is encouraged in a world where everything and everybody exists to become the equipment of others and to become consumers for the sake of consumption, rather than to take a stand on their own temporality and to understand their possibilities for themselves.

This third mode of time, world time, clock time, is the world of consumerism, where we use up time to secure the benefits we desire to be at home, unquestioningly as any other within our consumer societies. In educational terms time is an obstacle to be overcome so more consumption can take place. This requires shorter courses, the rejection of un-assessed work (for time is wasted in lingering), immediate feedback and precisely defined clusters of knowledge to be identified and consumed. There is no time to become, only time to be what we have consumed.

In summary, for Heidegger, there are three modes of being, each associated with a distinct notion of time. By temporalising being, Heidegger offers a basis for understanding how practices engage us with our worlds. Moreover, should we fail to recognise these differences and confuse their temporal forms, we run the risk of saying that temporality is something which is ' "earlier" and "later", "not yet" and "no longer". Care would then be conceived as an entity which occurs and runs its course "in time". The Being of an entity having the character of Dasein would become something *present-at-hand*' (1962: 375). Thus Heidegger allows us to conclude that if the temporality of being becomes that of the present-at-hand our being as Dasein is violated. Table 5.1 summarises these concepts.

The difference between ordinary (Mode 3 time), the abstract measurement of the flow of time and Mode 2 is that Mode 2 is relational to the events

Table 5.1 Heidegger's notions of Time and Being

Time	Modes	Examples
Originary or primordial time	Mode 1 time	Time of authenticity facing the everydayness of the world free from the time of other, seeking to become what one might be rather than being what others determine one to have become
Datable time, that is events located in relation to others. It is the shaping of separated notions of past, present and future	Mode 2 time	Time is located, not specific in terms of clock time more attuned to events and feelings
Time reckoning or clock measured linear time	Mode 3 time	Calculative time, sequential clock time, time is consumed and used

themselves based on their temporal significances, whereas Mode 3 is an external linear time within which the events can be externally measured. For instance, the great lecture is remembered as preceding the disappointment of the final exam result (Mode 2) and not that it occurred at 9.33am on 31.12.07 (Mode 3). We coordinate in abstract Mode 3 time.

Indeed all three modes of time are bound together degeneratively and dependently; ordinary time is a degenerative form of world time, and world time a degenerative form of originary temporality. Thus, the distinctive existential meaning of our being that is our originary temporality is levelled off. In allowing this we have an option to resist and so are culpable if we do not. We risk losing our essential being and become no more than resources to be packaged and consumed; that is our being ceases to be Dasein and we adopt the being of ready-to-hand or present-at-hand entities.

In the face of this, educational institutions are presented with a gigantic challenge to enable them to understand themselves and then foster the integrated notion of originary temporality if they see as their mission the development of humanistic values in addition to more practical ways of earning a living.[3] This requires them to encourage all their stakeholders – students, faculty and donors of funds – to be open to their world and not to encourage thought-less responding to the needs of others and in turn treating others and themselves as reservoirs of resource. Our individual historicality and our future possibilities need to be disclosed so that Dasein might truthfully take a stand on itself and our formal education ought, amongst its other functions, to facilitate this. It will require encouraging a stringency and resoluteness in educational institutions' activities through which they reveal the importance to our being of the originary future. In so doing they need to disclose a way of being in the present which is not the generalised way being of others which, I perceive, they currently do through notions such as performativity. I am looking towards the university to revitalise primordial temporality. If education institutions do not take up the challenge, but dwell in the tranquillity of external directives, always ready-to-hand to shape a Mode 2 or 3 future, they contribute to the nihilism currently manifest in consumerism and it becomes ever more inevitable.

Consumerism and the changing notion of time

Heidegger does talk about how the 'circularity of consumption for the sake of consumption is the sole procedure which distinctively characterizes the history of a world which has become an unworld' (1973: 107). However, the worldhood of consumerism is subsumed in his later works where he sees *technology* as totalising our practices and potentially our being. His solution is to understand how this occurs and to find ways of living with technology without taking on a technological way of being (see Dreyfus and Spinosa 2003). For instance, Heidegger says that technology is no mere means but that it is a way of revealing; a way of seeing the true meaning of an entity. If we give heed to this, then another whole realm of the essence of technology will open itself to us. It is the realm of revealing, i.e. of truth.

(Heidegger 1977: 12)

Moreover, Heidegger argues that we need to be struck by the strangeness of this statement and be drawn to understand what technology means. I will borrow his way of thinking but revert to Heidegger's initial concern with consumerism. How can we live within a consumerist society without being restricted in our openness to people and things? It is in this sense of its education's revealing purpose that I intend for us likewise to be struck by the consumerism now implicit in our higher educational system. To reinforce and sustain the background of consumerism, marketing management shapes the significance of our world.

Marketing is a grasping of the needs of consumers. It provides the structure for the development and promotion to consumers of products and services to perpetuate consumerism. Thus marketing provides both a hermeneutic to understand consumerism and a way of shaping it. To reinforce and sustain the background of consumerism, the university's marketing management shapes the significance of our academic world to all its audiences. This gives a common, circumspective meaning to equipment's function of encouraging the practices of consumerism and identification of entities as commodities and consumers. Indeed, for Norris, advertising and marketing 'become the signs and language and entire communicative structure within society, which come to dominate all other forms of discourse and significance' (2006: 466). They may also dominate world time by changing the everyday datability of events by crowding their relative pace, their rhythm and their expected duration. It has accelerated the rate at which these events are sequentially located in the temporality of originary time, bringing the future to us faster, allowing us to linger less in the present and requiring us rapidly to forget entities in the past. The increased density of our present takes away our time to act from our originary temporality of our authentic being and replaces it with the reckoning of ordinary time of a successive future, present and past.

This gives a common, circumspective meaning to equipment's function of encouraging the practices of consumerism and identification of entities as commodities and consumers. As I have already indicated, if our world view becomes one of things whose purpose is to be consumed, the very nature of their being and time is challenged and levelled down as Heidegger has suggested to a single dominant form of time, Mode 3 time.

This provides the context for the everyday datability of events to change their relative pace, their rhythm and their expected duration. It allows a measure to judge the accelerated rate at which these events are sequentially located, bringing the future to us faster, allowing us to linger less in the present and requiring us rapidly to forget entities in the past. The increased density of our present takes away our time to act from our originary temporality of our authentic being (Mode

1 time) and replaces it with the reckoning of ordinary time (Mode 3 successive future, present and past.

In our everyday mode of being we get swept up, irresolutely, in th understand ourselves in terms of these encounters which are thrust upon us. We busily lose ourselves in dealing with the rapidly changing events that concern us. This leads us in a certain way of talking: 'I have no time' (Heidegger 1962: 463). The time Heidegger means here is the notion of primordial temporality, lost to Mode 3, ordinary time. This may be willingly accepted in order to make sense of a world in our everydayness, but such an acceptance must be informed by its alternatives. This is a role education can play, awakening us to the possibility that we can take a stand against accepting the role 'for-the-sake-of' acquisition of commodities that can often, unquestioned, define our everyday practices.

Education as consumption

Is this what consumerism is doing, pressing us to turn away from knowing ourselves by taking a stance on ourselves and accepting the being of another consumer entity? Furthermore, if education institutions fully embrace consumerism, where 'for-the-sake of which' is immediate consumption, will it level down the potential for *us to* develop our own authentic Dasein with the help of higher education institutions? If it does not resist consumerism by developing our authentic being through its ordinary temporality, we need to question whether institutions are offering a distinctive mission of challenging society or whether they are just delivering consumer ideology and practice. This interpretation is very important, for our being is constituted as primordial temporality and is evident by our practices. If we act as consumers in the world of consumer time, what does it make of our being? Does it lead to the commodification of being, in such a way that it risks ceasing to be 'Dasein'?

Universities who promote education as a commodity by offering hedonistic gratification and routes to careers reduce our existential potential to be, into a fixed social status designed to assist us to consume. Klassen reports, for example, that in the marketing of higher education institutional values and priorities are usually symbolised by the message 'that students will not need to change in order to be successful' (2000: 21). Even more disturbingly, he concludes that for the students in half his sample, 'the perspective of college life offered is practically devoid of commitment and loyalty to anything beyond having a good time while waiting to graduate'. The impact of these changes is summarised by Hassan, who observes

> the commercialization of the university is primarily an economic and political process of transformation that has little if anything to do with education, knowledge production and the well being of either staff or students. What is more, these changes are all being refracted through the prism of neo-liberal ideology.
>
> (Hassan 2003: 77)

How might we resist a contemporary focus on instrumentality and restore a notion of time for both thought and thoughtfulness in our students? To use the terminology of Giroux and Giroux (2004), how do we restore the public time gifted for the use of the university for thinking, reflection and critical appraisal of society, its knowledge and its moral positioning? As they insightfully reflect, time 'refers not only to the way in which temporality is mediated differently by institutions, administrators, faculty and students, but also how it shapes and allocates power, identities, and space through a particular set of codes and interests' (2004: 226). This is an ontological approach and more like the education suggested by Barnett (2007). It has not the linearity of production, but a grasping of meaning in terms of temporality. The difference is that, instead of the being of objective presence, it is being that can project its own possibility.

In allowing a consumer marketing concept to create a form of educational experience appropriate for marketing techniques, then well-being unconcealed through education is potentially compromised by the totalisation of the marketing concept. This is a process where we become something rather than someone and where consumption of the known holds sway. Marketing is not the only technology which is enframing of education – it is being forced by policy makers to do something for which it was not intended – but neither is it benign. If we continue to market education through the temporality required by the market then education will lose its transcendental potential and adopt a functionality of the market. So the irony is that by securing the resources for education, marketing changes the educational essence which these resources were intended to liberate.

The technological world of planning seeks to populate the future, to make it a linear extension from the past through present, usually by extrapolation. It owns time through the hegemony of determinism and it thus ignores the heuristics of the decision-making of a multifaceted potential student population. How else could we seek to *anticipate* rather than guess what will satisfy consumers' requirements? This rationality seeks to transcend the reality of these heuristics and stands as a signifier of reliability, competence and prudence. Such implicit application moves marketing away from a creative endeavour into the nihilism of determinism, of a time devoid of temporality and where the *techne* of planning is used without the need for the wisdom of experience as it relates the revelation of what is being marketed. This is the new educational marketing myopia.

My argument should not however be set against an educational system that has diverse institutions each offering a specific form of educational experience. My concern is with the practices employed, perversely, to encourage that diversity being used to totalise the actual educational offering, turning it into a commodity and changing student future possibilities into current cost benefits.

Concluding discussion

I have tried to suggest that consumption and education have, and ought to have, different temporal realities. Moreover, if consumption's time becomes the process which shapes the temporality of our educational goals, educational institutions cease to add significance to our world. The danger is that 'consumption of education' replaces our notions of education as a means to think of a future of imagination, hope and opportunities not yet known, with sequential and knowable 'nows' – a view of education based on our being in the world of consumption.

Further, I have suggested that when universities employ marketing techniques designed to perpetuate consumerism such an approach when adopted ought to create a dilemma for the university leadership: what are they seeking to achieve through marketing and why? The purpose of marketing is to achieve predetermined ends through the application of marketing skills and technologies. It has explicit goals – market share, sales volumes or profit, and an implicit desire to trap the consumer in their present 'in-order-to' buy – but at what cost? Naidoo and Jamieson have indicated that under a consumer notion of entitlement a student disposition 'may have negative ramifications for the development of higher order skills and more importantly, the dispositions and attitudes required for autonomous, lifelong learning' (2005: 273).

For Heidegger, in such a world 'the human is challenged forth to comport himself in correspondence with the exploitation and consumption: the relation to exploitation and consumption requires the human to be in this relationship' (2003: 63). Is this what education ought to be about? Or is it inevitable in these times of consumerism? Not according to Barnett, who offers a distinctive notion of education which needs its own time and is identified by him as 'pedagogical time' (2007: 53); a time for ontological change. It is defined by a time during which the institution can foster the willingness of students to 'venture forth' into the unknowable future beyond their studies with the confidence and trust nurtured in the academy to face the uncertainty of the future. It creates the time for the student to become, through the experience of higher education. In so doing so the student becomes able to confront the anxiety of the future with confidence, creativity and criticality. It does not achieve this by describing the unknowable as some form of predictable, yet inauthentic, anxiety-free extension of the present. Moreover, Barnett recognises the tension between this pedagogical time and the market's notion of consumable linear time, arguing that the market 'jostles with and even threatens to crowd out the pedagogical relationship' (2007: 9).

In conclusion, rather than rendering themselves up to the consumerism embedded in marketing, higher education institutions should attempt to promote a community where individuals seek to reclaim their existential temporalities through trust and meaningful engagement with their world. In the crowded world of skills, training and education providers, what would perhaps ironically give some universities 'a competitive edge' is to resist the tools and the consequences of consumerism. If higher education institutions continue to follow traditional marketing practices they will replace worthy education, as a facilitator of human experience, endeavour and imagination, with educational propaganda.

Marketing ought to be one of the concerns of higher education as it faces consumerism and I have attempted to illustrate this in terms of time. This is not an argument to bar the virtues of education from all those willing to benefit: quite the opposite. We need to increase the expansion and penetration of *paideia*, but not a consumerist education. We need marketers who are educationalists with understanding and belief in the value of education to promote it, even in the face of financial pressure from those who would turn the worth of education into a valuable, consumable commodity.

Notes

1   According to Kisiel, in his 1992 translation of Heidegger's *History of the Concept of Time, the* translation of '*ursprüngliches*' can equally be 'primordial' or 'originary'. I will use them as substitutes, making the choice on the basis of what seemingly suits best.
2   Heidegger contrasts the readiness-to-hand of equipment with the presence-at-hand of mere things.
3   I am reminded here of Buber's characterisation of educative relationships as 'in order to help the realization of the best potentialities in the pupil's life, the teacher must really mean him as the definite person he is in his potentialities and his actuality; more precisely, he must not know him as the sum of qualities, strivings and inhibitions, he must be aware of him as a whole being and affirm him in his wholeness' (1959: 131).

References

Barnett, R. (2007) *A Will to Learn: Being a Student in an Age of Uncertainty*. Buckingham: Society for Research into Higher Education and Open University.

Blattner, W. (1999) *Heidegger's Temporal Idealism*. Cambridge: Cambridge University Press.

Buber, M. (1959) *I and Thou*. Edinburgh: T and T Clark.

Clegg, S. (2003) 'Learning and teaching policies in higher education: mediations and contradictions of practice', *British Educational Research Journal*, 29(6): 803–19.

Dreyfus, H. L. and Spinosa, C. (2003) 'Further reflections on Heidegger, technology, and the everyday', *Bulletin of Science Technology Society*, 23: 339.

Giroux, H. and Giroux, S. (2004) *Take Back Higher Education*. New York: Palgrave Macmillan.

Guthrie, J. and Neumann, R. (2007) 'Economic and non-financial performance indicators in universities', *Public Management Review*, 9(2): 231–52.

Hassan, R. (2003). *The Chronoscopic Society: Globalization, Time and Knowledge in the Network Economy*. New York: Peter Lang.

Heidegger, M. (1962) *Being and Time* (trans. J. Macquirrie and E. Robinson). Oxford: Blackwell.

Heidegger, M. (1973) 'Overcoming metaphysics', in *The End of Philosophy* (trans. J. Stambaugh). New York: Harper & Row.

Heidegger, M. (1977) 'The question concerning technology', in *Basic Writing* (trans. D. F. Krell). London: Routledge, pp. 307–42.

Heidegger, M. (1992) *History of the Concept of Time* (trans. T. Kisiel). Bloomington: Indiana University Press.

Heidegger, M. (2003) *Four Seminars* (trans. A. Mitchell and F. Raffoul). Bloomington: Indiana University Press.

Klassen, M. L. (2000) 'Lots of fun, not much work, and no hassles: marketing images of higher education', *Journal of Marketing for Higher Education*, 10(2): 11–26.

Mandelson, Lord (2009) responding to questions at CBI launch of *Stronger Together* as reported by BBC News. Available from http://newsvote.bbc.co.uk/mpapps/pagetools/print/news.bbc.co.uk/2/hi/uk_news/education/8316658.stm?ad=1 (accessed 27 October 2009).

Naidoo, R. and Jamieson, I. (2005) 'Empowering participants or corroding learning? Towards a research agenda on the impact of student consumerism in higher education', *Journal of Education Policy*, 20(3): 267–81.

Norris, T. (2006) 'Hannah Arendt and Jean Baudrillard: pedagogy in the consumer society', *Studies in Philosophy and Education*, 24: 457–77.

Ylijoki, O.-H. (2004) 'Orientations of future in academic work', paper presented at the 20th EGOS Colloquium *The Organization as a Set of Dynamic Relationships*, sub-theme 22, July 1–3, Ljubljana University, Slovenia. Available from http://www.uta.fi/tasti/papereita/ylijoki_egos04_paper.pdf (accessed 18 February 2008).

Ylijoki, O.-H. and Mäntylä, H. (2003) 'Conflicting time perspectives in academic work', *Time & Society*, 12(1): 55–78.

Young, J. (2002) *Heidegger's Later Philosophy*. Cambridge: Cambridge University Press.

Chapter 6

Complexity theory – an approach to assessment that can enhance learning and transform university management

Lewis Elton

The Humboldtian model

That a Prussian civil servant's memorandum of nearly 200 years ago could be seriously relevant today needs justification. Humboldt's memorandum dealt with the political situation at the time – Prussia had suffered a total defeat at the hands of Napoleon, and so the proposed relationship of the new university to the state was crucial. Yet, I quote:

> The State must not treat its universities either like 'Gymnasia' – the most prestigious of the secondary schools – or as special schools, nor use them in either a technical or a scholarly manner. On the whole, it must not demand anything that is immediately relevant and directed towards them, but have an inner conviction that – when they achieve their own objectives – they will also fulfil those of the State, and from a much higher standpoint, a standpoint which makes it possible to cover far more and brings with it quite different strengths and levers than would be directly available to the State.
>
> (Humboldt 1810, my translation)

Thus, if universities are left to their own devices, they will pursue the wishes of the state (in addition to their own wishes) more successfully than if ordered by the state. In the recent past, this astonishing prescription has been interpreted in terms of complexity theory. Both complexity and collegiality are relevant to university assessment.

Complexity and collegiality

According to Stacey *et al.* (2000: 106), a complex adaptive system 'consists of a large number of agents, each of which behaves according to its own principles of local interaction'. What remains tacit is that this approach requires the 'agents', i.e. academics, individually and in small groups, to be in broad agreement concerning their aims and that those of the state should be among them, although not necessarily their only aims. However, if governments attack fundamental academic principles, such as academic freedom, the relationship between universities and government becomes fraught; the problem today is crass interference by government in a situation where less interference could lead to peaceful resolution of differences. Present problems are aggravated by the government 'buying off' academics at the top level through the encouragement of top-down management, to 'rule' their institutions, in contrast to their traditional role as the first servants of academia. There is a firm belief by government that in this age of the 'market', universities must be part of it and hence ought to be treated like a form of business.

According to Humboldt, universities best serve the community if governed collegially and left free from direct external interference. This apparent paradox has been interpreted in terms of complexity theory and, continuing Stacey's quotation,

> Coherent behavioural patterns of great complexity can emerge when large numbers of agents interact with each other in a self-organising way according to simple relational rules . . . In these systems, agents residing on one scale start producing behaviour that lies one scale above them: ants create colonies, urbanites create neighbourhoods.
>
> (Stacey *et al.* 2000: 154)

And, arguably, academics create disciplinary departments.

Assessment in universities and by the state

Let us consider this in the context of something that is at the heart of higher education. The relevance of the above to issues of assessment in universities – whether the assessment of students by universities or of universities by outside bodies – lies in the realisation by Humboldt that direct interference by outside bodies is counterproductive. Both have led to forms of assessment based on predetermined outcomes, i.e. in terms of so-called performance indicators (PIs), which conflict with the well-established consequences of 'Goodhart's Law' (Elton 2004) that 'when a measure becomes a target, it ceases to be a good measure'; as well as to the additional one of 'playing games'– from students concentrating on the examined as opposed to the taught curriculum, via plagiarism and other forms of cheating, to teachers teaching to the test.

Problems of traditional assessment often arise from a conflict between reliability and validity; in general, assessment in terms of predetermined outcomes is more reliable but less valid. All this has been known for the best part of a century; sadly, the interference by both governmental bodies and top-down management in educational processes, well understood for a long time, has now unnecessarily created these problems.

The real fault of much of the current assessment in universities is that much of it is in terms of predetermined outcomes and thus is unable to assess such important abilities as creativity – and also criticality (Johnston 2004) – which can only be assessed in terms of themselves. Creative work must be more than merely 'new'; it must show originality and it must in some way be significant. Furthermore, it cannot be produced under controlled conditions. While it is possible to lay down general rules for the recognition of creative work, it is not possible to specify these in detail. Each such piece of work has to be judged by experienced examiners on criteria which such examiners have developed through experience. Because the work is criterion referenced, norm-referenced methods of assessment, in which a candidate is compared with others in the group which is being assessed and grades are given accordingly, are inappropriate.

What all this has to do with complexity theory is that that theory provides a justification for keeping the state – and indeed any outside body – at arm's length.

Beyond complexity theory?

Unfortunately, keeping the state at arm's length is too negative an approach by itself, because many of the current deficiencies in university assessment arise from a lack of understanding within universities. Most academics do not consider university teaching and assessment researchable and teach as they were taught by people who taught as they had been taught, going back in an unholy pseudo-apostolic succession to the Middle Ages.

An additional explanation is provided by a misapplication of the concept of academic freedom, which makes it unprofessional to interfere with a colleague's teaching.

Modern developments in teaching and learning

While the Humboldtian University was revolutionary in other areas, it was conservative in its approach to teaching and learning. Major developments there in the past thirty years – none of which are part of the Humboldtian University – are:

- a move from teaching to learning
- the relevance of research into teaching and learning
- the scholarship of teaching and learning.

These have led to wholly new models of teaching and learning, such as, for example, problem based learning (PBL), with an adaptation to disciplines where problem situations are not provided by the applied nature of the discipline. Probably the first such approach was that of Hutchings and O'Rourke (2002), to English literature. They called it 'Enquiry Based Learning' (EBL), the principles of which are:

1 Start with a problem (given or discovered) within a field of knowledge.
2 The solution of the problem leads to disciplinary structure, not conversely.

3 Learning is initiated by students and facilitated by teachers, it is thus student centred.
4 Problems are derived from the discipline or from the situation – they are presented without previous information.
5 Students usually work in small groups, often with agreed different roles.
6 Resources are available.
7 Group sessions often occur with several groups in the same room (several groups in the same room have been found more effective than groups in separate rooms – the noise acts as stimulant, not distraction).
8 The resulting experience is satisfying both intellectually and socially.
9 The role of the teacher is as a facilitator, not an authority.
10 Materials may be provided, but often have to be searched for.
11 The result is often a group report, with all the implications for assessment.

While this may appear far from Humboldt's concept of university study, it is in fact a logical consequence of his fundamental concept of *Lernfreiheit* (freedom of learning) that the predetermination of managed performance indicators undermines.

Lernfreiheit and assessment

If students' freedom to learn is fundamental to the learning process, then the way that they are assessed must be part of that freedom and students must take part in the decision as to how they are assessed and what they are assessed on. Appropriate assessment methods, such as self, peer and group assessment, all lead to collegial student learning and assessment, on the basis of individual student interests.

How to assess work that does not lead to predetermined learning outcomes was discussed by Eisner (1985) in terms of what he called 'Connoisseurship', i.e. a general expertise in a field of study. Although always part of traditional art education, it first entered the field of traditional disciplines in the 1960s through 'project work'.

Professionalism in teaching and learning

The Humboldtian University never extended its ideas of professionalism to the teaching and learning process; University professors continue to teach as they have been taught. Routine lecturing continues as the basic teaching method, although redundant after the invention of moveable type in the fifteenth century! This situation is beginning to change through the recent movement of the 'Scholarship of Teaching and Learning', which for the first time treats university teaching as a researchable and researched discipline (Elton 2008). This has led to new and student-centred approaches to learning, such as Enquiry Based Learning, and new approaches to assessment; it has proved possible to introduce these even in otherwise very traditional universities (see e.g. Russell *et al.* 2002).

Consequences of this approach to teaching, learning and assessment

The primary consequence of such an approach to teaching, learning and assessment is that it leads to 'learning for the sake of learning' as opposed to 'learning for external purposes'. This raises two questions:

1   Will such a 'learning for the sake of learning' approach be in some way less effective than a 'learning directed to future use' approach?
2   Will it motivate students more or less in their studies?

This must be to some extent a matter for conjecture, but there is evidence that the excitement created by a 'learning for learning's sake' motivates both teachers and students. Furthermore, although employers often expect students in their first employment to 'hit the ground running', different employers seem to have different understandings as to what that ground is and good employers provide targeted training for their employees.

The scholarship of teaching and learning

A way forward into the future may come from the movement known as the Scholarship of Teaching and Learning (SoTL), together with a recognition of the importance of the continuing development of academics in teaching and learning (CPD in HE).

To understand the meaning of SoTL, one must understand the meaning of the word 'scholarship' more generally. Humboldt was concerned with both research and teaching, and he established a fundamental dichotomy – not between research and teaching, but between university and school – according to which the university, in contrast to school, treats scholarship always in terms of not yet completely solved problems, whether in research or teaching, while school is concerned essentially with agreed and accepted knowledge. The consequence, as he says in a most thought-provoking comment of his memorandum, is that in universities the teacher is then not there for the sake of the student, but both have their justification in the service of scholarship.

The arguably most regrettable feature of the dichotomy between research and teaching is that it has led to a skewed value system of by now long standing, with research being considered significantly more prestigious than teaching. In contrast, SoTL aims to achieve – in the service of scholarship – not only a unity between the practice of teaching and learning and research into teaching and learning, but an overall unity of teaching and research, i.e. disciplinary as well as generic teaching and learning, together with disciplinary research and research into teaching and learning; all in the service of scholarship *(Wissenschaft)*. It is this originally Humboldtian approach to the work of universities, which is fundamental to SoTL.

If teaching is as important as research, and research into teaching is as important as research in the disciplines, then we should demand a preparation for SoTL equivalent but not necessarily equal to the kind of preparation required for disciplinary research. Thus, while the latter is normally at the level of a first degree in the appropriate discipline, this would not be appropriate as an introduction to SoTL, which is not normally taken up by academics until after they are established in their disciplines. It should therefore be in the form of continuing professional development and involve a postgraduate qualification – Diploma or Master's degree.

Continuing professional development of the academic profession

Adults learn best if they are actively involved in their learning, so that they internalise it, and if they see it as relevant to their needs. For the continuing development of academics, these needs arise out of their practice and problems created by it. Hence a programme of CPD for academic teachers must convince them that university teaching is a problematic and researchable activity. It is reasonable to postulate that this is best achieved through academic teachers reflecting on problems in their own teaching and then to attempt to solve these problems.

One possible approach to CPD for academics is therefore through Problem Based Learning (PBL), with the additional requirement that the problems must arise from on-going practice. Such PBL is radically different from normal PBL in university courses in one respect: the problems are not selected in advance by the course designers, but are chosen through negotiation by the academics in question together with their course tutors. The fact that the whole CPD process is then initiated by the academic teachers undertaking it also means that their learning will be self-initiated and autonomous, and not prescribed by others. A course of this kind, which was accredited by the Staff and Educational Development Association (SEDA), was developed some years ago at UCL as a distance learning course (Stefani and Elton 2002).

The consequences of complexity

As far as complexity is concerned, we have so far been concerned with its direct effect on assessment. However, its effects are far more general and far-reaching.

The traditional world view is essentially based on the physics of Newton – the future is predictable on the basis of a full knowledge of the past – and all modern life, including effectively all management practices, are based on this view.

In contrast, complexity theory not only leads to the double conclusion that the future is unpredictable, but that its unpredictability is unpredictable. This does not mean that one should not plan for the future; it *does* mean that one must be prepared for the future not to correspond to one's expectations and include that contingency in one's plans.

In terms of a German saying, which long predates complexity theory, 'erstens kommt es anders und zweitens als man denkt' (firstly it will be different and secondly than one thinks).

Conclusions

Back to the educational world. The most important – and possibly least expected – conclusion relates to the primacy of scholarship in universities. Traditionally, there was always an expectation in Britain that scholarship would underlie all university teaching, but this was rarely formalised and, indeed, it often remained tacit. One central aim of SoTL is to formalise this primacy of scholarship in both research and teaching.

A second – and arguably equally important – conclusion relates to the provision of appropriate continuing professional development in teaching and learning. The traditional view, although not always expressed as blatantly, was that one improved in teaching through imitation of role models – one taught, as one had been taught by academics who taught, as they had been taught, by . . . an apostolic succession, going back to the Middle Ages. This extraordinary view of teaching was based on a firm, although tacit, conviction that university teaching was not a researchable subject and that improvement in teaching was largely a matter of imitation on the basis of role models. However, this view is becoming less acceptable and continuing professional development in teaching and learning is becoming respectable.

Finally – and perhaps the key point here in response to the managerialism of the 'marketised' university – the success of SoTL in all its aspects is possible only in a collegial environment in which collaboration at the lowest level of interaction is legitimised through its effect on higher levels: the basis of complexity theory.

References

Eisner, E. W. (1985) *The Art of Educational Evaluation: A Personal View*. London and Philadelphia: The Falmer Press.

Elton, L. (2004) 'Goodhart's law and performance indicators in higher education', *Evaluation and Research in Education*, 18: 120–8.

Elton, L. (2008) 'Collegiality and complexity: Humboldt's relevance to British universities to-day', *Higher Education Quarterly*, 62: 224–36.

Humboldt, W. von (1810, reprinted 1957) *Über die innere und äussere Organisation der höheren wissenschaftlichen Anstalten in Berlin*. Auswahl und Einleitung von Heinrich Weinstock. Frankfurt: Fischer Bücherei, pp. 126–34.

Hutchings, W. and O'Rourke, K. (2002) 'Problem-based learning in literary studies', *Arts and Humanities in Higher Education*, 1: 73–83.

Johnston, B. (2004) 'Summative assessment of portfolios: an examination of different approaches to agreement over outcomes', *Studies in Higher Education*, 29: 395–412.

Russell, J. *et al.* (2002) 'Using the online environment in assessment for learning: a case-study of a web-based course in primary care', *Assessment and Evaluation in Higher Education*, 31: 465–78.

Stacey, R. D. *et al.* (2000) *Complexity and Management: Fad or Radical Challenge to System Thinking*. Abingdon: Routledge.

Stefani, L. and Elton, L. (2002) 'Continuing professional development of academic teachers through self-initiated learning', *Assessment and Evaluation in Higher Education*, 27: 117–29.

The marketised higher education institution

Vision, values and international excellence: the 'products' that university mission statements sell to students

Helen Sauntson and Liz Morrish

Aims of this chapter

The past two decades have seen vast changes in the organisation and ethos of UK universities. Most apparent to those who work within the academy has been the emergence of a neo-liberal governmentality in university management that appears to place economic rationalism at the core of its operating philosophy. This is a key principle of 'neo-liberal' practice. Harvey (2005: 3) provides a useful working definition of neo-liberalism:

> Neoliberalism is in the first instance a theory of political economic practice that proposes that human well-being can best be advanced by liberating individual entrepreneurial freedoms and skills within an institutional framework characterised by strong private property rights, free markets, and free trade. The role of the state is to create and preserve an institutional framework appropriate to such practices.

At the insistence of Thatcher's Conservative government in the 1980s, neo-liberal reforms were imposed on institutions that hitherto had not prioritised issues of profitability or capital accumulation. Shumar writes that state-funded institutions were seen as inefficient and in need of market 'discipline', and so liable for 'hyper-commodification' (2008: 69). In the decades since, they have been required to reposition themselves as simulacra of business, with annual appraisals, audits of teaching hours, transparency reviews of work practices, peer teaching evaluation, teaching quality and research audits. Central to neo-liberal and managerial reform has been an increased emphasis on personal responsibility (Ong 2006: 14); the objectives of the institution appear to be ordered around the benefit of managers (Clarke *et al.* 2000: 9); and there is an over-arching focus on capital accumulation (Harvey 2005: 160). Indeed, so far has the association cemented itself in the governmental mind that universities in 2009 became the provenance of the newly formed Department for Business, Innovation and Skills (BIS). The fact that there is no mention of education in its title at all is surely not a coincidence. This new climate has been described by Slaughter and Leslie (1997) and Canaan and Shumar (2008).

This chapter aims to examine the impact of mutually reinforcing discourses of capitalism, neo-liberalism, managerialism and marketisation on universities in the UK. We take as a particular case study – mission statements – what they represent and what they communicate, and we present as evidence the analysis of a detailed corpus linguistic analysis of all of the available mission statements for UK universities in the Russell Group, 1994 Group and Million+ group. We will examine the extent to which marketisation, commodification and globalisation play key roles in the university's construction of its own identity and 'brand'. We will also consider the ways in which students are positioned, simultaneously, as consumers, units of profit, and as 'products' of the university. Furthermore we question the extent to which mission statements represent uniqueness, or whether this claim is tempered by a kind of discursive uniformity and standardisation. Finally we will discuss whether there is any evidence of resistance or challenge to dominant discursive constructions of the neo-liberal university.

Marketisation, branding and mission statements

As discussed above, there are clear links between capitalism, neo-liberalism and managerialism. As governments in the US, UK, Australia and Canada have reduced their block grants to universities, academics have been forced to compete for scarce research funds, and these have increasingly been targeted towards areas seen to sustain economic priorities. In this way, faculty have been coerced into academic capitalism in order to maintain their research (Slaughter and Leslie 1997: 113–14). Shumar describes another market force – the 'mallification' of US universities, where campus bookstores have been turned over to chains such as Borders (in the US) or Blackwells (in the UK), and food services and halls of residence have been privatised. This has had the effect of blurring the boundary between public and private space, and of the purpose of academic space, and even education itself (Shumar 2008: 71–4). Of course, such a turn to capitalism has consequences for the system of values held by most academics. Slaughter and Leslie provide evidence that many academics have subordinated a philosophy of altruism in favour of the values of the market. This change, they note, has been driven by a dependence upon resources which are controlled by government priorities.

University managers have also sought to deliberately transform academic values, and this has largely been effected by a change in discourse. Fairclough provides one of the first critical studies of this new discourse in universities, referring to a concept he calls 'the technologization of discourse' (1995: 102). This he defines as:

> a process of intervention in the sphere of discourse practices with the objective of constructing a new hegemony in the order of discourse in the institution or organization concerned, as part of a more general struggle to impose restructured hegemonies in institutional practices and culture.

To this end, departments have been replaced by 'cost centres' which are headed by 'team leaders' whose duties resemble those of accountants rather than academics. Students have been repositioned as 'customers', who must be placated in the pursuit of a high ranking in the student satisfaction survey. Universities have recognised that a calculated redesign of discourse can be transformative of social and cultural relations within their walls, and this is embedded in mission statements. Administrators have mastered these discourses and demand to be spoken to in their own language by academics who are required to justify their working practices on a frequent basis. A large part of this managerialist redesign is carried out by retraining personnel in the new standardised and normalising discourses.

According to Harvey (2005), marketisation is a key principle of neo-liberalism, and despite universities offering what Mighall (2009) calls an 'immaterial product', they have been obliged to engage in self-promotion and marketing much more intensively than in the past. Mission statements are traditionally seen as part of an organisation's 'strategic plan' (Cochran et al. 2009; Pearce 1982; Pearce and David 1987), but in their haste to construct a unique appeal, universities have attempted to express their claims to purpose and distinctiveness through these documents. Such 'branding' remains an article of faith with senior managers, despite some doubt about whether, in the context of limited student finance and a fee cap of £3,000, there exists any significant competition in the 'marketplace' of universities. And, in the face of scepticism from their academic staff, who are often alienated by both the discourse and ethos of marketisation, what might be the appeal of branding to vice chancellors?

Mission statements for universities were almost unknown until the late 1980s, but are near universal in 2010. There were very few of our sampled websites where we failed to locate one. Pearce and David (1987: 109) provide the following definition of a mission statement:

> An effective mission statement defines the fundamental, unique purpose that sets a business apart from other firms of its type and identifies the scope of the business's operations in product and market terms . . . It specifies the fundamental reason why an organization exists.

Falsey expresses their purpose even more concisely 'A mission statement tells two things about a company: who it is and what it does' (Falsey 1989: 3, cited in Williams, 2008: 96).

The data and methods of corpus analysis

In this current study we assembled a corpus of university mission statements, accessed between April and June 2009. The corpus amounted to 13,630 words. Within this corpus, we identified three sub-corpora, representing the three earliest 'mission groups':

- Russell Group of the twenty major research intensive universities of the UK (16 universities sampled)[1]
- 1994 Group: nineteen smaller, internationally renowned, research-intensive universities (15 universities sampled)[2]
- Million+ group defines itself as a university think-tank. It mainly comprises post-1992 universities. (http://www.millionplus.ac.uk/who/index) (22 universities sampled).[3]

According to the Universities UK website: 'The Universities in the UK are diverse in their missions and location. A number of these have formed groups with common interests. These include the various regional university associations and also the so called "mission groups".'[4]

Sinclair (1991: 171) defines a corpus as 'a collection of naturally-occurring language text, chosen to characterize a state or variety of a language'. Corpus linguistics involves using a computer-held body of naturalised texts and a range of computerised methods, to explore aspects of language and language use. A main advantage of using corpus linguistics is that it enables us to make observations about language use which go beyond intuition and, because it is computer-based, it allows the exploration of patterns of language use which are not observable to the human eye.

Corpus analysis often starts with a simple analysis of word frequencies across the whole corpus or, as in our case, within each of the three sub-corpora which comprise the whole corpus. A word frequency list is a useful starting point for word-based corpus analysis as it can begin to reveal information about themes within the texts comprising the corpus. This can then provide a basis for further analysis. We compiled a list of words which had at least ten instances within each corpus, and then made a comparison of the word frequency lists across the three sub-corpora. This was a useful way of enabling us to see different themes and priorities across the three groups.

A next stage commonly used in corpus analysis is to consider the semantic environment of some of the most frequent lexical words in each corpus by examining their collocations. Sinclair (1991: 170) defines collocation as 'the occurrence of two or more words within a short space of each other in a text'. Examining a word's collocations can help to build up a semantic profile of that word which can contribute to revealing any underlying discourses and ideologies in the corpus. Using word frequency and collocation analysis together can provide a fairly good overview of the main themes, discourses and ideologies prevalent in each of the sub-corpora and can reveal the main discursive similarities and differences between them.

It is standard practice in corpus linguistics to remove the grammatical words from a word frequency list, so that the words presented are the lexical, or content, words. In our lexical word frequency lists for the three sub-corpora, we have additionally separated the frequent lexical words into word classes: nouns, verbs and adjectives. These frequency tables are presented as Tables 7.1 and 7.2.

Table 7.1 Noun frequency lists for the three sub-corpora

Russell	1994	Million+
1 University	1 Research (used as noun)	1 University
2 Research (used as noun)	2 Student*	2 Student*
3 World	3 University	3 Research (used as noun)
4 Student*	4 Mission	4 Learning (used as noun)
5 Vision	5 Teaching	5 Knowledge
6 Mission	6 Staff	6 Education
7 Activities	7 Quality	7 Vision
8 Excellence	8 Knowledge	8 Mission
9 Teaching (used as noun)	9 Learning	9 Staff
10 Staff	10 Academic (used as noun)	10 Academic (used as noun)
11 Knowledge	11 World	11 Commitment
12 Society	12 Excellence	12 Quality
13 Learning (used as noun)	13 Vision	13 Values
14 Environment	14 Environment	14 Teaching (used as noun)
15 Education	15 Education	15 Excellence
16 Quality	16 Development	16 Development
17 Impact	17 Statement	17 Community
18 Academic (used as noun)	18 Work	18 Needs (used as noun)
19 Innovation	19 Areas	19 Environment
20 Goal	20 Industry	20 Organisation
21 Future (used as noun)	21 Community	21 Institution
		22 Innovation
		23 Individuals
		24 World
		25 Statement

Table 7.2 Adjective frequency lists for the three sub-corpora

Russell	1994	Million+
1 International*	1 Highest	1 Social
2 Leading	2 Leading	2 Academic
3 Highest	3 Committed	3 New
4 Future	4 Social	4 Higher
	5 International*	5 Professional
	6 Intellectual	6 Educational
	7 Cultural	7 Cultural
		8 High
		9 Committed
		10 Potential
		11 International*
		12 Inclusive

Universities – marketing the product

When we examine the word frequency list for all three mission groups we find that *research* is a frequent item in all groups (most frequent for 1994 Group, second most frequent for Russell Group and third most frequent for Million+ group). This reveals some of the concerns about the 'product' of each group of universities. The high ranking of *research* in the 1994 Group suggests that research is presented as a priority in this set of statements. This perhaps reflects this group's anxiety with foregrounding and enhancing their research profile as part of their overall strategic plans. Clearly, this also applies to Russell Group universities for which *research* is the second most frequent noun.

One lexical item – *student*[5] – is positioned differently across the three groups, and therefore emerges as being of particular concern for this chapter, because it offers itself as an alternative commodity and product of universities. *Student* is the second most frequent noun for the 1994 and Million+ groups but occurs only fourth on the list for the Russell Group (after *university*, *research* and *world*). This suggests that students are given more prominence in the 1994 and Million+ statements, and the fact that *learning* and *education* are also high on the Million+ list (4th and 6th respectively), and *teaching* and *learning* are higher on the 1994 list than they are on the Russell Group list, also reflects the greater priority given to teaching in these universities, as opposed to the primary emphasis on research in Russell Group universities. The positions of frequent nouns such as *research*, *student*, *learning* and *teaching*, therefore, arguably reflect the relative priorities of the three groups of UK universities with the Russell Group prioritising research, the 1994 Group prioritising research and teaching, and the Million+ group being more concerned with teaching. These are the products being marketed through the mission statements.

In the Russell Group statements, *student* also collocates with words which indicate something to do with 'quality' and which often have a superlative meaning, for example, *high-quality*, *best*, *most able*, *talented* and *excellence*. Just as research is frequently described in terms of its high quality in the Russell Group statements, students seem to be constructed as another 'high quality' product which is being used to market the university. In fact, this type of collocation is rarely found in the 1994 Group and Million+ group statements.

Knowledge is a word which is fairly frequent in all three sub-corpora, although it appears with the highest frequency in the Million+ group (11th in Russell Group, 8th in 1994 Group and 5th in Million+ group). *Knowledge* comes below prestige and ranking markers such as *world* and *excellence* in the Russell Group list but a considerable way above them in the Million+ group. *Quality* and *knowledge* have a similar frequency in the 1994 Group list (appearing in 7th and 8th positions respectively). *Knowledge* has a similar frequency to *education* in the Million+ list (appearing in 5th and 6th positions respectively).

What is clear from the concordance list is that *knowledge* does not collocate with *student*. This suggests that the way knowledge is being presented in the mission statements has little to do with students creating or developing knowledge. Instead, knowledge is treated as a 'product' which the university owns as a commodity, and which can, therefore, be 'sold' and marketed to potential students and perhaps other stakeholders. So the frequency of collocations such as *dissemination* with *knowledge* and *knowledge transfer* suggest that knowledge is being constructed as a fully formed product which can be passed on by the university – knowledge is a product rather than a process in which students are invited to become engaged. *Knowledge* also collocates with other commodities and products which the university is offering in its mission statements such as *skills* (especially in Million+ group statements), *learning* and *research*.

The high value of knowledge as a commodity is often emphasised through frequent collocating modifiers such as *cutting-edge, exemplary* and *highest quality* – these modifying adjectives collocate particularly frequently with *knowledge* in the Russell Group statements. In the 1994 Group statements, there appears to be more emphasis upon what can be done with knowledge, so we see it collocating more frequently with verbs such as *increase* and *exploit* and nominalisations such as *advancement, dissemination, application* and *communication*.

In the Million+ statements, *knowledge* collocates more with *skills* than it does in the other two groups. *Skills* seem to be marketed as a product in the Million+ group whereas the other two groups place a greater emphasis on marketing *research* and *learning*. *New knowledge* is a collocation which occurs a number of times in the Million+ statements but which does not occur at all in either of the other two groups of statements. *New* is a frequent adjective in the Million+ group which does not appear in the other two adjective frequency lists. Again, as the Million+ universities are not in a position to be able to use markers of prestige and quality to sell themselves, the newness and originality of their products is perhaps being used as an alternative marketing strategy in this group of mission statements.

From these findings, it seems that nouns appearing in the semantic field of what we might term 'pedagogy' are the main 'products' which are being marketed in the Million+ statements whilst research and prestige and rank markers are the main products being marketed by the Russell Group universities. The 1994 Group statements seem to draw on a combination of both.

Universities – marketing prestige and rank

Indicators of prestige and rank are evident when we examine the relative frequencies of *world* across the three groups. A key concern of Russell Group universities is proving that they are world leading (as will be shown later, *leading* collocates frequently with *world*, particularly in the Russell Group statements) and these universities are increasingly positioning themselves towards an international market. Globalisation is a feature of neo-liberal discourse so the frequent use of *world* in Russell Group statements contributes to this theme. *World* does also appear in the other two lists but lower down (11th in 1994 and 24th in Million+) suggesting that prioritising globalisation and internationalisation in mission statements is not so important for these universities as it is for the

Russell Group ones. This is reinforced through *international* being the most frequent adjective for the Russell Group statements but not for the other two sub-corpora. *World* (especially when collocating with *leading*) appears to be used as a marketing strategy, as a means of signalling the high quality of the work of the university. Other frequent nouns also appear to serve a similar function, for example, *excellence, quality, impact. Excellence* is used most frequently in the Russell Group statements, followed by the 1994 Group and then the Million+ group. *Quality* is used most frequently in the 1994 Group statements, followed by the Russell Group and then the Million+ statements. *Impact* only occurs as a frequent noun in the Russell Group statements (17th on the list). Universities in all three groups, therefore, seem concerned with marking out the standard of their work in their mission statements.

Next, we considered the collocations of *leading* which appeared as the second most frequent adjective for both the Russell and 1994 groups but which appeared only five times in the Million+ frequency list. What is clear from examining collocations is that *leading* is being used in both groups to advance a claim about quality. A common left collocate in the Russell Group statements is *world* which further emphasises the Russell Group's preoccupation with globalisation and with using its international status as a marketing tool. *Leading edge* and *leading role* are common right-hand collocations in both the Russell and 1994 groups. There are very few occurrences of *leading* for the Million+ group, and the ones that do occur collocate quite differently from the other two groups. For example, *leading technologies* and *leading contribution* are collocations which do not occur in the 1994 or Russell group statements.

As we have seen in the previous section, Million+ group statements privilege *knowledge* above the overt quality and ranking markers evident in the other two groups. Clearly the Million+ universities can make no claims about being 'leading' universities in their statements, but it is interesting that so many of the Russell and 1994 group statements do make claims about being 'leading' and amongst the 'highest' universities in the UK. The frequent use of such superlatives has the effect of a 'corporate boast' (Johnson 1995) in many of these mission statements and reflects the fact that universities view themselves as operating in an increasingly competitive environment (this itself is a feature of neo-liberalism).

Universities – the brand

In the introduction, we asked what might be the value to vice chancellors of mission statements. Their value seems to rest in the belief that branding commodifies some indefinable quality of a university which nevertheless constitutes a 'unique selling point' (USP). Moore (2003: 331) argues that in late capitalism, value no longer attaches to the product itself as:

> a tangible thing; rather, value inheres in something else, something less tangible: the aura, the simulacrum, the reproduction (as opposed to the

original), the brand. The attempt to replace value with symbolic meaning grows out of a sense that production has been transformed, or replaced, by signification.

Branding claims to secure 'uptake' of the product, to the extent that Kalia and Bangar (2002) assert that in the twenty-first century, brands have become an indispensable asset of an organisation. However, brands are inherently fragile, which is no doubt why university mission statements, an arm of the branding process, are in a constant state of amendment and change (Morphew and Hartley 2006: 456).

In terms of the self promotion function of branding, this rests for most universities on some rather abstract claims for uniqueness, which takes place through a recycling of essentially the same few nouns and adjectives (see Tables 7.1 and 7.2), though their relative order may vary for each mission group. The teams of managers who write these documents are charged with propounding a particular institutional narrative recounted through the lexicon of business and industry. Common to each of the mission groups are *quality*, *excellence* and *vision* which serve to attach themselves to the products available for student consumption, particularly in the Russell and 1994 group mission statements. It is interesting to note that these frequent nouns are abstract and semantically vague. It could be argued that, because nouns such as *excellence* and *quality* are used so frequently in the statements, that their meanings start to become questionable. With so many universities claiming 'excellence', how can one tell which ones really are the most excellent? Urciuoli (2000) refers to such words as strategically deployable shifters (SDS). Because SDSs are multi-functional and polysemic, they are not always the sites of overt struggle (Sauntson and Morrish, forthcoming). Davies and Bendix Petersen argue that a characteristic of neo-liberal discourse is that it disguises its own negative impact and so forestalls resistance (2005: 85). In our corpora we can see that branding cements itself through these unarguable, but indistinct virtues.

For Russell Group universities, their claim to distinctiveness is based on excellence of research and students. There is a discourse of competitiveness, with assertions of world-leading quality, and boasts of ordinal ranking. For 1994 Group universities, their appeal is to research and teaching quality, while the Million+ group prioritise learning, students and knowledge. Universities undergo frequent comparisons (e.g. through league tables, RAE submissions etc) therefore it is not surprising to find such competitiveness inserting its way into the discourse of the Russell and 1994 group statements.

Resisting neo-liberalism?

However, in addition to examining some of the most frequent words (especially nouns and adjectives) and collocations, and how these reflect the predominant neo-liberal concerns of many of the mission statements, we also wanted to look for evidence of any counter-hegemonic resistance to neo-liberalism in the corpus.

Some words which appeared extremely infrequently in the corpus, and which seemed somewhat at odds with the thematic priorities embodied by the most frequent words, included *radical* (1 occurrence in each group), *intellectual* (1 occurrence in 1994 Group), *liberal* (1 occurrence in 1994 Group), *freedom* (1 occurrence in 1994 Group) and *public* (1 occurrence in Million+ group). In fact, all but one of these words (1 occurrence of *radical* in a Russell Group statement) occurred in only two of the total number of mission statements in the corpus (1 each from 1994 and Million+ groups) suggesting that these two universities were relatively isolated in containing words which challenged and resisted the neo-liberal hegemony. These kinds of words arguably appeal less to a neo-liberal rhetoric and more to the kinds of 'traditional' academic values which typified UK universities prior to the neo-liberal turn. The rarity of such challenges points first to the dominance of neo-liberal discourse in the whole corpus of mission statements and, second, suggests that university mission statements are fairly uniform in their foci, especially *within* each group.

There were also some frequent adjectives, largely in the Million+ statements (*social, academic, new, professional, educational* and *cultural*) which also appear to reflect a different focus from the other two groups, especially the Russell Group. These adjectives seem less explicitly to do with competitiveness and standards and more to do with promoting learning (*academic*), providing careers opportunities (*professional*) and making a contribution to social life (*social*). In this sense, it appears that students are being constructed as more than mere consumers in the Million+ statements but are instead being presented with opportunities which they, as learners, must actively take up with a view to playing a part in the social world after graduation. The chapter that talks about student as citizen develops these thoughts further. This provides some challenge to Shumar's observation that the purpose of higher education has been constructed as a form of consumption, and no longer for the enlightenment of the individual (2008: 74). The use of *new* as a frequent adjective in the Million+ list may also be a result of these universities not being in a position to compete with those in the 1994 and Russell groups. Perhaps the strongest claims that the Million+ universities can make is that they offer something 'new' and different to prospective students, employees etc. These might perhaps blend the traditionally held self-evident purpose of a university with some neo-liberal values of personal responsibility and consumer choice.

From these few examples, it seems there are some instances where the dominant neo-liberal discourse of the mission statements is being challenged by an alternative discourse, based on a different set of values. This insight offers the possibility of wider resistance. First architects of these documents should reconsider the potential audience for their mission statements. Perhaps, given their current uniformity, the branding function might be abridged in favour of the function identified by Pearce and David (1987: 109) that a mission statement 'specifies the fundamental reason why an organization exists'.

A salutary lesson to writers of mission statements was reported in the *Times Higher Educational Supplement* in January 2010. A businessman complained to the Advertising Standards Authority, stating that the University of Plymouth's claim on its website that it was 'the enterprise university' was misleading.[6] Via the Freedom of Information Act, this individual ascertained that, indeed, only two of Plymouth's graduating class had gone on to start businesses with the university's support, and only one member of staff had formal expertise in enterprise. Furthermore, only one out of the 275 academics he claimed to have contacted approved of the slogan. This case study is a warning to authors to consult more widely throughout institutions where they would find widespread concurrence among staff and students, and possibly even employers, about why universities exist. One certain point of agreement is that they do not exist for the benefit of managers and their *visions*.

Concluding remarks

We find these mission statements to be dominated by neo-liberal discourse which extols marketisation, commodification and globalisation. Here we see an extension of what Slaughter and Leslie (1997) termed 'academic capitalism'. In an era of global markets, declining block grants and ever increasing competition for research monies, universities have embraced the profit motive and turned to market-like behaviours (Slaughter and Leslie 1997: 11). The key purpose of mission statements appears to be an indefinable kind of 'branding' in which concrete purposes and achievements are replaced by a symbolic avowal of the values of business and industry. What we view as a re-packaging of students as (simultaneously) consumers and products of universities is a logical extension of this philosophy.

Within its mission statement, the neo-liberal 'business-facing' university discursively constructs its identity, at least in part, by use of a small set (21–25 items) of nouns and adjectives which have an indeterminate semantic range. These lexical items are designed to propound a managerialist institutional narrative designed to forestall challenge, precisely because it is impossible to contest the positive images they invoke. In this way, universities construct themselves, their students and graduates in the desired corporate image. Students, but also knowledge, research and teaching/learning are all offered as products of the university. Students are somewhat ambiguously positioned as, simultaneously, consumers, units of profit and as products of the university.

Furthermore we find that the aim of university mission statements to represent uniqueness is displaced by a tendency to discursive uniformity and standardisation. We can clearly identify a genre of university mission statements in terms of their thematic components and discursive similarity, however, there emerge some significant differences between the mission groups. Lexical items of *research*, *student**, *learning* and *teaching* reflect the relative priorities of the three groups of UK universities. As expected, we see the Russell Group places emphasis on research, while the 1994 Group prioritises research and teaching, and the Million+ group identifies its focus on teaching. Russell Group institutions portray themselves on a world stage, and claim an impact for their research and scholarship. 1994 Group and Million+ group universities are more modest in their claims, but all attend to the hierarchy suggested by their relative positions in league tables. Million+ universities also portray themselves as being beneficial to the individual and society. The adjectives in this domain seem less explicitly to do with competitiveness and standards and more to do with promoting learning (*academic*), providing career opportunities (*professional*) and making a contribution to social life (*social*).

In some instances, though, we do see glimmerings of resistance to the dominant discursive constructions of the neo-liberal university. Adjectives such as *intellectual*, *liberal*, *freedom* and *radical* occur very infrequently in any of the corpora. There are very few universities, it seems, that choose to portray themselves in harmony with the ethos of those academics who work within their walls. This suggests that the narrative insistences of neo-liberal rhetoric do not sit entirely comfortably or without challenge within the HE context. We live in the hope that this particular historical moment, when neo-liberal policies are emerging as tainted, may offer the promise of further discursive, structural and agentive resistance.

Notes

1   Further information about the Russell Group is available from http://www. russellgroup.ac.uk/ (accessed 2 August 2009).
2   Further information about the 1994 Group is available from http://www. 1994group.ac.uk/aboutus.php (accessed 2 August 2009).
3   Further information about the Million+ group is available from http://www. millionplus.ac.uk/aboutus.htm (accessed 2 August 2009).
4   Further information about Universities UK is available from http://www. universitiesuk.ac.uk/UKHESector/FAQs/Pages/About-HE-Sector-and-Universities. aspx (accessed 2 August 2009).
5   The convention of using a * indicates that all forms of the word are included in this search, e.g. 'students', 'student's' etc.
6   The University of Plymouth's mission statement was not included in our database because it only appears in the University Alliance group.

References

Canaan, J. and Shumar, W. (eds) (2008) *Structure and Agency in the Neoliberal University*. London: Routledge.
Clarke, J., Gewirtz, S. and McLaughlin, E. (eds) (2000) *New Managerialism, New Welfare?* London: Sage Publications Ltd.
Cochran, D., David, F. and Gibson, C. (2009) 'A framework for developing an effective mission statement', *Journal of Business Strategies*, 25(2): 27–39.
Davies, B. and Bendix Petersen, E. (2005) 'Neo-liberal discourse in the academy: the forestalling of (collective) resistance', *Learning and Teaching in the Social Sciences*, 2(2): 77–97.

Fairclough, N. (1995) *Critical Discourse Analysis: The Critical Study of Language*. Harlow: Longman.

Falsey, T. (1989) *Corporate Philosophies and Mission Statements: A Survey and Guide for Corporate Communicators and Management*. Westport, CT: Greenwood.

Harvey, D. (2005) *A Brief History of Neoliberalism*. Oxford: Oxford University Press.

Johnson, R. (1995) *Inaugural Professorial Lecture*. Nottingham Trent University

Kalia, A. and Bangar,V. (2002) 'Branding in the 21st century: important issues', *International Journal of Communication*, 12 (1).

Mighall, R. (2009) 'What sets you apart?' *Times Higher Education Supplement* (23 July). Available from http://www.timeshighereducation.co.uk/story.asp?sectioncode=26& storycode=407458 (accessed 2 August 2009).

Moore, R. (2003) 'From genericide to viral marketing: on "brand"', *Language and Communication*, 23(3): 331–57.

Morphew, C. and Hartley, M. (2006) 'Mission statements: a thematic analysis of rhetoric across institutional type', *The Journal of Higher Education*, 77(3): 456–71.

Ong, A. (2006) *Neoliberalism as Exception*. Durham, NC: Duke University Press.

Pearce, J. (1982) 'The company mission as a strategic goal', *Sloan Management Review* (Spring): 15–24.

Pearce, J. and David, F. (1987) 'Corporate mission statements: the bottom line', *Academy of Management Executive*, 1(2): 109–16.

Sauntson, H. and Morrish, L. (Forthcoming) Gender and Sexuality: The Discursive Limits of 'Equality' in Higher Education. Introduction to a Special Issue of *LATIS: Learning and Teaching: The International Journal of Higher Education in the Social Sciences*.

Shumar, W. (2008) 'Space, place and the American university', in J. Canaan and W. Shumar (eds) *Structure and Agency in the Neoliberal University*. London: Routledge: pp. 67–83.

Sinclair, J. (1991) *Corpus, Concordance, Collocation*. Oxford: Oxford University Press.

Slaughter, S. and Leslie, L. (1997) *Academic Capitalism: Politics, Policies and the Entrepreneurial University*. Baltimore: The Johns Hopkins University Press.

Urciuoli, B. (2000) *Strategically Deployable Shifters In College Marketing, or Just What Do They Mean by 'Skills' and 'Leadership' and 'Multiculturalism'?* Available from http://language-culture.binghamton.edu/symposia/6/index.html (accessed 2 August 2009).

Williams, L. (2008) 'The mission statement: a corporate reporting tool with a past, present, and future', *Journal of Business Communication*, 45(2): 94–119.

Chapter 8

From Accrington Stanley to academia? The use of league tables and student surveys to determine 'quality' in higher education

Stella Jones-Devitt and Catherine Samiei

Introduction

This chapter propels the higher education domain into a future dystopian world. It is now 2020 and the Leitch Review of Skills (2006) has driven the agenda for higher education in the UK for the last two decades. Beyond the impervious elite, many learned institutes have reinvented themselves accordingly or failed to survive. By adopting a futuristic polemic approach this chapter will consider some of the outcomes and potential unintended consequences of imposing explicit and implicit marketisation on higher education. Specifically, it explores the shift towards viewing the higher education experience as synonymous with a competitive 'outputs' model. This is becoming more evident with the prevalence of university league tables and student surveys, as characterised in the UK by the National Student Survey (NSS) initiative.

These league tables and surveys are used increasingly as primary tools for assessment of quality, premised on the primacy of the consumer – formerly the 'student' – voice. This chapter will explore assumptions underpinning the use of league tables, originally used to determine competitive sports outcomes, but increasingly used as key arbiters of 'quality' in higher education. The inclusion of 'Accrington Stanley' within the title is apposite for the perspective adopted throughout this chapter. Sadly in 1962, this north-west England football club resigned from the English Football League for financial reasons in the middle of the competitive season. This caused mayhem still referred to romantically in popular sporting folklore, when – despite the town's best intentions and good performances – the club could not generate the required income and folded. This irony can be applied to a contemporary higher education context where one measure of performance – namely income generation – supplants all other assessment of quality.

This informs the discourse of neo-liberalism, examined by Clarke (2004: 31) in which:

> The 'private' means a number of inter-locking things, each of which is naturalised by being grounded in extra-social or pre-social forms. First,

it designates the market as the site of private interests and exchange. Private interests in this sense are both those of the abstract individual (known as 'economic man' for good reason) and the anthropomorphised corporation, treated as if it was an individual. This personifying of the corporation extends to it having needs, wishes, rights and even feelings. Corporations are, in a sense, doubly personified – both in the persons of their heroic leaders (Chief Executive Officers) and in the corporate entity itself.

This is characterised in higher education by an individualised behavioural focus in which the consumer is sovereign in theory and rhetoric, if not practice. This is illustrated by the resultant shift from positioning the individual as passive student learner, towards one in which seductive notions of 'active consumer' prevail.

We use the four central presuppositions underpinning neo-liberalism, as identified by Olssen and Peters (2005). These comprise: promoting the concept of global choice for individuals, organisations and multinational corporations; minimising the role played by the State in everyday life; the privileging of individualism; escalating regulation, audit and public accountability. Despite numerous critical voices (Barnett 2005; Carnoy 2005; Tierney 2006) the neo-liberal agenda for higher education continues to gather momentum. As Brown and Scott (2009: 2) state:

> The 'marketisation' of higher education – the application of the economic theory of the market to the provision of higher education – seems unstoppable. Market entry is being liberalised. Tuition fees are being introduced or raised. Grants for student support are being supplemented by loans. Institutional rankings and 'league tables' to guide student choice are proliferating. Institutions are devoting increasing energy and resources to marketing, branding and customer service. Nor is this phenomenon confined to student education. Much academic research and scholarship is subject to market or 'quasi-market' coordination as, increasingly, is the recruitment and remuneration of academic and other staff.

It has redefined accountability in terms of commercially oriented 'visible' outputs, cost and quality. These four presuppositions are used as a basis to take neo-liberal ideology in higher education to a 'logical' conclusion.

We illustrate the changing role of higher education by exploring how, in 2020, one institute in particular, New Liberalia University, has wholeheartedly incorporated competency-based curricula, within the context of commercial and consumer-led adjudication of quality. Each of Olssen and Peters' (2005) key facets of neo-liberalism are presented in relation to a New Liberalia University scenario and these scenarios are considered in turn to provide a critique of the neo-liberal agenda.

The chief executive's address for the new academic year for 2020/21 at New Liberalia University characterises the zeitgeist:

The Chief Executive's Welcome for 2020

Welcome to New Liberalia University (NLU) and thank you for making such an informed choice. I can assure you that our mantra *NLU for a New You* will be followed assiduously by our team of enablers, dedicated to fulfilling your investment for future economic prosperity. This university has a proud reputation, built from successes gained since being awarded university status in 1992. Originally a vocationally oriented institute, NLU has now grown into one of the leading niche providers of employer-sponsored curricula as demonstrated in the recent Moving Industry Forward Decisively (MIFD 2019) league table. NLU stands proudly at the top of the 'Learning for Earning' category for the third year running.

Whilst delighted, I am not surprised that NLU enjoys this accolade. Just look at the key features that make NLU so distinctive: all our learning products can be accessed *when* you like, *how* you like and facilitated by *whom* you like. You choose the preferred mode of transmission and you choose and hire the tutor-enabler from our list of retained facilitators. You choose whether to pay on acquiring your specific learning outcomes or when you have completed a set of profession-specific skills *and* the full range of NLU services are guaranteed for twelve months. This embeds our contractual obligation for your success by the swiftest possible route, comprising '*a 100% pass rate or get your money back*'. (Please refer to written terms and conditions in the latest Co-Consumer Learner Charter.)

I personally pledge that everyone at NLU is on message about your learning; indeed all of our human capital is employed on a retained contract basis, subject to regular stakeholder review of meeting crucial performance indicators to satisfy your happiness and employability prospects. If you do not like the staff, NLU does not retain them. It is that simple. As an accountable and transparent chief executive, I will always take pragmatic steps to assure you that your faith in NLU is well-rewarded and that your investment is protected.

You are now part of our growing global family of co-consumer learners. This applies whether you are joining NLU for one of our very popular week-long 'Skills Fest' units or taking our one-year Advanced Standing Employability Study (ASES) option as part of the industry-led innovation in doctoral future proofing. I am delighted to share with you the very exciting news that NLU can now offer an employability internship scheme to all co-consumer learners who pay full 'Learning for Earning' fees in advance for the ASES year long doctoral programme. NLU tutor-enablers will match you carefully with a sponsor company, which then guarantees a probationary year of employment for each co-consumer learner. On successful completion of your internship, your Learning for Earning fees will be reimbursed (dependent on meeting agreed weekly performance indicators as assessed by the sponsoring company).

I am confident that you will have a very productive time at NLU. This confidence is strengthened by the knowledge that all of our learning products are continually quality assured by external scrutiny and regulation. In addition, all of the available human capital is dedicated to enabling you to become ready to take your place in tomorrow's economy, today. Gone are the days of the ivory tower and the unaccountable and complacent university sector. Thank you again for choosing New Liberalia University. NLU for a New You!

Carl P. Da Foo (Chief Executive, New Liberalia University)

We are going to take issue with the assumption that a neo-liberal present and future for higher education – as espoused by the chief executive above – represents an irresistible inevitability. This approach follows an established line of critical discourse explored by Clarke (2004), Olssen and Peters (2005) and Barnett (2005).

Promoting the concept of global choice for individuals, organisations and multinational corporations

The New Liberalia University Vision and Mission Statement (2020)

Our Vision – Any time, any place, anywhere. There's a wonderful world you can share. You're the bright one, we're the right one. Join NLU.

Our Mission – As the leading niche provider of employer-sponsored curricula, New Liberalia University's mission is to:

- Provide opportunities of 'Learning for Earning' at individual, organisational and trans-corporate level, removed from direct state intervention.
- Guarantee a responsive and agile service that provides bespoke learning products, dedicated to facilitating your success.
- Develop the global branding of NLU for a New You by ensuring transparent reporting of quality performance measures that ensure that you are ready to take your place in tomorrow's economy, today.

The positioning of neo-liberalism as one of the key global economic drivers has resulted in an escalating cultural drift – demonstrated by the NLU mission statement – that accepts the inevitability of fragmentation and the devolution of mainstream public services. Jones-Devitt and Smith (2007) assert that the emerging neo-liberal citizen is increasingly immersed in ideological resentment of the state, making them less likely to comply with one of the key agencies of social mobility, namely state-sponsored higher education. The customer or, in NLU parlance, the co-consumer learner, is apparently able to shop around for the *right* product, at the *right* price, with the *right* quality. Olssen and Peters (2005) note that this is premised on the assumption that globalised forms of competition in higher education will increase productivity, accountability and control, which inevitably lead to improved quality.

However, Deacon (2000: 9) refutes the assumption that all co-consumer learners benefit from global choices, arguing that:

> Services for the poor run the danger of becoming poor-quality services, precisely because the middle class is no longer willing to pay taxes for services from which it does not directly benefit.

This emphasis on choice is evident in the New Liberalia University where 'all our learning products can be accessed *when* you like, *how* you like and facilitated by *whom* you like'. Significantly, choice has been extended not only to the timing and mode of study but also to 'who' delivers the learning. However, whilst ostensibly appearing to provide flexibility in learning this 'choice' is illusionary. This idea of student as choice-maker is picked up in great detail in the chapter by Nixon *et al.* later in this book. The privileging of individualism and the emphasis on individual choice is based on the assumption that an individual is placed in the best position to determine their needs. It assumes a level of informed choice that students beginning a course may not possess. Also, as Lynch (2006) argues, this choice does not account for those who are not able to make 'active consumer choices' due to time or financial restrictions. Hartley (1997) suggests that the implied logic of this position indicates that the poor have simply 'chosen' poverty. Additionally, on a larger scale, this emphasis on the individual as the 'author of their life' ignores any notions of collective engagement or social responsibility and 'public good' and assumes the permanence of values based on market forces. Yet as Hartley (1997) implies, the seductive nature of choice replaces the worthiness of 'public good' by attaching emotive meanings to consumption rather than in privileging benevolent behaviour.

Furthermore, whilst appearing to offer individual choice, the focus of responsibility for success is placed firmly with the university as the provider of the education. The student as consumer becomes expectant of the receipt of an appropriate product and consumer satisfaction must be guaranteed; hence the '100% pass rate or get your money back'. However, in the neo-liberal university, these consumer promises are qualified and come with built-in get out clauses that demonstrate the hollowness of these guarantees: 'Please refer to written terms and conditions in the latest Co-Consumer Learner Charter'. Similarly, the neo-liberal university is characterised by rhetoric, which superficially appears to promote inclusivity and participation – 'the growing global family'. The false promises of the neo-liberal university simultaneously offers the promise of everything and nothing; representing rhetoric without substance. Beck and Beck-Gernsheim (2002) contend that social infrastructures, built on such neo-liberal assurances, place more pressure on individuals to become judicious consumers, regardless of ability and capacity. They define this paradox as 'individualization', characterised as:

A social condition, which is not arrived at by a free decision of individuals. To adapt Jean-Paul Sartre's phrase: people are condemned to individualization. Individualization is a compulsion, albeit a paradoxical one, to create, to stage manage, not only one's own biography but the bonds and networks surrounding it and to do this amid changing preferences and at successive stages of life, while constantly adapting to the conditions of the labour market, the education system, the welfare state and so on.

(Beck and Beck-Gernsheim 2002: 4)

This demands an active contribution by individuals when navigating through the numerous array of choices and is based on the assumption that students possess the appropriate skills to make these choices.

Minimising the role of the State

Excerpt within product brochure (2020) of the media interview with Barbara N. Petty, co-consumer learner representative on the Stakeholder Board at New Liberalia University.

Q. So, Barbara, why did you choose NLU as the place to be for a New You?
A. I was attracted to NLU because of its demonstrable commitment to reducing nanny state interference whilst making sure that I am looked after as a paying customer who gets value for money.

Q. How did you find this out?
A. It was easy. I accessed the 'How is NLU doing for you?' site to check out the percentage of social education still funded at NLU. When I compared it with other sector competitors, I was delighted to find that the University has now stopped such subsidised schemes for so-called disadvantaged groups. It really did slow everything down for responsible citizens and it damaged the reputation of NLU with employers and customers alike. The rest is history. I simply contacted one of the tutor-enablers, told them what I wanted, and here I am, ten months into my learning, on the brink of my ASES doctorate.

Barbara's uncomplicated analysis of her needs indicates several flaws in assumptions made about state involvement in higher education. The scenario above implies that the market is a self-regulating force beyond compare, regulating itself and her aspirations far more effectively when removed from any state-sponsored intervention. However, Clarke (2004) argues that the avowed purpose of neo-liberalism is to dissolve the public realm by presenting a crude dichotomy of choice between public and private. He contends that the schism of public and private is not synonymous with state and market as defined by neo-liberal advocates. 'Private' is taken to mean individual/familial/domestic spheres, whilst 'public' equates to market/state/policy/bureaucracy. Yet the 'market' is often categorised as both private and public to suit ideological purposes; hence, the market functions within the public domain but is also recognised as supporting the private, non-collectivised ambitions of economic prosperity and personalised self-fulfilment.

This crude dichotomy is then located within an unhelpful framework of binary opposites. The choice is between a muscular, responsive and desirable globalisation of capital, transformed by corporate ambitions and personal prosperity, contrasted with a weak, static, parochial and ill-located nation state in which nobody competes to survive. As Harman (1996) notes, the assumption that globalisation – due to effective powers of self-regulation and governance – has reduced reliance on nation states for economic support is flawed. His evidence suggests that many multinational organisations would not have survived without state subsidies and intervention.

In New Liberalia University, Barbara has internalised the message that fragmentation of services and movement away from state intervention is desirable. As an active co-consumer learner, she expects to access an array of publicly digestible, transparent and sector-comparable quality indicators, in order to adjudicate performance.

Notions that higher education provision should be increasingly accountable to quasi-market forces and less reliant upon state funding are signposted within the recently updated Higher Education Funding Council for England (HEFCE) Strategic Plan 2006–2011 which asserts that:

> Private and public sector employers want H.E. to produce rounded, highly skilled graduates, who are readily employable and can play their part in helping their organisations adapt to changing customer, stakeholder and economic demands. Employers also need access to HE to support the ongoing development of their existing staff to meet changing priorities. Sector Skills Councils have been assigned a role in articulating employers' needs and we will continue to work with them and other relevant bodies, together with the HE sector, to promote engagement with employers.
>
> (HEFCE 2009: 6)

However, the co-funding initiative for employer engagement, initiated by HEFCE as part of the neo-liberal ethos of 'agile' economic responsiveness has achieved minimal success with both universities and employers. While this intervention sought to supplant state subsidy with employer sponsorship, the resultant lack of engagement indicates that the higher education 'market' is not yet the viable and preferred choice assumed within the New Liberalia scenario.

Clarke (2004) argues that economic calculations premised on the supremacy of the 'market' to regulate effectively – from the ideologically neutral stance of pragmatism – have led to the creation of different routes of public service delivery and operational design. Approaches include direct privatisation, cross-sectoral partnerships, outsourcing and contracting, new market creation, internal market conflation, creating new conditions for competitive success. Arguably, the two latter approaches have had the most direct influence on public service delivery of higher education. In New Liberalia University, the conflation of an internal market with quality constructs only that which is measured as worthwhile, logically ensuring that all which is immeasurable is deemed worthless in both economic and educational terms.

Olssen and Peters assert that this ascendant neo-liberal form of higher education has borrowed from Agency Theory and Cost-Transaction Economics (developed in the 1950s) to exert market techniques for institutional governance. Hence, the inclusion and costing of human actions that can be counted and 'performed', resulting in fragmentation and removal of state-sponsored intervention at collectivist level; elaborate performance management systems and overtly managerial perspectives in universities:

> Rather than specify a broad job specification based on a conception of professional autonomy and responsibility, it specifies chains of principal-agent relationships as a series of contracts as a means of rendering the management function clear and accountable. Agency Theory theorizes hierarchical work-relationships as contracts where a principal becomes a commissioning party to specify or delegate work to an agent to perform in return for some specified sanction or reward.
>
> (Olssen and Peters 2005: 320)

Privileging individualism

Important media communiqué from Don Toogood-Tobetrue, Acting Director of the Total Co-Consumer-Learner Experience (TCCLE) at New Liberalia University:

> New Liberalia University (NLU) has just reached the 2020 play-off finals due to achieving excellent League Table positions in the following TCCLE components: Total Self Esteem Rating, Elevated Prosperity Scale, Hedonism in Higher Education, and finally triumphing in the Anti-Altruism Depression Score. This is a testament to the global family approach embraced by all at NLU. If successful in the play-offs, the institute hopes to secure sufficient funding to guarantee the continued employment of all acting directors – including myself – for at least another year . . .

Olssen and Peters (2005) argue that neo-liberal privileging of individualism is a construct of the state that uses auditing, accounting and management to achieve the end goals of freedom, choice, customer sovereignty, competition and individual initiative as well as compliance and obedience.

In the neo-liberal approach, there is an explicit focus on outcomes determined by market forces such as 'future economic prosperity'. For the student, the approach could result in many unintended consequences. This runs the risk of leading to an outcome-focused student body who rely on extrinsic motivation and who regard failing as an impossibility. This approach could also have potential unintended consequences on the level and nature of student engagement, possibly resulting in students whose learning is focused solely on achieving and demonstrating skills and competencies. Within the neo-liberal university of 2020, students are increasingly seen as co-producers of knowledge, albeit as 'co-consumer learners'. This redefinition of roles appears to offer choice, accessibility and opportunity but simultaneously disregards the inherent power dynamic in the academic–student relationship and fails to recognise that students may not always be in the best position to individually determine and inform all aspects of modes and methods of learning.

The underlying message of the neo-liberal agenda is an emphasis on the quick, easily digested and accessible education which does not acknowledge the commitment, challenges and hard work required for genuine academic engagement with ideas and ways of thinking. The recent UK government sponsored consultation document *Higher Education at Work: High Skills, High Value* (published by the now obsolete Department for Innovation, Universities and Skills (DIUS)) recommends an acceleration of graduate status for business purposes:

> We are promoting the availability of two year honours degrees. These are an important component of the HEFCE flexible pathways programme, for which the target is to have at least one thousand enrolled students during 2008/09. HEFCE is examining the early results from pilots of two year compressed degrees. The experience has been encouraging and HEFCE are looking to increase their spread and take up. They can be an attractive option – particularly for learners with strong study skills, including mature full-time learners studying in mid-career.
>
> (DIUS 2008: 30)

The implicit message of New Liberalia University schemes like 'Learning for Earning' is premised on assumptions that are outcome driven and that are measured by performance indicators that reinforce the notion of academic engagement as a product to be purchased. Many universities privilege a flexible approach that allows learners to work whilst studying yet Callender (2008) indicates that there is demonstrable evidence to show that this often has a detrimental effect on academic achievement.

Escalating regulation, audit and public accountability

As indicated by the results shown in Table 8.1, the University of New Liberalia sits proudly at the top of the Good University TCCLE League Table for 2020, qualifying for a further round of income-generating play offs. In 2020,

Table 8.1 Good University TCCLE League Table for 2020

Total Co-Consumer Learner Experience (TCCLE) Good University Table for 2020					
Maximum % Scores	TSER	EPS	HHE	AAD	Total
1 New Liberalia University	92	87	89	99	91.75
2 Accrington Stanley Academy	90	89	88	91	89.50
3 University of Human Capital	90	86	89	92	89.25
4 Enterprise Aspiration University	89	88	86	90	88.25
↑ TCCLE Good University League Play Off Qualifiers ↑					
5 University of Naff Crafts	89	85	86	89	87.25
6 T. K. Macks Plank Institute	87	86	87	85	86.25

Key
TSER – Total Self-Esteem Rating
EPS – Elevated Prosperity Scale
HHE – Hedonism in Higher Education
AAD – Anti-Altruism Depression

the concept of 'employability' (embodied within the TCCLE ratings) embraces criteria previously attributed to the private – rather than public – domain; the 'individualization' alluded to by Beck and Beck-Gernsheim (2002) – in which individuals navigate and interpret social infrastructure in increasing isolation – now requires extension into cultivating specific traits and abilities to produce the corporate citizen rather than the individual, per se. Carnoy describes this as a process in which 'identity is defined in terms of the way that global markets value individuals' traits and behaviour' (2005: 18).

This is evident in the current increasingly fragmented delivery of higher education and the drive for outputs which has resulted in an increased array of audit tools and mechanisms for measuring and guaranteeing quality. Numerous bodies have emerged as the arbiters of quality including the Quality Assurance Agency (QAA) and HEFCE government-supported initiatives as well as public-based audit such as the *Times* league table.

There has been much detailed criticism of these measures employed as audit tools. A general criticism of audit and the link to coercive and authoritative governmentality is presented by Shore and Wright (1999). Similarly, Blackmore (2004) provides a critique of academic internal audit by both HEFCE and QAA based on the problematic nature of measures focused on outcomes. Specific criticism is also considered by Laughton (2003) who considers why the QAA Teaching Quality Assessment (TQA) has been rejected by academics. Interestingly, Yorke (1998) notes that the financially linked research assessment tools have not received as much of a challenge. Yorke (1997) also points to the arbitrary nature of the measures employed by the *Times* league table, citing the lack of detail, technical deficiencies, arbitrariness of weightings and high levels of intercorrelations as fundamental weaknesses which challenge the validity and meaning of the league table. Similarly, Alderman (1997) points to the lack of a 'gold standard' for benchmarking and O'Leary, the original author of the table, acknowledges inaccuracies in the data of the 1997 table. Despite amendments made to the 1997 league table in response to criticisms, Yorke in an article written in 1998 concludes that the league table has become 'progressively more strongly unidimensional' and that changes to the measures have resulted in 'no progress with respect to diversity' which 'if anything . . . has regressed' (1998: 60).

Brown (2006) identifies three key misconceptions of current quality measures in higher education. These misconceptions include the association between access to information and 'quality' and students' ability to make meaningful judgements based on the information provided. The final misconception relates to the notion that quality is all about consumer satisfaction (as measured by the National Student Survey) rather than in recognising the intrinsic value of education as a transformative experience.

In addition, problems associated with defining measure and measurement audits do not address implicit outcomes. The limited measurement of visible outputs leaves many hidden unmeasured values. Put simply: what cannot be easily measured is often valued as worthless. Brown and Scott extend this debate by suggesting that there is difficulty in measuring the resonance of even 'visible' outputs or, as they prefer to name them, 'experience goods':

> Economists sometimes make a distinction between 'search goods' and 'experience goods', the difference being that the customer can only judge the quality of experience goods after purchase, as they are consumed. But higher education is actually a 'post-experience good', the effects of which may not be discoverable until well afterwards. The information has also to be accessible and fair but there is plenty of evidence that students from less favoured backgrounds are even more disadvantaged in making judgements than those from more favoured ones.
>
> (Brown and Scott 2009: 5–6)

The neo-liberal approach is frequently presented in direct opposition to the elitism of the 'ivory tower', which is seen as unaccountable and complacent. In contrast, the assurances given, regarding the external scrutiny and regulation of the neo-liberal university, claims to promise accountability and transparency. However, this accountability and transparency is measured by selective perform-ance indicators that are determined and set to meet the narrow needs of specific market-forces; one value-laden judgement has simply replaced another. Whilst rejecting the elitism and exclusion of the traditional university system, neo-liberalism effectively creates and supports a new two-tiered system with more traditional universities able to disengage from the audit and performance indicator culture of neo-liberalism (for example, Oxford and Cambridge opting to remove themselves from *The Times* league tables) whilst the post-1992 universities are forced to justify their status by engagement and compliance with the neo-liberal agenda. Within traditional universities, the dynamic of student as consumer is reversed. As Marginson (1997, cited by Olssen and Peters 2005: 327) states 'these institutions choose the student-consumer more than the student choosing them'.

However, the neo-liberal assertion of choice is actually based on a limited range of options that is subject to the vested interests of stake-holders and which can actually lead to what Lynch (2006) identifies as a 'culture of compliance'. As noted within New Liberalia University, staff can become merely a 'tool' by which to achieve the goals of the individual – with a shift away from the emphasis on the effort and commitment required for effective academic engagement. Staff become 'enablers' facilitating learning rather than supporting risk-taking and creating possibly 'uncomfortable' learning spaces where students are challenged.

This model leaves no room for the challenge of academic debate and reinforces a culture of compliance which is bolstered by the emphasis on corporate values with all staff 'on message about your learning'. As Olssen and Peters (2005: 313) assert:

> The traditional professional culture of open intellectual enquiry and debate has been replaced with an institutional stress on performativity, as evidenced by the emergence of an emphasis on measured outputs: on strategic planning, performance indicators, quality assurance measures and academic audits.

Staff become 'human capital' resources to be exploited to meet the vested needs of an employer-led curriculum and to generate economic value. The contract based nature of their employment and its reliance on successfully meeting performance indicators further engenders compliance and reduces the willingness of staff to challenge the approach. Spaces for dissent are reduced and audit and surveys become tools for justifying the removal of non-compliant staff. As Olssen and Peters (2005) argue, contractual models of employment challenge the notion of professionalism, limiting freedom and autonomy within the workplace.

This emphasis on performance outputs can also be seen to result in a competitive individualism based on insecurity, characterised by an inherent conflict between neo-liberal values of individualism and corporate responsiveness as tensions emerge between the personal and the organisational. Holley et al. (2006) describe how performance output approaches – underpinned by micro-managed set targets within a context of reduced resources – create tensions for staff and students alike in both interpretation and practice. They note:

> The university and its practices had no space to recognise that the student (any student) might be able to define and articulate his own needs – nor even to have his own wants and needs . . . we have found that as lecturers our strategies for responding to students are not governed by student need – but by management and government targets – and in the end, the students are further unsupported and silenced.
>
> (Holley et al. 2006: 40–1)

Conclusion

We have provided an interpretation of the logic of neo-liberalism in higher education – when taken to its extremes – via the 'futureshock' which embodies New Liberalia University in 2020. The unchallenged acceptance of a neo-liberal approach threatens the autonomy and independence of the university and may result in unintended consequences that compromise the fundamental principles and values surrounding the purpose of higher education. If universities are to be, as Lynch (2006) argues, sites of universal learning and public engagement and places to challenge received orthodoxies, perhaps neo-liberalism should not be accepted unquestioningly. When addressing the key facets of neo-liberalism as identified by Olssen and Peters (2005) and exploring the logic of its purported quality measurement tools in the context of higher education, several flaws appear:

- There is less choice – rather than more – for specific groups. Both Deacon (2000) and Lynch (2006) found that people from the poorest socio-economic sectors were disproportionately disadvantaged in a higher education context.
- Neo-liberal assumptions which privilege reduced state intervention in higher education are premised on crude and unhelpful dichotomies. Notions of 'private' as good and 'public' as bad are too simplistic when scrutinised. As Harman (1996) noted, notions that market force regulation would enhance quality, whilst reducing reliance on the state, are not substantiated by available evidence. Furthermore, Brown and Scott assert that removal of state-sponsorship may inhibit academic risk-taking. They note that 'higher education confers both collective (public) and individual (private) benefits. Without public subsidy these would be under-supplied because of the risk that the costs could not be recouped by the provider' (2009: 4).
- Privileging individualism can dislocate the learner in higher education. Olssen and Peters (2005) contend that the consumer focus actively rewards individual compliance and adherence to a corporate message. This is reinforced by Beck and Beck-Gernsheim (2002) who argue that pressure is exerted on individuals to become judicious consumers, regardless of personal motivations and ability to comply.
- Increasing amounts of regulation, audit and public accountability within higher education have not secured higher standards of sustainable quality. Yorke (1998) found that many of the criteria used in league tables and surveys to determine quality for the consumer were spurious. Lynch (2006) and more recently Brown and Scott (2009) suggest that many marketisation approaches ignore very important implicit measures of higher education quality and worth due to lack of visibility and unsophisticated analyses.

To avoid the dystopian future world of New Liberalia University from becoming a reality, we contend that the application of some judicious critical thinking principles would ensure a more considered debate, rather than eschewing discussion of the influence of marketisation and its influence on quality in higher education. We suggest that a meta-cognitive approach should be adopted to explore definitions of the higher education 'offer'; including considering competing conceptualisations and possible boundaries of market-located provision. The emerging knowledge economy should be recognised alongside the potential contribution of higher education by examining the privileging of knowledge and exploring the relationship between knowledge production and wider ownership. Any appraisal should consider the underpinning assumptions of a marketised system of higher education in light of validity and enduring nature. Notions of present-day and anticipated future contexts could help define the key issues, including evaluating the different forms of evidence offered as justification for the marketised university. All stakeholders should examine ways of ensuring which ideas are translated into action, which ideas remain as prevailing wicked issues and which are consigned to history alongside the original Accrington Stanley.

References

Alderman, G. (1997) 'League tables merit improvement', *The Times Higher Education Supplement*, 1298 (19 September): 14.

Barnett, R. (2005) *Reshaping the University: New Relationships between Research, Scholarship and Teaching*. Maidenhead: The Society for Research into Higher Education and the Open University.

Beck, U. and Beck-Gernsheim, E. (2002) *Individualization*. London, Thousand Oaks and New Delhi: Sage Publications Limited

Blackmore, J. A. (2004) 'A critical evaluation of academic internal audit', *Quality Assurance in Education*, 12(3): 128–35.

Brown, R. (2006) 'Never mind the feel', *Academy Exchange*, 4 (Summer): 12–13.

Brown, R. and Scott, P. (2009) *The Role of the Market in Higher Education*, report for the Higher Education Policy Institute (HEPI). Available from http://www.hepi.ac.uk/files/01Highereducationandthemarket.pdf (accessed 27 October 2009).

Callender, C. (2008) 'The impact of term-time employment on higher education students' academic attainment and achievement', *Journal of Education Policy*, 23(4): 359–77.

Carnoy, M. (2005) 'Globalization, educational trends and the open society', paper at OSI Education Conference *Education and Open Society: A Critical Look at New Perspectives and Demands*. Budapest: Open Society Institute Education Support Program.

Clarke, J. (2004) 'Dissolving the public realm? The logics and limits of neo-liberalism', *Journal of Social Policy*, 33(1): 27–48.

Deacon, R. (2000) *Globalization and Social Policy: The Threat to Equitable Welfare*, Occasional Paper No. 5. Geneva: United Nations Research Institute for Social Development.

Department for Innovation, Universities and Skills (DIUS) (2008) *Higher Education at Work: High Skills, High Value*. Consultation document available from http://www.dius.gov.uk/consultations/~/media/publications/H/Higher_Education_at_Work (accessed 27 October 2009).

Harman, C. (1996) 'Globalisation: a critique of a new orthodoxy', *International Socialism*, 2(73): 3–34.

Hartley, D. (1997) 'The new managerialism in education: a mission impossible', *Cambridge Journal of Education*, 27(1): 47–57.

Higher Education Funding Council for England (2009) *HEFCE Strategic Plan 2006–11: Updated June 2009*. Bristol: Higher Education Funding Council for England.

Holley, D., Sinfield, S. and Burns, T. (2006) '"It was horrid, very, very horrid": a student perspective on coming to an inner-city university in the UK', *Social Responsibility Journal*, 2(1): 36–41.

Jones-Devitt, S. and Smith, L. (2007) *Critical Thinking in Health and Social Care*. London, Thousand Oaks, New Delhi and Singapore: Sage Publishers.

Laughton, D. (2003) 'Why was the QAA approach to teaching quality assessment rejected by academics in UK HE?', *Assessment & Evaluation in Higher Education*, 28(3): 309–21.

Leitch Review of Skills (2006) *Prosperity for All in the Global Economy – World Class Skills*. London: HMSO.

Lynch, K. (2006) 'Neo-liberalism and marketisation: the implications for higher education', *European Educational Research Journal*, 5(1): 1–17.

Olssen, M. and Peters, M. (2005) 'Neoliberalism, higher education and the knowledge economy: from the free market to knowledge capitalism', *Journal of Education Policy*, 20(3): 313–45.

Shore, C. and Wright, S. (1999) 'Audit culture and anthropology: neo-liberalism in British higher education', *Journal of the Royal Anthropological Institute*, 5(4): 557–75.

Tierney, W. G. (2006) *Trust and the Public Good: Examining the Cultural Conditions of Academic Work*. New York: Peter Lang.

Yorke, M. (1997) 'A good league table guide?', *Quality Assurance in Education*, 5(2): 61–72.

Yorke, M. (1998) 'The *Times* "league table" of universities, 1997: a statistical appraisal', *Quality Assurance in Education*, 6(1): 58–60.

Chapter 9

Branding a university: adding real value or 'smoke and mirrors'?

Chris Chapleo

Introduction

The UK higher education (HE) market has seen institutions seek to differentiate from one another, often utilising the practice and techniques of branding as part of this process.

Whilst there is a general consensus among university management (Chapleo 2004) that this is a necessary and legitimate process as part of the marketisation of higher education that universities have to embrace (Maringe 2005), this view is not without its critics; Jevons (2006), for example, argues that branding often has an unclear purpose and that large quantities of money are spent on branding activity without publicly available research on the efficiency or the outcomes of these investments.

The overall aim of this chapter is to examine both sides of this debate, considering the extant literature, and examining the findings of recent research by the author that explored the rationale for branding UK universities, and the views of senior management of UK universities on issues surrounding branding their institutions.

Specific objectives of the chapter are to critically examine the rationale for branding UK universities, in particular to examine whether current approaches and techniques of branding are applicable to the UK university sector. This work is intended to further the debate on branding in the UK university sector.

Literature review

Branding in higher education

There is a growing body of work involving marketing in higher education (Hemsley-Brown and Oplatka 2006) that focuses on 'sub areas' such as marketing communications (Klassen 2002), marketing planning (Maringe and Foskett 2002), positioning and corporate identity (Gray *et al.* 2003; Melewar and Akel 2005) university selection requirements (Beerli Palacio *et al.* 2002; Veloutsou *et al.* 2004) and, to some extent, the related discipline of branding. The academic literature concerning branding in higher education does seem to be limited (Hemsley-Brown and Oplatka 2006; Waeraas and Solbakk 2008) despite branding's rise up the strategic agenda for UK universities (Rolfe 2003). Certain aspects of branding have been explored however, including the role of the web in university branding (Opoku *et al.* 2006), the role of heritage (Bulotaite 2003), the emergence of brand identities (Lowrie 2007) and brand architecture 'harmonisation' of UK universities (Hemsley-Brown and Goonawardana 2007).

It seems that university branding is an issue of strategic importance and universities are expending considerable amounts of resource on branding their institutions (Rolfe 2003) but the literature on branding in higher education is limited, despite the view that higher education and branding go back a long way (Temple 2006).

Objectives of branding in higher education: why is there a need to brand UK universities?

Any examination of the objectives of branding for UK universities should involve the role of branding in a commercial context. Initially, branding was conceived as a means to establish a product's name and to convey the legitimacy, prestige and stability of the product. However, this evolved into the modern brand paradigm built upon abstraction and cultural engineering, where products embody ideal lifestyles and may be only tenuously linked to functional benefits (Holt 2002).

Most conceptualisations of brand are reasonably explicit when it comes to the advantages of branding, but generally relate more to a commercial arena. De Chernatony and McDonald (2005) assert that a successful brand delivers sustainable competitive advantage and invariably results in superior profitability and market performance. These concepts, whilst arguably challenging to quantify in any sector, may be particularly so when applied to higher education. It may of course be argued that UK universities have always been branded to some extent (e.g. logos and heraldic crests), but most writers on branding would concur that true UK HE branding in its wider context (including external and internal branding) is a comparatively recent phenomenon.

Can branding in HE be measured through current models?

An examination of the benefits of branding may lead to the seemingly complex area of brand evaluation and metrics. It is generally agreed that it is important to measure brand performance, but that monitoring systems should suit the organisation in question (De Chernatony and McDonald 2005; Keller 2003). Keller offers the *brand value chain* as a means to ultimately understand the financial impact of brand marketing expenditure and other models such as Millward Brown's *criteria to assess the strength of a brand* (1996) and Young and Rubicam's *brand asset valuator* (1994) are widely known. However, whilst these models have a degree of applicability to the HE sector they are primarily focused on commercial brands and may not wholly suit the particular situation of universities. Variables such as 'market share', 'price premium' and 'loyalty' are examples of the metrics alluded to, which may need a degree of re-conceptualisation for the HE context.

The marketisation of UK higher education (Stamp 2004) may change the way that branding activity is quantified, as price comes into the equation. When consumers have limited prior knowledge of a service category, brand name may be the most accessible and diagnostic cue available. Strong brands get preferential attribute evaluation, generally higher overall preference and can charge price premiums (Hoeffler and Keller 2003). One key argument for brand expenditure in HE is that of price premiums (Ambler *et al.* 2002) that may become increasingly relevant as many countries, including the UK, adopt a market system for university tuition fees.

Despite the wealth of research on strong or successful brands, the literature is more limited when it comes to discussing the specific area of brand metrics or objectives of brand spending. This situation is exacerbated when it comes to considering specific objectives in less traditional marketing fields such as education. This is perhaps surprising when one considers that spending university budgets on branding activity can be controversial (Jevons 2006).

It may be argued that the better university brands gain in terms of 'quality of student' and raise the overall academic standing (Bunzel 2007). Bunzel associates branding in US universities with enhancing reputation and possibly positive influence on university ranking but concedes that there is little evidence in rankings to support a close link to branding activity.

However, one cannot ignore the relationship between university brands and league tables, particularly the extent to which branding activity seeks to influence league table position. Indeed the issue of league tables and their consequences are picked up in several other chapters in this book. It is debatable whether the presence of league tables changes the conception of branding in the sector, as there is an increasing focus on league table position as a measure of success among some target groups (HEFCE 2008).

Effective branding can use considerable resources and it is therefore important for managers to use such resources effectively and monitor their brands. However, brands are complex, and any monitoring system should be tailored to suit the organisation's environment (De Chernatony and McDonald 2005). Whether we should seek to quantify all branding activity in universities is therefore debatable, but it seems evident that whilst commercial branding techniques are utilised in HE, some appropriate metrics are desirable.

In summary, the literature reveals some work on measurement of branding activity in general, but very little for university branding programmes. The competitive situation in UK higher education has arguably forced UK universities to adopt a more professional approach to marketing activity (Bakewell and Gibson-Sweet 1998) but whether this extends to explicit objectives for branding is debatable. Whilst it is conceded that not all branding activity can be quantified, surely when it has been claimed that 'vast sums are spent without clear purpose' (Jevons 2006) a clear rationale and linked metrics are necessary.

Branding as part of the 'marketisation' of the UK university sector

Before branding's role in UK higher education institutions (HEIs) can be examined, the implicit market principles that underpin it may be explored. The idea of offering higher education as a commodity is fundamentally questioned by Gibbs (2001) who argues that the adoption of a commercial market model for HEIs can be seen in the move towards consumable education through modularisation, semesterisation and self-directed learning and manifests in the current accompanying 'discourse of marketing'. This view of the prevalence of the market and the ultimate quest for individual fulfilment conceives brands as tools to help one create the self one desires (Holt 2002). A market view may turn students into consumers and educators into service providers but, Gibbs (2001) argues, misses the point that higher education contributes to the social well-being of its society, and that this ought to be preserved outside the market. It may be that if universities wholly adopt market forces and therefore offer purely what the current market demands rather than to 'stretch the thinking' of a society, then they will have failed in a fundamental role and compromised a key part of their distinctive benefits to society by becoming 'a sponsored training park for accountants and gardeners' (Gibbs 2001: 91).

Whatever the view of marketisation of UK HE, it does seem that a marketing culture has yet to really permeate universities (Jevons 2006) and it is open to conjecture whether this is due to a fundamental unsuitability of such a view of HE, where many believe that universities should not be in the business of marketing (Bunzel 2007). Against such critique, it is arguable whether branding activity is simply part of the discourse of marketing or can seek to offer wider benefits for HEIs.

Within examination of the applicability of marketing concepts in HE, there is a growing body of work that questions the suitability of commercial branding concepts in this sector (Jevons 2006; Temple 2006; Johnston 2001; Waeraas and Solbakk 2008) and indeed whether commercial style branding in universities can actually challenge their institutional integrity (Waeraas and Solbakk 2008).

Branding may even be considered 'a hollow deception or superficial indulgence' (Mighall 2009) where university customers 'are *vulnerable*, especially if they are in an overseas country, to *branding* which is conveyed only through a web site or a prospectus and not by personal experience'. 'Universities in the heart of cities can arguably seek to brand themselves as havens of rural peace without immediate repercussion' (Temple and Shattock 2007).

The very effectiveness has also been challenged; in particular, whether university branding is worth the time and cost, as there is little evidence to show that a university branding program really creates a change in perception (Bunzel 2007).

What benefits can branding offer a university?

A cynical view may consider branding as something that is done 'to' an institution without any necessary responsibility to reflect a reality. A more sympathetic view would advocate, however, that if we think of 'brand' as the sum of ideas, emotions and associations evoked by an institution, then it appears less sinister, arbitrary or extravagant (Mighall 2009).

Various arguments have been offered for branding including congruence between student's values and those of the university, leading to reduced drop out rates (Jevons 2006). Branding may be a shorthand measure for the whole range of criteria that go to make up the quality of the university (Jevons 2006) and universities require strong brands to enhance awareness of their existence and course offerings, to differentiate themselves from rivals and to gain market share (Bennett *et al.* 2007).The concept of differential pricing strategies, linked to expansion of tuition fees, has also been offered as an argument to support the application of commercial branding approaches (Ambler *et al.* 2002).

Improved league table positions have been offered as an objective of branding but there seems to be a role over and above a focus on league table positioning alone. HEFCE (2008: 54) argue that 'league tables may be influential, but only part of the complex decision making process and often used to confirm a decision already made'. A strong brand should communicate far more about strengths in key areas than the often narrow indicator of league table placing. If used appropriately, branding could build upon league table positioning by emphasising unique selling points but it may be argued that an institution that is comparatively lowly placed in the league tables can nevertheless have a successful brand with niche target audiences.

Whilst there may be arguments for and against investing in branding, these may be superfluous to some extent, as universities may have brands whether they like it or not if branding is the effective expression and management of how people think and feel about the institution. This conceptualisation is not about dreaming up hollow promises, but defining what an institution can authentically offer (Mighall 2009).

A rationale for branding activity in HE can, it seems, be coherently argued for, but the more fundamental issue may be what society requires of HE. All of the forgoing arguments for branding UK HEIs are to some extent reliant upon an implicit assumption that the adoption of market forces in the HE sector is a positive thing, and this, it seems, is still open to some debate.

In view of the limitations and seeming contradictions in the literature, it seems appropriate to examine the views of those with influence on the branding strategy of UK HEIs.

Methodology

An inductive approach was at the core of the empirical work seeking to explore UK university branding activity through a 'deeper understanding of factors' (Christy and Wood 1999; De Chernatony *et al.* 1998).

Specific objectives of the research were explored earlier, but ultimately the aim was to investigate the degree to which branding is seen as an important strategic activity in UK universities, and the extent to which the value of such activity can be articulated by those who often drive it: university leaders and marketing professionals.

The sample involved two distinct stages: initially fourteen interviews with vice chancellors, followed by eighteen interviews with university heads of marketing or external relations, completed in 2008. The sample size is broadly in line with McGivern (2003) as appropriate to understand interviewees' collective views on a topic but it is conceded that results can only be argued to offer indicative results (Miles and Huberman 1994).

The sample in this research broadly reflected that in Chapleo (2005) where UK universities were segmented into three sub-groups based on incorporation date and comprised new universities (1992 and post-1992), 'red-brick' middle group universities (1950s–1960s) and older universities (incorporated before 1950). Universities from these three disparate sectors were included in order to identify similarities and differences (Bennett *et al.* 2007). Within these categories the sample was one of convenience, making the most of opportunities to ask potentially useful informants where access can be difficult (Daymon and Holloway 2004). University leaders, senior marketing and careers personnel were selected as they represented experts who can draw on their specialist knowledge to define the fundamental characteristics of relevant matters (Tremblay 1982; De Chernatony and Segal Horn 2003).

Semi-structured interviews were utilised, as complex issues can be penetrated (Gummesson 2005; Chisnall 1992) in line with other branding studies (Hankinson 2004). Whilst an interview guide was used, respondents were invited to expand upon ideas and concepts as they wished. The average duration of interviews was 37 minutes. The interviews were transcribed to assist content analysis (Goodman 1999). Analysis was informed by Miles and Huberman (1994) and Schilling (2006), who advocate coding that attaches each statement or phrase to defined dimensions derived from theory and prior research. The results were assessed by an independent research assistant to maximise the benefits of qualitative research by allowing a degree of subjective judgement from the researcher (Flick 2006) and hopefully therefore data of a 'richer' nature (Daymon and Holloway 2004).

It should be stated that the anonymity required by some participants (in discussing specific details of marketing activity, for example) made the attribution of direct quotes awkward. A number of pertinent quotes were assigned by age category of university, however, in an attempt to address this issue.

Findings and discussion

Rationale for branding UK universities

There was a wide variance in the responses among senior marketing personnel, from broad benefits ('to achieve clarity' or 'to be more competitive') to far more specific ('for stakeholders to recognise the university'). Several respondents talked of trying to 'change a negative' or 'undesirable' position. This has resonance of parallels with 'place brands' (Hankinson 2004; Mighall 2008), as institutions concerned also mentioned the negative or erroneous perception of their location city/town. Whilst not the same, it seems there may be possibilities for universities to learn from work on place brands.

Respondents suggested a role for branding at a time when institutions may merge or be involved in takeovers (Manchester was suggested as an example) and another of the wish 'to position the institution as world class in an international arena' indicative of the international competition UK universities now face (Binsardi and Ekwulugo 2003). Warwick was often mentioned as a successfully branded institution in this context.

Some senior marketers discussed the role of branding in their institutions in broader terms. There was talk of 'communicating what the university does in all its breadth' (middle university), and one particularly interesting objective was to 'capture stakeholders and get them "on brand"; in other words to enable and encourage them to communicate the brand message' (new university). The new university marketer summarised this as 'the role of branding used to be to try to maintain consistency of imagery and message, and to communicate to people what the university stands for, but today the aim is to get the stakeholders of the university to communicate the brand'.

Finally, the need to 'establish a unique/clear position' was expressed by several institutions, seemingly driven by recent UK government policy (Stamp 2004).

Among HEI leaders there was also some variation in the understanding of the rationale for branding in the sector. The facts that they defined brand in slightly different ways, and sometimes overlapped it with 'reputation' are perhaps symptomatic of the differences in understanding of the purpose and rationale of branding activity. There was, however, a consensus that it is an important strategic activity for a university (and likely to remain so), driven by government agendas, funding issues, tuition fees and mergers/alliances. It seems that leaders and senior marketing personnel can, as would be expected, argue a coherent rationale for university branding activity in their institution, but that there is a variety in the understanding of why this is necessary and what it can/should achieve. The key reasons for branding a university evident in this work are summarised in Figure 9.1.

Is the purpose and value of branding clear?

The predominant view of senior marketing personnel was that the sector enerally was not consistent concerning the objectives of branding, with talk of 'misconceptions, even at a senior level' (new university) or that 'the sector is totally unclear about it' (new university).

However, a number of respondents gave more positive responses about clarity of objectives, with views that 'there has been improvement, but there is still a

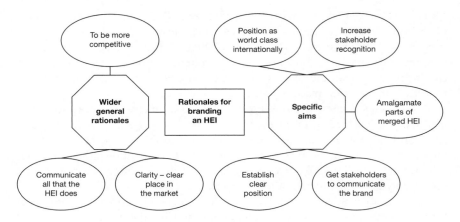

Figure 9.1 Identified rationales for branding a UK HEI

long way to go' (new university). It may be argued that, whilst sector marketers suggest a rationale for branding this is by no means unanimous, especially outside marketing staff.

There was a sense among UK university leaders that branding was a necessary reaction to macro factors such as 'tuition fees, funding issues, government push to differentiation and mergers'. The idea of institutions wishing 'to occupy a clear place in the market' was offered as the clearest purpose for branding among UK university leaders. A question that is seemingly evident is whether the rationale for branding HEIs is to some extent particular to the political landscape in the UK in the first decade of the twenty-first century, and therefore assumptions that these driving forces translate internationally, or will persist in the UK are risky.

It is perhaps indicative of the sample, but there was a limited sense of questioning the value of branding among either group of interviewees. This perhaps demonstrates the widely varying expectation of what branding activity can and should achieve for the university. However, it was interesting (and surprising) that there was, despite these widely varying expectations of branding's benefits, comparatively little mention of linking back to overall university strategic objectives among senior marketing personnel (although university leaders were more inclined to make this link).

Does branding a UK university add 'real value'?

The majority of senior marketing respondents unequivocally thought that it is a necessary process given current government HE policies (middle university) or that, 'whilst it can be seen as superficial, it is actually a necessary long-term process' (new university). Several others were a little more ambiguous but were generally supportive of some aspect of the long-term value of branding activity, or saw it as closely related to reputation management.

However, a number of marketing respondents were more cynical, with one new university in particular arguing that it was 'a fad'. This is interesting when it is considered that the respondents are those who in general are likely to be 'championing' branding at the university management level but even here there was a degree of cynicism on the value of the branding process.

The other group perhaps likely to be critical to the branding agenda within universities are the leaders, but they generally viewed branding as an activity of strategic importance, and likely to remain so unless government policy changes dramatically.

Ultimately, a key question in the applicability of branding concepts may be how they are conceived and conceptualised, which inevitably leads to questions on the applicability of the current branding models to the UK HE context.

Are the current approaches and techniques of branding applicable to the UK university sector?

When senior marketing professionals were interviewed on this topic, there were interesting comments that university branding 'probably does not borrow or learn enough from commercial approaches' (middle university) although it was conceded by several respondents that there is a danger of trying to use inappropriate models for university branding, typified by a new university view that 'some lessons can be learned', but that 'intelligent application of branding theory' is important due to the nature of the higher education sector.

Several marketing respondents suggested that some universities have tried simple application of commercial branding models, but that these are not wholly appropriate. UK university leaders echoed this view to some extent, suggesting that there is little evidence of a convincing model to construct and manage a brand in institutions such as universities. One chief executive of a 'middle group' university asked 'do we build one overall institutional brand that encompasses all we do, or do we have a series of strong sub brands which have a stronger profile than the overall institutional brand?' It seems reasonable to conclude that whilst a lot can be learned from commercial branding practice, the particular nature of HEIs as large, complex, quasi-commercial organisations founded on the principle of academic freedom means that a branding approach that takes account of these qualities, whilst not easy to design or indeed to implement, is required.

Limitations and criticisms of branding activity in UK universities

As well as the discussed 'lack of a clear model to build an HE brand', other views of respondents on the general limitations of branding activity in UK universities were explored. Both senior marketing personnel and leaders were generally

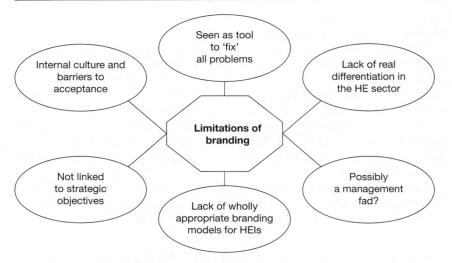

Figure 9.2 Perceived limitations of the branding concept in university sector

supportive of branding but it was conceded that it was a problematic business, with factors such as 'the lack of real differentiation in the sector', 'internal barriers to acceptance' and 'the particularly diverse nature of universities that is hard to encapsulate' being widely cited, particularly among university leaders. Some of these factors were discussed by senior marketing personnel, but this group were perhaps more consistently supportive of branding activity, although several did suggest that the current spate of branding activity was a 'management trend'.

It was notable that no one talked of any inherent unsuitability of marketing concepts; although it was conceded that within their universities others questioned the suitability. In reality some leaders hinted at questioning aspects of branding but suggested that the agenda was driven at a government policy level. The criticisms and limitations of branding as applied to universities are summarised in Figure 9.2.

Conclusions

Overall, many of the issues identified in relation to branding UK HE are seemingly influenced by UK political and economic agendas at the time of the research. This obviously makes conclusions UK specific to some extent and limits the extent to which they can be taken as representative for HEIs internationally. However, many countries are experiencing the marketisation of HE to some extent and therefore, whilst generalisations should be treated with caution, the issues should resonate with HEIs outside the UK. As long ago as 1999 it was suggested that the USA had already been through the clash of cultures that led to greater marketisation (Sanders 1999) but many European countries are in a similar position to the UK to some degree.

Leaders of UK universities seemingly saw branding as an activity of strategic importance, and likely to remain so. There was a degree of overlap in their understanding of brand with that of reputation, but most were able to articulate a rationale for branding, albeit often in broad terms. The sector marketing professionals were also able to articulate *a* rationale, as one would expect, but do not necessarily have a consistent view of this rationale. Whilst it is conceded that branding in any sector does not always have the same objectives, there seems to be a danger that in UK HE it becomes seen as a tool to fix all problems, or something that 'we should be doing'.

It was notable that there was limited mention of linking branding programmes to overall university strategic objectives, particularly among the senior marketing personnel. A link to institutional strategy would seem to be a natural underpinning of branding and although the sample was exploratory (and therefore to assume that this is always the case would be unfair to the HE marketing profession), it does seem curious and should perhaps be further investigated.

On the question of whether the current techniques of branding are applicable to the UK university sector, the lack of a clear model to facilitate building a brand in a university was identified as a problem. Any consensus seemed to suggest that simplistic application of commercial approaches is not helpful.

Overall, whilst there seemed to be broad support for branding as a strategic activity and a general understanding of benefits, the consistency of views on this were limited. Many aspects of any degree of consensus, however, rely upon the implicit assumption that marketisation of UK HE is a good thing; an assumption that may be robustly challenged (Gibbs 2001: 93). A counter argument, however, may be underpinned by looking towards American Ivy League institutions and their market 'success'; perhaps UK HE can learn from aspects of their approach applied in a UK context.

Whilst UK government policies push HE towards a market system, it seems reasonable to argue that aspects of branding can be beneficial in specific areas such as awareness of course offerings, differentiation and communicating strengths (Mighall 2009). What is required, however, is perhaps a subtler bespoke approach to branding based upon an understanding of the diverse, complex and unique nature of UK universities. To simply apply commercial branding techniques and approaches without consideration of the nature of HE would logically seem to be inappropriate, and findings in this research seem to support this suggestion. This 'failure to domesticate marketing' and the corresponding simplistic use of borrowed wisdom from business may threaten the viability of activities such as branding and has contributed to negative attitudes, particularly among academics (Maringe 2005).

The debate over branding in UK HE continues, but the fact that spending money on branding activity can be contentious suggests the need for further empirical investigation of both the suitability of many of the concepts and appropriate ways to measure the value of branding a university. This has to be based upon a fundamental examination of branding's role within the equally contentious trend towards the marketisation of UK higher education.

References

Ambler, T., Bhattacharya, C. B., Edell, J., Keller, K. L., Lemon, K. N. and Mittal, V. (2002) 'Relating brand and customer perspectives on marketing management', *Journal of Service Research*, 5(1):13–25.

Bakewell, J and Gibson-Sweet, M. F. (1998) 'Strategic marketing in a changing environment – are the new UK universities in danger of being "stuck in the middle"?', *International Journal of Educational Management*, 12(3):108–13.

Beerli Palacio, A., Diaz.Meneses, G. and Perez Perez, P. J. (2002) 'The configuration of the university image and its relationship with the satisfaction of students', *Journal of Educational Administration*, 40(5): 486–505.

Bennett, R., Ali-Choudhury, R. and Savani, S. (2007) 'Defining the components of a university brand: a qualitative investigation', paper presented at *International Conference of Higher Education Marketing*, 2–4 April, Krakow, Poland.

Binsardi A. and Ekwulugo F. (2003) 'International marketing of British education: research on the students' perception and the UK market penetration', *Marketing Intelligence & Planning*, 21(5): 318–27.

Bulotaite, N (2003) 'University heritage – an institutional tool for branding and marketing', *Higher Education in Europe*, 28(4): 449–54.

Bunzel, D. (2007) 'Universities sell their brands', *Journal of Product and Brand Management*, 16(2): 152–3.

Chapleo, C. (2004) 'Interpretation and implementation of reputation/brand management by UK university leaders', *Case International Journal of Educational Advancement* (June), 5(1): 7–23.

Chapleo, C. (2005) 'Do universities have "successful" brands?', *The International Journal of Educational Advancement*, 6(1): 54–64.

Chisnall, P. (1992) *Marketing Research*. Maidenhead: McGraw Hill.

Christy, R and Wood, M. (1999) 'Researching possibilities in marketing', *Qualitative Market Research: An International Journal*, 2(3): 189–96.

Daymon, C. and Holloway, I. (2004) *Qualitative Research Methods in Public Relations and Marketing Communications*. London: Routledge.

De Chernatony, L. and McDonald, M. (2005) *Creating Powerful Brands*. Oxford: Elsevier.

De Chernatony, L., Dall Olmo Riley, F. and Harris, F. (1998) 'Criteria to assess brand success', *Journal of Marketing Management*, 14: 765–81.

De Chernatony, L. and Segal-Horn, S. (2003) 'The criteria for successful service brands', *European Journal of Marketing*, 37(7/8): 1095–1118.

Flick, U. (2006) *An Introduction to Qualitative Research* (3rd edn). London: Sage Publications.

Gibbs, P. (2001) 'Higher education as a market: a problem or solution?', *Studies in Higher Education*, 26(1): 85–94.

Goodman, M. R. V. (1999) 'The pursuit of value through qualitative market research', *Qualitative Market Research: An International Journal*, 2(2): 111–20.

Gray, B. J., Fam, K. and Llane, V. (2003) 'Branding universities in Asian markets', *Journal of Product & Brand Management*, 15(7): 466–7.

Gummesson, E. (2005) 'Qualitative research in marketing: road-map for a wilderness of complexity and unpredictability', *European Journal of Marketing*, 39(3/4): 309–27.

Hankinson, G. (2004) 'Relational network brands: towards a conceptual model of place brands', *Journal of Vacation Marketing*, 10(2): 109–21.

HEFCE (2008) *Counting What is Measured or Measuring What Counts? – League Tables and Their Impact on Higher Education Institutions in England*, HEFCE Issues Paper, April 2008/14. Bristol: HEFCE.

Hemsley-Brown, J. and Goonawardana, S. (2007), 'Brand harmonization in the international higher education market', *Journal of Business Research*, (60): 942–8.

Hemsley-Brown, J. and Oplatka, I. (2006) 'Universities in a competitive marketplace – a systematic review of the literature on higher education marketing', *International Journal of Public Sector Management*, 19(4): 316–38.

Hoeffler, S. and Keller, K. (2003) 'The marketing advantages of strong brands', *Brand Management*, 10(6): 421–45.

Holt, D. (2002) 'Why do brands cause trouble? A dialectical theory of consumer culture and branding', *Journal of Consumer Research*, 29: 70–90.

Jevons, C (2006) 'Universities: a prime example of branding gone wrong', *Journal of Product and Brand Management*, 15(7): 466–7.

Johnston, A. (2001) 'Branding – the key to student recruitment (or maybe not)', *Education Marketing*, HEIST, March: 28–9.

Keller, K. L. (2003) *Strategic Brand Management*. New Jersey: Prentice Hall.

Klassen, M. (2002) 'Relationship marketing on the internet: the case of top and lower ranked universities and colleges', *Journal of Retailing and Consumer Services*, 9: 81–5.

Lowrie, A. (2007) 'Branding higher education: equivalence and difference in developing identity', *Journal of Business Research*, 60(9): 990–9.

Maringe, F. (2005) 'Interrogating the crisis in higher education marketing: the CORD model', *International Journal of Educational Management*, 19(7): 564–78.

Maringe, F. and Foskett, N. (2002) 'Marketing university education: the South African experience', *Higher Education Review*, 34(3): 18.

McGivern, Y. (2003) *The Practice of Market and Social Research: An Introduction*. London: FT Prentice Hall.

Melewar, T. C. and Akel, S. (2005) 'The role of corporate identity in the higher education sector', *Corporate Communications: An International Journal*, 10(1): 41–57.

Mighall, R. (2008) 'Rewards for town and gown', *Brand Strategy*, July: 34–5.

Mighall, R. (2009) 'What exactly *is* the purpose of branding the university?', conference presentation at *Discovering Futures*, 23 April, London.

Miles, M. B. and Huberman, A. M (1994) *Qualitative Data Analysis: An Expanded Sourcebook*. Thousand Oaks, CA: Sage.

Millward Brown International (1996) *The Good Health Guide*. Warwick: Millward Brown International.

Opoku, R, Abratt, R. and Pitt, L. (2006) 'Communicating brand personality: are the websites doing the talking for the top South African business schools?', *Brand Management*, 14(1–2): 20–39.

Rolfe, H. (2003) 'University strategy in an age of uncertainty: the effect of higher education funding on old and new universities', *Higher Education Quarterly*, 57(1): 24–47.

Sanders, C. (1999) 'Universities go for a spin', *Times Higher Education Supplement*, (10 December): 8.

Schilling, J. (2006) 'On the pragmatics of qualitative assessment: designing the process for content analysis', *European Journal of Psychological Assessment*, 22(1): 28–37.

Stamp, R. (2004) 'The new challenge of branding buy-in', *Education News* (Winter), Euro RSCG Riley: 7.

Temple, P. (2006) 'Branding higher education: illusion or reality?', *Perspectives*, 10(1): 15–19.

Temple, P. and Shattock, M. (2007) 'What does "branding" mean in higher education?', in B. Stensaker and V. D'Andrea (eds), *Branding in Higher Education: Exploring an Emerging Phenomenon*. Amsterdam: EAIR.

Tremblay, M. (1982) 'The key informant technique', in R. Burgess (ed.), *Field Research: A Sourcebook and Field Manual*. London: Allen and Unwin.

Veloutsou, C., Lewis, J. W. and Paton, R. A. (2004) 'University selection: information requirements and importance', *The International Journal of Educational Management*, 18(3): 160–71.

Waeraas, A. and Solbakk, M. (2008) 'Defining the essence of a university: lessons from higher education branding', *Higher Education*, 57(4): 449–62.

Young and Rubicam (1994) *Brand Asset Valuation*. London: Young & Rubicam.

Chapter 10

Access agreements, widening participation and market positionality: enabling student choice?

Colin McCaig

Introduction

This chapter presents an alternative view of marketised higher education from much of this volume: not only does it focus on how HEIs use marketing strategies to position themselves ethically in relation to competing HEIs of the same type, it also uses the concept of widening participation (WP) as a specific arena of institutions' marketing strategies and discusses the impact on student choice. It will locate evidence for increasing market positionality among HEIs within both marketing theory and in the historical development of widening participation policy in the English HE sector. More specifically this chapter will discuss how Office for Fair Access (OFFA) access agreements came to reflect the marketing positionality of institutions.[1] It will present an analysis of bursary and additional support regimes and types of outreach activities that reveal a tendency for more prestigious and less prestigious institutions to engage in quite different forms of widening participation activity. It will conclude that, paradoxically, the increasingly sophisticated use of widening participation as an arena for market differentiation reduces rather than increases applicants' ability to make informed choices given the complexity of student support arrangements.

Widening-participation-focused marketing activity designed to realise differentiation can be observed in many aspects of institutional behaviour, including marketing and the centralisation of admission practices (SPA 2008; Adnett and McCaig 2010), much of which can be construed as a logical response to the growth of state WP incentives. The following analysis concentrates specifically on how pre- and post-1992 institutions use access agreements to promote visions of widening participation that suit their own recruitment needs rather than to promote recruitment to the sector as a whole. In so doing such institutions perpetuate pre-existent differences between institutions in relation to access to HE.

The growth of English higher education

Three major themes emerge from an examination of the history of higher education development in the English context: first, it becomes clear that the episodic expansion of the sector in response to the needs of national economy has always been accompanied by calls to widen participation to under-represented groups; second, in most episodes of expansion, the traditional research universities have been left unaffected by the requirement to widen participation or engage in reform of any kind; historically, technical colleges and mechanics' institutes met the demand for new advanced-level curricula and absorbed most of the increased student numbers. The third major theme has been the increasing role of the central state in higher education.

The English higher education system, though highly stratified in terms of institutional history, mission and prestige, is a unitary one. Successive waves of expansion, most notably in 1965 when the government created 30 polytechnics, has seen the number of higher education institutions reach 130 in England by 2010. At the time polytechnics were created, largely from former technical colleges or mechanics' institutes, they were established as a *public sector* of higher education funded by local authorities; along with colleges of higher education (usually teacher-training colleges) and further education (FE) colleges, this sector was intended to be responsive to regional and national employment needs. A binary divide, then, with universities awarding their own degrees on one side and polytechnics and colleges delivering courses leading to degrees awarded by a state body (the Council of National Academic Awards) on the other, existed until 1992 when public HE and FE institutions were freed from local authority control and set out to diversify their missions.

The increasing role of the central state is crucial in any understanding of the development of higher education in England since the nineteenth century, particularly in relation to the increasing application of human capital concerns in response to national economic needs. Throughout the nineteenth century pressures to reform the universities by producing scientists, engineers and graduates suited to the new professions met with resistance from the traditionalists who believed that that a university education should have no market value; instead the universities' role was to develop a disinterested culture (Lyons 1983). This was challenged towards the end of the nineteenth century by the development of civic 'red-brick' universities (Briggs 1983), the funding of which was later taken on by the state.

Two world wars in the first half of the twentieth century further demonstrated the failings of the nation's higher-level scientific and engineering education. In response, successive post-war governments became more committed to education as a tool of workforce planning, and the route towards a coherent and more centralised HE system was signalled by a series of governmental reports calling for expansion of places, particularly in science and engineering (Allen 1988; Stewart 1989). Overall, successive governments increased higher education places from 50,000 in 1938–9 to 100,000 in 1958–9 (Allen 1988: 41).

Centralisation and expansion

Economic expediency and the need for a more highly trained workforce, coupled with unmet social demand for higher education, were also reflected by political pressures. The incoming Labour government in 1964 believed that higher education was not only good for the nation, but could also produce material and cultural benefits for an ever growing proportion of the population. Labour's promise of 'a programme of massive expansion in higher, further and university education' allowed them to be radical, yet firmly within the consensus of the times around the Robbins Report (Report of the Committee of Higher Education 1963). The Robbins Committee's first priority was for instruction in necessary skills, but that was buttressed by the other, more liberal, major aims of the report: to produce not just specialist but cultivated men and women; to further the advancement of the idea of learning as a good; and the transmission of culture.

Robbins was responding to calls for expansion from two directions, the politically desired science and technological imperative, and the twin social effects of 'bulge' (increased birth rate which increased demand for places) and 'trend' (more students staying on at school and taking A levels following the 1944 Education Act which delivered secondary education for all (Ashby 1983, cited in Nuttgens 1983)). Perhaps the main feature of the expansionist consensus was the perceived need to make higher education more accountable to the state: Robbins' recommendation that the funding of higher education came under the control of the Department for Education and Science was introduced by the outgoing Conservative government in 1963 (Simons 1991). This new public sector of higher education, with polytechnics delivering CNAA accredited degrees, allowed the traditional liberal universities to continue unmolested even as places expanded (McCaig 2000).

Expansion was also anticipated under the incoming Conservative government after 1970, with the 18-year-old cohort in HE predicted to rise to 22 per cent by 1981 (from 7 per cent in 1961 and 15 per cent in 1971, Kogan and Kogan 1983: 22). However, economic difficulties changed the funding environment and expansion was curtailed and the 18-year-old cohort attending HE fell from 14.2 per cent in 1972 to 12.4 per cent in 1978 despite steady rises in the numbers suitably qualified (Kogan and Kogan 1983: 25). Changing demographic factors noted by the 1978 Brown Paper *Higher Education into the 1990s* drew attention to the fact that there would be a decline in the 18-year-old cohort from 1985 until the mid-1990s when demographic growth would begin again (DES 1986: 7).

Expediency and the pressure to widen participation

Among solutions to address the falling cohort sizes discussed within the Employment Department was the (temporary) expansion of places for women, mature students and the working classes and for an increase in places to study vocational qualifications (DES 1986; Fulton and Ellwood 1989). Thus expanding opportunity through widening participation, though encouraged by such expediencies, was largely a by-product of demographics and the changing nature of the demand for labour. The fact that, as the DES noted, many of the universities did not fear a dilution of standards suggests that they expected to attract the same proportion of students with the best A level results, while the colleges of education and the polytechnics would again absorb these new kinds of students (DES 1986).

As long as the public sector reacted to the new conditions and widened access to pick up the slack in demand, the universities could maintain their supply at the prestige end of the market. While this might have satisfied those concerned with the needs of the national economy and those wishing to preserve standards at the universities, it fell short of the demands of egalitarian reformers who increasingly throughout the 1980s began to equate widening access and participation with social justice. This took the form of academic pressure: the Leverhulme study for the Society for Research into Higher Education presented evidence that proved to be influential in justifying expansion and widening access into the 1990s and beyond (SRHE 1983).

The Education Reform Act (ERA) of 1988 opened up new possibilities for course and institutional flexibility by abolishing tenure for academic staff at the established universities (Robertson 1995: 45). Expansion was also relaunched with a doubling of the age participation ratio (APR, of 18-year-olds attending HE) from 15 per cent to 30 per cent between 1988 and 1992, presenting the higher education system with a new set of problems: a mass system would henceforth be funded on the same basis as an elite system, which would inevitably increase social demands for accountability. The Conservative government's solution to this new set of conditions was to begin the process of transferring the costs from the state to the individual by the introduction of student loans to cover maintenance. Another act, the Further and Higher Education Act (1992), introduced further competition into the system by abolishing the binary divide and allowing former polytechnics and (some) colleges to become universities awarding their own degrees and compete openly for students (McCaig 2000).

Widening participation as a political and educational phenomenon clearly developed largely in response to expansion, and was rooted as much in the needs of the economy as in social demand although the fact that the huge increase in participation had not widened the social base was increasingly seen as inequitable as well as a waste of potential. During the 1980s and 1990s the expediency of expansion was matched by social justice arguments that could be traced back to Robbins, and these were reflected by key policy changes. Widening participation premia (additional funding per student from selected under-represented groups) were first introduced in the early 1990s and have been the subject of a period of sustained growth since 1997/8; WP performance indicators (PIs), introduced in 1999, have also been a factor along with other non-financial measures (for example the introduction of the *Statistical Bulletin on Widening Participation*, issued by the Universities and Colleges Admissions Service, UCAS). More recently government has introduced targets for participation (Pugh *et al.* 2005) that have made WP a mainstream activity for all kinds of institutions, particularly since the Labour party came into power in 1997 with a social justice agenda. While people from lower socio-economic backgrounds constitute around half of the population of England, they account for just 29 per cent of young, full-time, first-time entrants to higher education (National Audit Office 2008), a proportion that has not grown despite the growth in places.

In 1999 the government required all HEIs to issue statements outlining what they were doing to widen participation, and in the same year launched the Excellence Challenge programme (later rechristened Aimhigher) designed to widen participation in higher education by raising aspirations among young people from under-represented groups with the ability to benefit from it (echoing Robbins). Much of the funding was delivered through university-led regional Aimhigher partnerships (of HEIs, colleges and schools) ensuring the engagement of the whole sector in WP for the first time. In 2001 all HEIs were asked for widening participation strategies that set out plans, targets and activities to be undertaken during 2001–4. Changes to the funding of English HE announced in the White Paper *The Future of Higher Education* (DfES, 2003) introduced the requirement for institutions that wished to charge more than the standard fee of £1,225 per annum (they could and mostly did charge up to £3,000 pa from 2006/7) to outline, in an access agreement to be lodged with the OFFA, the combination of bursaries and outreach that would offset the effects of the higher fee on applicants from under-represented backgrounds. This combination of state interventions by the Labour government introduced real financial incentives for all institutions not only to take WP seriously but also opened up the opportunity for WP to become part of institutional market positioning.

The English higher education market

Traditional marketing theory would anticipate that HEIs try to differentiate themselves from competing institutions. Gibbs and Knapp identify two key aspects of market differentiation: the product (in higher education, the programmes on offer) and the image of the institution. For the 'right image' it is important for institutions to be firmly located in a 'choice set' (Gibbs and Knapp 2002); choice sets are those few clear-cut and instantly recognised groupings, for example the 'prestigious research university' choice set, or the 'accessible to all' choice set. Location within a choice set makes it easier for consumers to make application or acceptance decisions. From the institutional perspective, prestigious HEIs may wish to *consolidate* a position within their 'choice set' by emphasising the high entry requirements for its programmes of study and emphasising the values of excellence and global reputation. However, by definition not all institutions can be prestigious. Alternative competitive strategies might include re-engineering institutional processes in relation to admissions, outreach and WP policies in order to affect demand to *alter perceptions* about the institution (Gibbs and Knapp 2002).

For example a post-1992 institution may wish to portray itself as more prestigious by withdrawing sub-degree qualifications such as Higher National Diplomas (HNDs) and Foundation degrees and concentrating on degree and postgraduate programmes. Alternatively post-1992 institutions may choose to make a virtue of their inclusiveness and consolidate their position by offering more transitional support and encouraging applicants by offering different types of higher education experience. Maringe (2005) has identified a series of distinct but interrelated conceptualisations of marketing used by HEIs, of which two are of interest here. One is the *production* view of HE marketing which sees institutions striving to promote the product (programmes of study) as widely as possible and at the lowest possible costs for the consumer (for example by offering part-time or distance learning programmes), or by increasing production by providing additional programmes of study that attract students with additional WP funding attached.

The other concept is the *selling philosophy* of marketing where the emphasis is not so much on the product but on the image of the institution (for example, as a prestigious institution). However, widening participation, with its attendant 'socially just' and 'open access' image also presents post-1992 institutions with an opportunity to engage in the *selling philosophy* even without having to move into another choice set. We can see examples of this kind of 'image selling' marketing strategy in recent changes to institutional admissions practices introduced since the *Fair Admissions* report by Schwartz in 2004 (DfES 2004). A review of the impact of Schwartz four years on found that many institutions were absorbing once autonomous admissions functions within central departments primarily responsible for marketing or WP (SPA 2008; Adnett and McCaig 2010). More overtly, OFFA access agreements provide state-sponsored opportunity for institutions to demonstrate market differentiation and burnish their WP image. The remainder of this chapter looks in detail at how such agreements reflect marketing positionality.

Differentiation: the role of OFFA access agreements in shaping the English HE market

There are two main tools of differentiation that OFFA access agreements contain: targeted additional financial support (over and above mandatory means-tested bursaries) for certain applicants on certain courses; and targeted outreach and support activities for applicants from certain under-represented groups. Both can have a significant impact on the shape of an institution's student body and send or reinforce key messages about the nature of the institution. Marketing theory suggests that market efficiency in higher education systems requires full information being available to consumers (Gibbs and Knapp 2002). In HE systems where students contribute to their fees and maintenance costs (such as England, Australia and the US) the notion of full information should include bursary and other financial support levels for the purpose of comparison. However, the limited research carried out thus far suggests that the access agreement bursary/support regime introduced in England after 2006/7 is too complex for consumers to make application decisions based on the level of support available in the marketplace.

This is partly because, in addition to bursaries available to all applicants within residual income bands, institutions offer a variety of additional financial support scholarships for particular groups (e.g. for mature applicants, those with dependants, those from local low participation neighbourhoods, those from poor backgrounds that display merit, etc.) and then often to only a few applicants each year, making comparison between offers problematic (McCaig and Adnett 2009; Adnett and Tlupova 2007, Davies *et al.* 2008, Callendar 2009a, 2009b).

Evidence in this part of the chapter comes mainly from a content analysis of two sets of a sample of twenty access agreements; one set from 2006 (original access agreements) and one set from 2008 (revised access agreements). The same sample of institutions was used on each occasion and contained ten pre-1992 institutions, all members of the Russell Group of research universities, and ten large post-1992 institutions (McCaig 2006; McCaig and Adnett 2009). The analyses suggest that, first, targeting additional financial support and outreach varies between HEI types; second, that the incidence of targeting increased between 2006 and 2008; and third, that the shift of funding towards discretionary support represents a reduction in the amount of mandatory support for all students given the same overall spend.

While both institution types spent a similar proportion of the additional fee income by sample average (25 per cent for pre-1992s; 23.5 per cent for post-1992s), pre-1992s accepted far fewer applicants from lower social classes – a sample average of 18.9 per cent compared with a sample average of 41.6 per cent among post-1992s (McCaig and Adnett 2009: 23). Note that these proportions are significantly below benchmark for pre-1992s and above benchmark for post-1992s. This means that pre-1992s can offer far more generous bursaries and additional financial support to applicants from under-represented groups (NAO 2008). On average maximum bursaries from our sample of pre-1992 institutions in 2006 was £1,625 per annum; for post-1992s it was £865 per annum (the minimum amount specified by OFFA was £300, raised to £310 by 2008). Analysis of the revised 2008 agreements, however, showed a slight decline among both sectors' bursaries: the pre-1992s' sample average was £1,521, the post-1992s' average £678 (a slightly larger decline) (McCaig and Adnett 2009: 28). The reason for this is a shift to additional financial support targeted at specific groups institutions wished to recruit, as we shall see.

These findings suggest that institutions are in fact engaged in a process of using agreements to shape the nature of their student body in the way marketing theory would describe. Indeed, prior to the introduction of the variable fees/bursary regime the DfES baseline assessment of institutions' planning found that many were already targeting under-represented groups in an attempt at institutional repositioning (Temple *et al.* 2005). Nor was this a surprise to government: the Department for Business, Innovation and Skills (BIS, the government department responsible for HE policy since 2009) launched a review of tuition fees with a brief to explore the potential for further targeting of bursaries in the name of supporting fair access (BIS 2009: 6) presumably as a means of ensuring greater differentiation. It should also be noted that government and the sector ignored a swathe of advice to introduce a national bursary scheme that would have obviated the inequalities and confusion for consumers highlighted by this and other analyses (see Callender 2009a, 2009b; Chester and Bekhradnia 2008).

Research into institutional differentiation research in the United States of America, with a longer history of tuition fee/bursary regimes, points to the dangers inherent in replacing mandatory aid with discretionary aid. Levels of aid granted on the basis of merit (rather than need) have become more important over time. In the US context, competition between institutions leads to a drive to enrol 'desirable' students (those with good SAT scores and grades) which can raise institutions' position in league tables (Heller 2006). Thus discretionary merit aid, by offering disproportionate support to middle-class applicants from families too well off to get federal and state aid, can work against system-wide widening participation outcomes for under-represented groups that bursaries were designed to support.

In the English context institutions are using an ostensibly generic WP resource (the additional fee income derived from the variable tuition fees) to reshape specific patterns of recruitment. These typically include scholarships and special bursaries on the basis of: merit or excellence; applications to shortage subjects; applicants from partner institutions; on the basis of age (i.e. mature students); having responsibility for dependents; being in financial hardship; or demonstrating potential (McCaig and Adnett 2009).

Such discretionary and highly targeted support, of course, adds layers of complexity to the bursary market applicants are supposed to be able to negotiate. A fully functioning market with perfect information would clear applicants and places, with those most in need of additional support able to access that support; however due to the variability in bursary/support regimes the English HE market cannot clear in such a way. Potential applicants may be aware that University X offers a bursary of £1,000 per year of study (while University Y offers the minimum £310), but they almost certainly will not be aware that University Y is also offering £1,000 for 25 locally based applicants over the age of 30 with family responsibilities willing to study a shortage subject. So how did this situation come about?

Access agreements were not designed to strengthen the market in higher education: the then Secretary of State, Charles Clarke MP, 'hoped that price should not affect student choice of whether to go to university, where to study or what course to take' (Callendar 2009a). However, many pre-1992 institutions chose to apply the requirement to offer bursary support to students with non-needs based bursaries offered on top of the basic mandatory £310 bursary, thereby creating a bursary/support market based on their own recruitment patterns and needs that other institutions were not slow to take advantage of.

Additional financial support and outreach changes between 2006 and 2008

Comparative analysis of the 2006 and 2008 agreements shows that pre-1992 institutions remain more likely to offer additional financial support in the form of targeted bursaries and scholarships. However, there is evidence to suggest that post-1992s have shifted some of their standard bursary support to funding additional financial support in the manner of pre-1992 institutions in their 2006 agreements and become more sophisticated in their marketing (McCaig and Adnett 2009). Targeted discretionary bursaries and scholarships on offer from our sample of pre-1992s grew from a maximum of £1,468 to £1,527 per annum between 2006 and 2008; however, post-1992 institutions' maximum support grew from £633 to £1,147 per annum (McCaig and Adnett 2009: 30) thereby significantly closing the gap with, or aping the marketing strategies of, pre-1992s.

The profile and criteria for the selection of those groups offered additional financial support also varied by HEI type, as do the types of activities offered. Generally, pre-1992 institutions focused on *individuals with potential* to succeed, while post-1992s focused on tackling *socio-economic barriers* to accessing higher education. Overall, pre-1992 institutions appeared to become more plural between the 2006 and 2008 agreements in the range of categories supported, with more offering additional financial support for mature students and for those enrolling in shortage subjects, merit based and financial hardship. The patterns identified in the 2006 analysis remained, however by 2008: pre-1992s were more likely to offer additional support for shortage subjects, those demonstrating 'potential' or merit, those on PGCE courses and for those with financial hardship; while post-1992s were more likely to offer support for students enrolling from local schools and colleges linked by formal progression arrangements and those undertaking vocational programmes. Overall post-1992s engaged with a wider range of age groups and a wider range of social groups, and were more likely to be engaged with learners with disabilities.

This is supported by findings from other research (e.g. McCaig *et al.* 2007) which also found clear variation by institution type in the nature of WP engagement with under-represented groups. Data from the Educational Providers Survey (part of the National Evaluation of Aimhigher) in 2006 reveals that not only do post-1992 institutions engage with a wider range of social groups (e.g. work-based learners, parents/carers, looked-after children), they are also more likely to engage with most of the groups that pre-1992 institutions also engage with (the exception being people from lower social classes; HEFCE 2006).

In access agreements, pre-1992s are more likely to concentrate on activities relating to the potential applicant to higher education (mentoring, summer schools, tariff points achieved), and especially those with financial circumstances that might discourage entry to HE. These may come from those who are first generation of their family to go onto HE, those from low participation neighbourhoods or lower socio-economic classes; pre-1992s also concentrated their efforts on high achievers amongst those from groups associated with low entry rates, i.e. those who would enter HE but be more likely to choose a post-1992 institution in the absence of such interventions by pre-1992s. These would include taster events, mentoring, residential schools and outreach activities with schools, emphasising help for *individuals* from under-represented groups.

By contrast post-1992 institutions were more likely to highlight curriculum development and progression arrangements between the institution and the local colleges and schools (such as compact schemes) and also to enhance vocational progression in conjunction with Local Learning Networks (LLNs). Post-1992s were also more likely to offer pre-entry information advice and guidance (IAG), events for parents and carers, sector-related HE taster events and promoting vocational routes to HE all of which are aimed at under-represented *groups* or supporting national economic needs; often this amounts to the same thing as students from under-represented groups are more likely to enrol on vocational HE programmes (Archer 2003; Sutton Trust 2004).

Given this systemic and vocational focus, post-1992 institutions remained more likely to engage in a range of activities that none of the sample pre-1992s were engaged in: the mapping of apprenticeship routes to HE, collaborative curriculum development, mapping of vocational/non-traditional routes to HE and offering non-residential schools. Widening participation for post-1992s can therefore be characterised as concerned with encouraging a wider uptake of HE in vocational subject areas and meeting the needs of employers; while for pre-1992s WP can be characterised as about identifying, encouraging and selecting talented individuals suitable for high academic achievement.

In both cases the main focus of activities and under-represented groups targeted seems to be involvement with specific institutions rather than general aspiration-raising and thus exemplify the selling philosophy of institutional marketing. This focus is also apparent in the sophisticated maneuvering of bursary pricing among institutions in the absence of a national bursary scheme that would have reduced complexity for consumers (Callender 2009a, 2009b; Chester and Bekhradnia 2008).

Discussion

Overall the introduction of OFFA access agreements, recent changes to admissions policies and outreach priorities seem to have reinforced the notion that there are two distinct types of institutions working towards their own conceptions of widening participation. In access agreements pre-1992 institutions offer larger bursaries to fewer potential students, and engage with fewer disadvantaged groups in a more restricted way. Pre-1992 institutions thus use state WP funding to reinforce their choice set image as 'selecting' institutions with high entry standards, but willing to take high-achieving students from poor and under-represented groups. Partnership outreach work is more often with non-statutory bodies concerned with identifying excellence among the under-represented, such as the National Association of Gifted and Talented Youth and the Sutton Trust. In marketing terms, pre-1992 institutions use widening participation to soften their reputation as austere, elitist institutions closed off to the needs and desires of the majority. Such institutions appeal to the meritocratic instinct: they sell the message that, if you are good enough you can get in here, whatever your background.

Meanwhile, post-1992 institutions as 'recruiting institutions' use state WP funding to increase student numbers which they do by promoting their product, and even by tailoring their product by designing programmes that are attractive to a wider cohort of potential students. They offer lower bursaries and less additional financial support, but to a wider group of potential applicants and from roughly the same proportion of additional income derived from variable fees as pre-1992s (McCaig and Adnett 2009). Outreach is similarly plural and more likely to involve collaborative work with state funded partnerships such as Aimhigher and Lifelong Learning Networks designed to foster vocational progression routes. The emphasis here is necessarily about raising awareness and fighting cultural resistance to accruing debt to fund higher education participation, rather than spending on direct recruitment to the institution (though of course they benefit as most WP students study at their local post-1992 institution). In marketing terms, widening participation allows such institutions to present themselves as socially aware providers of opportunity for all social types in a supportive student-friendly environment and responsive to the needs of the local/regional economy.

This latest example of central state involvement, combining financial incentives (the ability to charge more per student) with a weak form of accountability (the need to use access agreements to justify the additional money in WP terms) reinforces the historical tendency to reform English HE while at the same time retaining institutional autonomy for the most prestigious universities. In the last 15 years we have witnessed another of the episodic periods of expansion of the sector noted earlier (again largely in response to the needs of national economy), and once again this has been accompanied by calls to widen participation to under-represented groups. However, because the government and powerful research institutions among the HE sector chose not to introduce a national bursary scheme, providing means-tested support to any applicant offered a place anywhere in the system, the state has provided the setting for a sophisticated marketplace in which widening participation is invited to play a prominent part.

Institutions have therefore adapted the state interest by focusing (in some cases refocusing) their marketing strategies, in effect playing the game. Was this inevitable? Access agreements offered an opportunity for all institutions to portray themselves as WP institutions and they would have been foolish to turn this down. However, the state's hands-off approach to access agreements has resulted in such a degree of complexity for consumers that many of these market signals seem to have (so far at least) gone unnoticed. Another effect has been that, overall, as in previous periods of expansion, the traditional research universities have been left unaffected by the requirement to widen participation or engage in reform of any kind, beyond offering a few bursaries to poor but bright applicants; once again it is the post-1992 institutions that have adapted to calls for a new kind of HE by providing the most imaginative outreach and support package and by engaging in vocational curriculum design. Meanwhile, prestige institutions use state WP funding to market themselves as meritocratic bastions of quality and tradition – but have they done anything to enable student choice?

Notes

1   The Office for Fair Access (OFFA) was established by the Higher Education Act (2004) which also introduced variable tuition fees. Institutions wishing to charge more than the standard fee rate (£1,225 per year of study) had to submit Access Agreements to OFFA outlining how they would use some of the additional fee income to support applicants from under-represented groups who might otherwise be deterred (OFFA 2004).

References

Admissions to Higher Education Steering Group (2004) *Fair Admissions to Higher Education: Recommendations for Good Practice* (Schwartz Report). London: Department for Education and Skills.

Adnett, N. and Tlupova, D. (2007) *Variable Tuition Fees and Widening Participation: Issues and Some Early Evidence*, paper to *BERA Annual Conference*, September.

Adnett, N. and McCaig, C. (2010) 'Achieving transparency, consistency and fairness in English HE admissions: progress since Schwartz?' *Higher Education Quarterly* (forthcoming).

Allen, M. (1988) *The Goals of Universities*. Milton Keynes: The Society for Research into Higher Education and The Open University Press.

Archer, L. (2003) 'Social class and higher education', in L. Archer, M. Hutching and A. Ross (eds), *Higher Education and Social Class: Issues of Exclusion and Inclusion.*, London and New York: Routledge Falmer.

BIS (2009) *Higher Ambitions: The Future of Universities in a Knowledge Economy. Executive Summary*, BIS, November.

Briggs, A. (1983) *Tradition and Innovation in British Universities, c.1860–1960*, in N. Phillipson (ed.) *Universities, Society and the Future*. Edinburgh: Edinburgh University Press.

Callendar, C. (2009a) 'Institutional aid in England: promoting widening participation or perpetuating inequalities', in J. Knight (ed.) *Financing Equity and Access in Higher Education*. Rotterdam: Sense Publishing.

Callendar, C. (2009b) *Institutional Bursaries in England:Findings from the Latest OFFA Research*, paper to the *Nuffield Foundation Seminar Institutional Aid for Students in the UK and USA*, London, May 19.

Chester, J. and Bekhradnia, B. (2008) *Financial Support in English Universities: The Case for a National Bursary Scheme*. Oxford: Higher Education Policy Institute.

Davies, P., Slack, K., Hughes, A., Mangan, J. and Vigurs, K. (2008) *Knowing Where to Study? Fees, Bursaries and Fair Access*. London: Sutton Trust.

Department for Education and Skills (2003) *The Future of Higher Education White Paper*, Report of the United Kingdom Government.

Department for Education and Skills (DfES) (2004) *Fair Admissions to Higher Education: Draft Recommendations for Consultation*. London: DfES.

Department of Education and Science (DES) (1978) *Higher Education into the 1990s*. London: HMSO.

Department of Education and Science (DES) (1986) *Projections of Demand for Higher Education in Great Britain 1986–2000*, DES 2904/8. London: HMSO.

Fulton, O. and Ellwood, S. (1989) *Admissions to Higher Education: Policy and Practice*. Sheffield: Training Agency.

Gibbs, P. and Knapp, M. (2002) *Marketing Further and Higher Education Research: An Educators' Guide to Promoting Courses, Departments and Institutions*. London: Kogan Page.

HEFCE (2006) *National Evaluation of Aimhigher: Survey of Higher Education Institutions, Further Education Colleges and Work-based Learning Providers*. London: Higher Education Funding Council for England.

Heller, D. (2006) *Merit Aid and College Access*, paper presented at the *Symposium on the Consequences of Merit-Based Student Aid*. Madison: University of Wisconsin

Kogan, M. and Kogan, D. (1983) *The Attack on Higher Education*. London: Kogan Page.

Lyons, F. S. (1983) 'The idea of the university from Newman to Robbins', in N. Phillipson (ed.) (1983) *Universities, Society and the Future*. Edinburgh: Edinburgh University Press.

Maringe, F. (2005) 'Interrogating the crisis in higher education marketing: the CORD model', *International Journal of Educational Management*, 19(7): 564–78.

McCaig, C. (2000) *Preparing for Government: Educational Policymaking in the Labour Party, 1994–1999*. University of Sheffield (unpublished PhD thesis).

McCaig, C. (2006) *Variable Tuition Fees: Widening Participation and Institutional Marketing Strategies*, paper to the *Annual Conference of the British Educational Research Association*, September.

McCaig, C. and Adnett, N. (2008) *Variable Tuition Fees and the Impact of Access Agreements on Widening Participation and Fair Access*, paper presented to *BERA*, Edinburgh, September.

McCaig, C., Stevens, A. and Bowers-Brown, T. (2007) 'Does Aimhigher work? Evidence from the national evaluation', *Higher Education Research Network 2006 Research Report*. Sheffield: Sheffield Hallam University

McCaig, C. and Adnett, N. (2009) 'English Universities, additional fee income and access agreements: their impact on widening participation and fair access', *British Journal of Educational Studies*, 57(1): 18–36.

National Audit Office (2008) *Widening Participation in Higher Education*. London: The Stationery Office.

Nuttgens, P. (1983) 'Technology and the university', in N. Phillipson (ed.) *Universities, Society and the Future*. Edinburgh: Edinburgh University Press, pp. 167–85.

OFFA (2004) *Producing Access Agreements: OFFA Guidance to Institutions*, 2004/01. Bristol: OFFA.

Pugh, G., Coates, G., and Adnett, N. (2005) 'Performance indicators and widening participation in the UK', *Higher Education Quarterly*, 59(1): 19–39.

Report of the Committee on Higher Education appointed by the Prime Minister. Volume I: Report, *The Robbins Report*, 1963, Report of the United Kingdom Government.

Robertson, D (1995) 'Universities and the public interest: time to strike a new bargain?', *Renewal*, 3(4), October.

Simons, B. (1991) *Education and the Social Order*. London: Lawrence & Wishart.

The Society for Research into Higher Education (1983) *Excellence in Diversity: Towards a New Strategy for Higher Education*. University of Surrey: SRHE.

Stewart, W. A. C. (1989) *Higher Education in Postwar Britain*. London: Macmillan.

Supporting Professionalism in Admissions (SPA) (2008) *Fair Admissions to Higher Education: A Review of the Implementation of the Schwartz Report Principles Three Years On*. Cheltenham: SPA.

Sutton Trust (2004) '3,000 state school students each year missing from our top universities'. Available from http:/www.suttontrust.com/news.asp#linkone (accessed 11th December 2010).

Temple, P., Farrant, J. and Shattock, M. (2005) *New Variable Fee Arrangements: Baseline Institutional Case Studies for the Independent Commission; Summary of Research Findings*. London: Institute of Education Research report for the DfES.

Chapter 11

'This place is not at all what I had expected': student demand for authentic Irish experiences in Irish Studies programmes

Katherine Nielsen

Introduction

The North American style modularisation of higher education is creeping into universities in the UK and the Republic of Ireland. Nowhere is this more apparent than the targeting of international students by summer school programmes. Short courses which do not require the application for a student visa are quick, accessible and attractive to international students. While it can be tempting to evaluate the success of such programmes by the 'consumption' rate, or how students subscribe to the programme, it is important to note why students choose their educational 'destinations', incorporating both touristic and educational imperatives simultaneously.

This chapter uses an ethnographic method to gain insight from a snapshot of a summer school programme in order to examine the composition of the international student market in Ireland, the composition of curricula in these programmes and the impact of local resources on the attraction and satisfaction of international students in cultural studies programmes generally. Throughout the programme, students sought what they deemed to be authentic experiences of Irish culture. Their exposure inside and outside of the classroom often conflicted with preconceived ideas of the nature of Irish culture established in popular media, family traditions or community narratives.

Summer schools endeavour to meet both the disciplinary standards for Irish Studies and the experiential concerns of students. Increasingly these programmes have developed marketing schemes in the hope of attracting students using local history, urban attractions and rural settings to make their educational programmes more attractive than alternatives. The key feature of the programmes under consideration here are 'in-person' courses which Irish universities purposefully market as providing authentic experiences of Irish culture inherent in the physical locality on the island of Ireland. In contrast, other universities located throughout the world focus more on the impact Irish emigrants have had on international cultures and their experiences of cultural definition and assimilation rather than contemporary Irish culture. Sophisticated advertising campaigns are developed in order to lure these new consumer students away from competitors within

Ireland and abroad, and often use a unique feature of the locality of the school as a hook to attract students each year. Many summer school programmes have embraced marketing models in order to maximise enrolment. Summer schools are participating in larger, institutional level activities which effectively 'turn students into consumers, and educators into service providers' (Gibbs 2001: 87). These students generate not only tuition income, but also occupy student residences normally empty in the summer, purchase food from restaurants and catering services which might otherwise close and buy books for their studies all of which conforms to Slaughter and Rhoades' (2004) theory of academic capitalism. The metaphor of consumption is used in this chapter to challenge the distinction between *student* and *tourist*.

International students' consumption of higher education

International student mobility has increased in the past decade. In 2007, 2,048,189 international students were enrolled in courses (OECD 2007). As a result, universities are now competing on a global scale for students at various educational stages, offering a multitude of higher education programmes delivered both virtually and in classrooms. Many strategies have been employed to address these policy goals and innovative institutional programmes have been created which cater to students' interests and needs. Certainly paramount amongst these activities has been the development of strong, branded identities for individual institutions which form the foundation for marketing the university both locally and internationally. Although this practice is not new, increasingly universities are beginning to offer programmes specifically designed to recruit, and often retain, international students.

International students have far more choice than most students because of their willingness to move, and seek the best educational opportunities they can find. For example, Halliday notes that the allure of educational programmes is not solely the programme on which they study but also the opportunity 'to live in, and relate to, the country they are in. Students come to British universities for what we do well, and for the quality of the other students they find here' (1999: 113). While this chapter focuses on the experience of studying, most researchers have focused on the economic return of international studies, especially the social capital which these students gain on a globalised job market. For example, Waters (2006) demonstrated the social capital attributed to Canadian university degrees in Hong Kong where the propensity to offer jobs and promotions to those with foreign degrees disadvantages students who achieved significantly higher results in Hong Kong universities. McArdle-Clinton contests such findings in the Irish context, suggesting that the 'educated, socially aware, multilingual executives who can operate in diverse cultures with ease' are not the norm. Rather, companies seek to hire 'local labour, familiar with local culture and language, willing to work for lower wages' (McArdle-Clinton 2008: 25).

While theorists have focused on the outcomes of international education, this chapter examines how students choose educational programmes and what they hope to experience during their studies, noting how expectations are embedded in a marketised way of thinking.

The major driving forces in the choice of educational institution and programme include location, cost, academic quality of faculty and students, employment possibilities and the social life of the institution (Clarke 2007). The idea of students as consumers of academic programmes is gaining popularity in higher education discourse, as is their conceptualisation as educational tourists who move between institutions and indeed countries, to have 'authentic' educational experiences (Marga 2006; de Ridder-Symoens 2006). What is significant is the shift away from the focus on the institution in favour of a university where students are thought of as 'an important client (or even partner) of the university' (Oprean 2007: 95). Oprean's characterisation of the university/student relationship as a client or partner challenges marketisation discourse which legitimises students as the central driving force in higher education development through their perceived purchasing power. If supply and demand consumer models are applied to higher education, students must be accepted as 'the most important stakeholders and beneficiaries of the educational system' (Vlăsceanu and Voicu 2006: 40). Summer schools have difficulty in maintaining such a relationship with their students due to their transitory nature.

Whether students consider themselves to primarily be a student or a tourist, they purchase and consume not only educational products, but local products as well. Joenbloed suggests that there are 'freedoms' for student consumers: students should be able to choose their education providers, and products. They are entitled to complete and accurate information regarding cost and quality in order to make their choice and the modes of assessment. As a result, institutional marketing campaigns should clearly address who the institutional provider is, what product they offer, why this product is desirable and how this product is cost-effective (Jongbloed 2003: 114). Many summer school programmes do not offer courses recognised by their own institutions for credit accumulation, such as the Irish Studies courses offered in Ireland, and it is important for students to know this in advance in order to obtain recognition.

As institutions, summer schools offer short, easily digested programmes, where students have little opportunity to impact the instruction or institution. Gibbs' conceptualisation of the marketisation of higher education is fundamentally based on the unilateral relationship where educators produce goods in the form of courses, materials and degrees which students purchase for their personal use in relation to further study or employment opportunities. This characterisation, however, obscures the multi-directional nature of the educational relationship where educators also learn from students and together negotiate new understandings.

Irish Studies courses have been designed in Ireland to facilitate educational activity within programmes abroad. The major impediment to generating new courses in foreign universities is the accessibility to resources such as libraries and faculty who can sustain broadened course offerings. Summer school programmes have become one mechanism to address these problems in the short term. The only Institute of Irish Studies on the island, Queen's University Belfast (IIS QUB), seeks to capitalise on this market by offering a comprehensive introduction to the historical development and social conflicts which have made Northern Ireland a place of interest to both researchers and the general public. For example, the Director of the Institute of Irish Studies and of the Irish Studies Summer School claimed that:

> Northern Ireland has suffered in a way of being joined to both Britain and Ireland and all the resulting conflict that is attached to that relationship but there are some advantages in that many of the foreign students regard it as a British and Irish university at the same time which they find quite attractive.
>
> (cited in Smyth 2007: 13)

Research conducted

Field research for this chapter was undertaken employing mixed methods of data collection, while conducting participant observation at the Irish Studies Summer School, hosted by the IIS QUB in 2007. As an ethnographer, I was able to participate in the daily activities of the students, including discussions at daily meals, in the halls of residence, en route to the university, in the classroom and organised field trips. Such a technique combined informal interviews, classroom engagement, course evaluations and personal participation which allowed for a triangulation of data used to draw conclusions using multiple sources of information, either from an individual, a lecture, marketing material and interviews. This approach offers the opportunity not only to assess student motivation and satisfaction in a 'snapshot' at the beginning or end of the course, but also to examine how these perceptions changed on a daily basis in the lived experiences of students, faculty and staff. While each of these methods individually has limitations, their combination addresses the limitations of certain methods by relying on the strengths of others.

This was a comprehensive, three-week programme which presented a variety of disciplinary Irish Studies approaches, as well as providing a unique perspective on Northern Ireland and the historical trajectories of both the Republic of Ireland and Northern Ireland. The school consisted of a formal academic programme which included lectures, fieldtrips and social activities designed to introduce students with no previous experiences of Irish culture and the distinctions which exist between Irish culture and Northern Irish culture. Lecturers were drawn from local faculty and experts. This allowed the programme to incorporate anthropological, historical, geographical, political, literary, musical, theatrical, economic and linguistic disciplinary interpretations of Irish Studies at the same time. After attending the three weeks of sessions, students were then free to travel, or return home. The course was assessed by an essay due one month after the completion of the in-class component in order to obtain credit for the course. Those academic credits were not offered at the European Credit Transfer and Accumulation System (ECTS) standard. Instead, students who complete the assessment and attended the required classes received a letter recommending the awarding of credits sent to their home institution based on the North American 3-credit modularised system. It was left to the overseas institution to determine whether they would award credit for this programme. Because of this, domestic students had little incentive to participate in the course as a consequence. International students repeatedly expressed disappointment at the lack of interaction with local Irish students. Free time was built into the programme, however, and students could go into the community and meet local residents outside of the classroom.

By providing some methodological grounding and enabling students to experience first-hand Irish culture, it was hoped that students would return to the university for further academic study by formally enrolling on postgraduate programmes. With this aim in mind, a curriculum for the programme was designed to bring together a broad range of speakers in order to raise the profile of the university, lending authority to the lectures and potentially attracting new international students to the academic resources available at the university. For example, students participated in integrated workshops which enabled students to engage directly with archival material, politicians, entertainers and residents in order to learn how Northern Ireland has developed as a result of the peace process.

This combination of classroom activities and out-of-school learning allowed this programme to focus on Irish Studies as an emerging discipline as well as exploring Irish culture and the methodologies to study it. The QUB programme was innovative in the field in two respects: they provide a comprehensive presentation of disciplinary and interdisciplinary approaches to the study of Ireland, north and south, and they are packaging this curriculum for export. One 'student' participating in the programme was hoping to design a similar programme at their home institution where they were faculty in the US. Past exit surveys demonstrate that this is not an exceptional case. Rather, several students over the years have attended the programme with the intention of developing a similar curriculum at their home institutions. The physical presence of students in Belfast as part of this programme also offers students access to primary texts and library resources which they could not normally obtain at their home institutions. This monopoly on research resources is diminishing, however, as the JSTOR academic database is in the process of digitising the Irish Studies collection held in the QUB library. Students were also able to access other QUB faculty for the purposes of setting up further research visits, becoming visiting students or preparing applications for further formal studies in Belfast.

International student profiles

In 2007, the QUB summer school programme had fifty-eight students enrolled from seven countries: the United States, Canada, Spain, Bulgaria, Romania, Australia and Denmark. Students had chosen to participate in the programme for a variety of reasons, such as part of organised field trips through home institutions (mostly American), preparatory work for PhD research (mostly European) and for personal reasons, such as learning family heritages or experiencing Belfast after the implementation of the peace agreement. The prevalence of multiple student profiles suggests that there are several motivations for enrolling in studies in Ireland. These three groups demonstrate how different types of students are attracted to certain educational opportunities for different reasons. Students on organised field trips were enrolled as undergraduates taking the course as an elective module. A second group of postgraduates used the school as an opportunity to meet other students and faculty, and access research materials for their studies. Finally, a group of heritage tourists enrolled at the university in order to learn more about their family heritage as part of their holidays in Ireland. For all three groups the timing of the school was important as the summer had fewer academic and employment requirements than other times in the year.

The thirty-four students and three chaperones who participated in organised field school programmes through their home institutions constituted the majority of students in 2007. These courses were facilitated extensions of domestic courses offered through a US institution, which will grant students credits for participation. All those participating in these programmes were formal undergraduate students, in their second year of university, between the ages of 19 and 20. These students registered for the course both individually or as groups of friends, and while some had a family connection to the area which they met during the programme, many did not. The most popular destinations were Dublin and Scotland for further tourist travels during the programme on free weekends, which are both relatively close to Northern Ireland and several inexpensive airlines offer direct services. The proximity of Belfast to other destinations was an important motivation for enrolment on the programme. These students seemed to enjoy the programme overall, especially socialising in the pub in the evening and brewery tours.

There were fifteen students who had previously completed their undergraduate studies prior to attending the summer school. Some, mostly American, were interested in continuing their studies in Ireland, working outside the university. These students were predominantly female and slightly older than the undergraduate students, ranging from 24 to 34 years of age. Most had previously completed summer school programmes in the Republic of Ireland, and were particularly interested in what QUB had to offer in terms of postgraduate programmes. In fact, the Institute office depleted their supply of the advertising brochures for these programmes, which demonstrates an active interest in pursuing further studies in Ireland. Many European students were present as well, and were often interested in Belfast in particular as it related to their PhD research in conflict and peace studies. These students were keen to meet with local faculty to discuss visits and exchanges, but were not intent on undertaking full programmes at QUB as they were already enrolled on academic programmes elsewhere. These visitors endeavoured to make use of the library for further research materials unavailable elsewhere. Understandably, library access was problematic in that the hours of circulation were restricted to business hours and students on the programme were not allowed to borrow books as they were not formally registered students at the university, which provided challenges for the students to balance class attendance with library access. As well, many relevant texts were non-circulating, which forced these students to choose between class and the library.

Finally, a group of six heritage tourists participated in the school. While mainly from the US, many were school teachers in their forties and fifties, or retired, which offered them the time to attend the school. All had visited Ireland before, and many had previously attended summer school programmes in the Republic of Ireland. These students were very interested in cultural activities in Belfast, and outside of the formal programme organised independent trips along the notorious Shankhill Road, to small cities around Belfast which were hosting cultural festivals, and looking for traditional music sessions in the area. The prevalence of information on the internet and through guide books on activities in Ireland offered these tourists an opportunity to both learn about and participate in authentic experiences rather than performed ones. For example, often students were disappointed with the so-called 'authentic' jam sessions they found locally in which musicians were either American, or played American songs. Even with local, expert recommendations, many students were unable to locate what they considered to be authentic experiences. This is not an uncommon occurrence. For example, Kneafsey notes that the number of summer schools and festivals offering music and dance classes is increasing, representing an interest on the part of tourists in learning this aspect of Irish culture. This is in stark contrast to local perceptions of traditional music she collected during her ethnographic fieldwork, where she identified a sense of exclusion on the part of local residents from their local players as musicians move from playing loosely organised sessions to paid gigs for specific audiences (Kneafsey 2003: 39). As a result, the music local musicians play is not always what the students expected. Similarly, because of their representations of diasporic Irish experiences, the Ulster-American Folk Park was a favourite for this group of students. While most students wandered through the outdoor museum and gift shop, these students spent their afternoon in the archive of the Centre for Migration Studies also located at the park. One of these students remarked while visiting the indoor museum that they 'need to learn more about their heritage' and this museum offered a unique opportunity to do so. The comment is representative of a sentiment amongst heritage tourists to discover lost family histories.

Common to all students was an interest in wanting to learn more about Ireland. The QUB programme offered a unique focus on Northern Ireland and the historic religious conflict present was timely and cost effective. The course offered students the ability to meet local Irish citizens and gain access to local Irish resources. These students chose to attend the QUB programme, and most paid for this programme with personal financing. It is, therefore, worth noting how consumer behaviour theory helps us to understand how students chose this programme and how the marketing campaign the Institute of Irish Studies used to recruit these students tapped into the idea that their target audience of international recruits were as much tourists as students. The attraction of studying in Ireland and the opportunity to have apparently authentic Irish experiences were highlighted – hence a focus on things not available simply through the academic programmes.

Consumer choice for summer schools

Institutional marketing campaigns must clearly address who the institutional provider is, what product they offer, why this product is desirable and how this product is cost effective. This information should also include, wherever possible, information on the other students participating in the programmes as well because students learn not only from faculty but also from peers. In the case of the QUB summer school, the marketing materials designed to attract students significantly position the programme as unique in relation to other programmes in the Republic of Ireland because of curricular focus on Northern Ireland with respect to the Republic of Ireland and the UK, and the national and historic conflicts which have occurred in the island. For example, the 2008 guide answers the rhetotical question 'Why choose the IIS summer school?' by suggesting that:

> While images of Belfast and the troubled north have flooded the screens and newspapers of the world: for those who choose to live and work here, it is a fascinating place, a centre of diverse cultural activity enlivened by debate and discussion, a crucible for change. In one of the most popular sessions, Summer School participants have the opportunity to meet and dialogue with representatives of Northern Ireland's political parties and community leaders, enabling those who participate to take an active part in the unfolding of history as it happens.
>
> (QUB 2008)

While other institutions in Ireland certainly also have their own programmes, it is the conflicted culture in Northern Ireland which the programme markets to potential students.

The lectures which had the greatest student interest were those relating to the division between Protestant and Catholic communities as well as the lectures relating to popular culture such as theatre, film and music. What is striking about these lectures was that they all included some group activities and class participation. Rather than offering standard lectures, these experts allowed students to discuss in groups, participate in theatre and provide their impressions of film and bands, and their participation in these sessions allowed students to engage with the material, rather than simply listening. There was no required reading for the course; this was often the first introduction students had to the topics discussed. As a result, some lectures were difficult to understand. Many students independently found books to aid their understanding of the lectures during the first week, but as the course continued these students began to make their own connections between their lectures, and personal interactions developed their understanding of the conflict as a result.

Heritage centres have emerged in recent years as popular tourist destinations which the QUB programme incorporates into formal educational opportunities, such as the visit to the Centre for Migration Studies and the Ulster-American Folk Park discussed above. For Sheerin heritage has become Ireland's 'tourism *product:* a commodity to be marketed, packaged and sold to visitors' (Sheerin 1998: 39). He defines this product metaphorically as:

> A book containing chapters which relate the story of Ireland's heritage for the foreign and domestic visitor. It consists of a framework of themes and storylines to be developed at different heritage sites, around which Ireland's culture and heritage can be interpreted to visitors. The interpretive gateways into Ireland's heritage aim to heighten visitors' experience, to create a strong brand image of Ireland as a quality heritage destination with unique, distinctive attractions – all geared towards attracting more visitors and more visitor spending.
>
> (Sheerin 1998: 45–6)

Summer schools are similarly designed and incorporate these centres whenever possible. This multiplicity of histories negates the creation of an authentic history by tourism officials: the Irish tourist board Fáilte Ireland has established 'interpretive gateways' for Irish heritage. Johnson notes that 'time is obliterated by place as heritage mapping becomes a reference guide to spatialized storylines rather than to a series of localised yet interdependent histories' (1999: 194). The summer school sought to provide such a reference guide. The analytical framework developed in the classroom allowed students to interact with the history being represented there, and to critique those representations based on discussion with classmates, curators and experts. For example, during the walking tour in the Derry Bogside, local residents began to argue as to who should be acting as our tour guide, as the guide was a young man and one of the local street vendors had been present personally during the Battle for the Bogside which the guide was discussing. The students would have preferred a first-hand account of the clash rather than the neutral account presented by the registered tour guide providing authorised interpretive gateways discussed above. In this way a degree of scholarly identity and authentic tourist experience merged together.

The murals in Northern Ireland were of intense interest to the students in the programme. Whereas the murals in Belfast focus on representing the two opposing positions in the conflict (Protestant and Catholic), the Bogside murals were devoted to representing the Catholic version of the conflict. These murals are a major marketing feature for the programme to catch the attention of students and tourists more generally. There are two popular tours of the murals of Belfast, the bright red open-decked buses which provide rather politically neutral interpretations of the murals and also take tourists through the city centre and the shipyards. Many students in the summer school preferred the second option: Black Taxi Tours which were offered by both the 'loyalist' and 'republican' companies. Lisle considers these tours to be more authentic in that the drivers have obtained permission from the local residents to show tourists the murals, engage with them while tourists are taking photos, and will cater the tour to meet the interests of the tourists (Lisle 2006: 44–5). Also, tours in and around the city were organised by the summer school in order to highlight areas of significant mural activity, which allows students to make their own plans during their free time to visit those areas.

Discussion

Summer schools are a developing phenomenon in Northern Ireland. For example, 2007 marked the first year that the West Belfast Festival added a series of classes and lectures as part of their festivities. The Feile Summer School was also held at the university campus. Publicity noted that the:

> organisers are hoping the Feile Summer School will become one of its most popular events as it offers tourists the chance to take a crash course in Irish, visit public art installations and assess the Easter Rising of 1916 during a one-week school. Visitors will soon know all there is to know about Belfast, be familiar with its famous landmarks, speak the lingo and have an in-depth knowledge of the events surrounding Home Rule and partition.
>
> (McCrory 2007: 3)

As these independent dance, language and cultural schools grow in number, further research is required to examine how this experience differs from more traditional programmes in higher education institutions. The research discussed in this chapter reflects the varied discourses which have been developed in order to account for both educational and touristic experience of international students. What seems evident, however, is that through the purposeful design of summer school programmes which aim to cater to as many interests as possible, the students as a cohort participated in a large variety of touristic experiences that would not normally have been possible through traditional pedagogical delivery in universities. This at least suggests that conceiving of students as more than 'just' immersed in a scholarly discipline can be productive. In the case of the ethnographic data collected in Belfast, it seemed that students purchased all forms of tourism available, including both physical landscape through tours and literary landscapes in the Seamus Heaney Summer School, heritage tourism through a visit to the Ulster-American Folk Park, dark tourism through classroom learning and fieldtrips to sites of significance during the Troubles, and industrial tourism, focusing especially on the Harland and Wolff shipyards in Belfast Harbour and their connection to the *Titanic*.

Access to *authentic* locals is very difficult to accomplish in formal educational programmes and was often cited as a disappointment by students. Indeed, in spite of the invitation extended by a lecturer to join him at his musical gig later that evening, students did not do so and then complained that they had not had the opportunity to hear local music. What is striking here is that while this is an activity which one could conduct independently, there is an assumption that the school should provide this access as part of their purchase of an educational product. By inviting locals to participate as well in such events, this would increase the sense of participation in the local community.

As local residents develop their own short courses the value of higher education institutions' delivery of short courses for credit becomes a key component to the recruitment and retention of international students who have increasing customer choice in relation to educational products. The balance between education and tourism of international students is difficult for educational providers. While the university is responsible to present objective accounts for students, tour guides present commercialised representations, often advocating community interpretations of aspects of Irish culture and history. Many students prefer to purchase authentic local products in addition to the programmes at universities and institutions must balance the multifaceted nature of educational tourists in order to understand how to meet better the needs and desires of their students in the development and marketing of their products.

Increasingly, students pay fees to access higher education institutions, and summer programmes are becoming very popular and cost effective in providing educational opportunities for international student consumers. Universities are designing programmes with the explicit intent to market these programmes solely to international students, where domestic students cannot subscribe. As such some form of hybrid student-tourist or student as explorer is becoming an important segment for universities that seek to maximise revenue potential.

Conclusion

Conceptualising students as consumers is problematic, however. While some prospective students evaluate research institutions, consult league tables, talk with current and former students and visit campuses, many do not. This case study allows us to examine larger trends in the internationalisation of higher education, and what they hope to obtain from the providers of these programmes. Research is required on how students make choices in higher education institutions and programmes on an individual basis. This chapter has examined the consumer choices of Irish Studies students, who purchase short educational programmes and combine educational and touristic activities.

Consumption of educational products may be influenced by many factors, especially student preference, need and market competition between institutions for the best students. For example, different types of students will choose different types of academic programmes. Whereas domestic undergraduate students may choose to set off on an international adventure, geography and costs are real determining factors in the choice of programme and experience at an institution. Mature students and lifelong learners are more likely to study close to home in fields related to their previous or current occupations. Postgraduate students often move from one institution to another, be it nationally or internationally. The personal circumstances of students participating in these programmes are pivotal in understanding both student motivations and institutional responses to these motivations which are under examination in this chapter. Each academic institution must target particular types of students with marketing materials designed to entice enrolment in tailored programmes if they are to succeed both in terms of market viability and continued enrolments.

References

Clarke, M. (2007) 'The impact of higher education rankings on student access, choice, and opportunity', *Higher Education in Europe*, 32(1): 59–70.

de Ridder-Symoens, H. (2006) 'The university as European cultural heritage: a historical approach'. *Higher Education In Europe*, 31(4): 369–79.

Gibbs, P. (2001) 'Higher Education as a market: a problem or solution?', *Studies in Higher Education*, 26(1): 85–94.

Halliday, J. (1999) 'Political liberalism and citizenship education: towards curriculum reform', *British Journal of Educational Studies*, 37(1): 43–55.

Johnson, N. (1999) 'Framing the past: time, space and the politics of heritage tourism in Ireland', *Political Geography*, 18: 187–207.

Jongbloed, B. (2003) 'Marketisation in higher education, Clark's Triangle and the essential ingredients of markets', *Higher Education Quarterly*, 57(2):110–35.

Kneafsey, M. (2003) '"If it wasn't for the tourists we wouldn't have an audience": the case of tourism and traditional music in North Mayo', in M. Cronin and B. O'Connor, *Irish Tourism: Image, Culture, and Identity*. Clevendon: Channel View Publications, pp. 21–41.

Lisle, D. (2006) 'Local symbols, global networks: rereading the murals of Belfast', *Alternatives*, 31: 24–52.

Marga, A. (2006) 'The cultural legitimacy of the European university', *Higher Education in Europe*, 31(4): 425–38.

McArdle-Clinton, D. (2008) *The Consumer Experience of Higher Education: The Rise of Capsule Education*. London: Continuum.

McCrory, M. (2007) 'Tourists offered chance to go back to school', *The Irish News* (21 July), p. 3.

OECD (Organisation For Economic Co-operation And Development) (2007) *OECD Education Database*. Available from http://www.oecd.org/education/database (accessed 24 February 2010).

Oprean, C. (2007) 'Adequately responding to "Reform" and "Anti-Reform" pressures in the Romanian Higher Education system under the Bologna Process', *Higher Education in Europe*, 32(1): 91–7.

QUB, I.S.S. (2008) 'Why choose the IIS summer school', *QUB*. Available from http://www.qub.ac.uk/schools/IrishStudiesGateway/InternationalSummerSchool/Whychoose theIISSummerSchool/ (accessed 25 May 2010).

Sheerin, E. (1998) 'Heritage centres', in M. Peillon and E. Slater, *Encounters with Modern Ireland*. Dublin: Institute of Public Administration.

Slaughter, S. and Rhoades, G. (2004) *Academic Capitalism and the New Economy: Markets, State, and Higher Education*. Baltimore: The Johns Hopkins University Press.

Smyth, L. (2007). 'Students cross world for QUB school', *Belfast Telegraph* (20 July), p. 13.

Vlăsceanu, L. and Voicu, B. (2006) 'Implementation of the Bologna Objectives in a sample of European private higher education institutions: outcomes of a survey', *Higher Education in Europe*, 31(1): 25–52.

Waters, J. L. (2006) 'Geographies of cultural capital: education, international migration and family strategies between Hong Kong and Canada', *Transactions of the Institute of British Geographers*, 31: 179–92.

Chapter 12

The student as consumer: affordances and constraints in a transforming higher education environment

Felix Maringe

Introduction

The consumer metaphor in Higher Education (HE) rose to prominence following Deming's notion of Total Quality Management (TQM) in the early 1990s (Chaffee and Lawrence 1992). Under TQM, quality is defined in terms of conformance to the requirements of the customer (Kumar 2003). The student thus becomes the central focus for its determination. The metaphor experienced a further surge in significance following the emergence of marketisation in HE, an idea based on the notion of free trade in goods and services between countries encouraged and legislated for by the World Trade Organisation (WTO) and the General Agreement on Trade in Services (GATS) (Bassett 2006). In this 'free-market' environment (Ayal and Karras 1998), HE became a tradable service, based on demand and supply laws under which students became key consumers while universities and their staff were the providers. Consumerism is the central tenet of the free market in which business success depends almost entirely on satisfying customer needs and exceeding their expectations. Most recently, the notion of student as consumer has been highlighted following the move by many world governments to redirect the responsibility for funding HE in universities from central governments to individual students. This has been in response to the World Bank which has the view that the private benefits of a Higher Education experience are higher than its public benefits (Psacharopoulos 1994). Because students are now paying for their HE experience, directly or indirectly through 'learn now, pay later' loan schemes (AimHigher 2006), the notion of student as consumer has been brought into sharp focus.

The metaphor has had its fair share of supporters and critics alike over the years. At a time when the media is highlighting the increasing litigious nature of HE characterised by a surge in student complaints regarding the quality, quantity and sometimes even the relevance of their tuition and educational experience, it seems to be an apt time to revisit the concept and explore the extent to which its application in HE might contribute to or detract from the capacity of universities to deliver a quality experience to its students and to society. In focusing on this purpose, the chapter begins by examining the changing nature of the HE sector and explores the evolving role of university students in delivering a quality learning and educational experience. The key arguments for and against the consumer metaphor in HE are revisited. On the positive side the centrality of students in determining the nature and quality of their educational experience is highlighted. On the negative side, the pitfalls associated with the commodification of HE are explored. The chapter concludes with an evaluation of McMillan and Cheney's (1996) propositions against consumerism in HE in terms of whether the consumer metaphor: integrates students more strongly into the educational processes of HE learning and experience; enhances the quality of learning through its focus on consumer satisfaction; and supports or undermines the traditional values of HE learning. McMillan and Cheney (1996) are noted as having provided the most widely applied framework for critically engaging with the notion of consumerism in education (McEwan 2007).

But before we do all this, we need to clarify the concept of consumer and explore where it sits in relation to sister concepts such as customer and client as used in the context of business and education.

The notions of consumer, customer or client: business and HE perspectives

According to the Marketing Dictionary, the term consumerism has three fundamental meanings attached to it. The first meaning depicts a 'movement seeking to protect and inform consumers by requiring such practices as honest packaging and advertising, product guarantees, and improved safety standards'. This is what may be termed a consumer rights perspective. The second is a focus on consumerism as an economics theory in which it is suggested that a progressively greater consumption of goods is economically beneficial. The third is a values-oriented meaning in which materialistic values or possessions constitute an underlying approach to life in contemporary society. Therefore consumers have rights which need to be protected; they must be encouraged to purchase and consume more and finally they must be acculturated with materialistic values which place a greater premium on the instrumental value of things.

Consumerism and the consumer metaphor are used rather more loosely in HE. To begin with, students and potential students in HE are less protected and even less accurately informed about product quality to inform their participation, purchase and evaluation decisions. League tables which students are expected to use to make judgements and comparisons between institutional provisions are notoriously inaccurate and tend to be based on nebulous, difficult to quantify and culturally bound concepts (Cremonini *et al.* 2007). Bowden (2000) refers to league tables as offering a fantasy perspective of HE. On the other hand, university prospectuses tend to put a positive spin to things and have been found to be less trusted sources of information about the quality of an institution by prospective students (Foskett *et al.* 2008; Dyke *et al.* 2008). Although in the UK there is the Office for Fair Access (OFFA) which monitors student access to universities in order to minimise discrimination and other forms of unfair recruitment practice especially in view of the recent introduction of variable fees to HE, there are still many students who fail to gain access on grounds of financial difficulty (*The Guardian* 2009). Thus it can be said that consumer protection in HE is not a well-developed idea and seems to rest on rather shaky ground.

There seems to be a parallel of the economics theory of consumerism in HE. In a study for the Joint Economic Committee for the United States Congress, Saxton (2000) highlighted the enormous benefits associated with increased education. For example, investment in human capital enables individuals to increase their future earnings and enhance their experience in the labour market. These findings generally corroborate conclusions in what have come to be known as classic studies on the economic value of education (see for example, Carnoy and Dieter 1975; Gary Becker 1964; Theodore Schultz 1961; and most famously Adam Smith 1776). As a general rule therefore, and despite more recent World Bank economic adjustment driven studies, more education tends to be better for the individual, for society and for overall economic development. The British government has a target for 50 per cent of all adults to have university level education by 2020 (Denham 2008). Some countries especially in the OECD have already surpassed this target (OECD 2006).

It can be argued that the commodification of HE is the concept nearest to the idea of developing a value system in HE which prioritises the instrumental value of education ahead of everything else. Those who argue against consumerism in HE largely do so on the basis that there are strong moral arguments about making education a commodity in the same way fish and chips are a commodity purchased and consumed by an ever-willing public. In this sense, HE institutions become factories for the production of degrees which students can purchase using real money and their brains. Attempts by many universities to semesterise university calendars and to offer modules rather than units of instruction packaged at specific cost and transferable between degree programmes and institutions is increasingly being seen as evidence of the commodification of university instruction (Gibbs 2008). Access to prestigious institutions is protected by a requirement for high entry scores. Only the rich students can have access to grade boosting courses which charge huge sums of money. This however serves to give a false relationship between performance and social background and consolidates rather than limits the commodification of education in society. Commodification thus has potential to entrench rather than constrain inequality in society.

A consumer in HE is thus disempowered, poorly protected and subject to subtle machinations of powerful forces that seek to maintain the status quo through a covert process of guarded entry by ability to pay that guarantees grades by riches process.

The concept of a customer in HE became more prominently reflected in the HE lexicon as the marketisation of education grew. Having originated in TQM ideas, the idea that HE students were customers has received extensive critical review in the literature. By definition, a customer is someone who enters or has the potential to enter a purchase relationship with another person or organisation that may be selling or producing a service or product. In the business sense, the customer is everything because they are the ones who do the purchases and thus ensure business viability and profitability. The entire health of the organisation is measured on the extent to which the customers are happy. It is assumed that happy customers will ensure repeat business; will guarantee new business through word of mouth advertising; and will remain loyal to the business even in the face of stiff competition on aspects such as price. Although data is sometimes conflicting, the weight of evidence seems to suggest that customer satisfaction is positively related to business performance indicators such as sales, profits and share margins (Boselie *et al.* 2008). In regard to TQM, it has been argued that the only view of quality that matters is that of the customer (Gerson 1993). TQM is fundamentally an organisational mindset focused on continuous improvement of products and processes with an underlying aim to 'delight the customer' (Janpen *et al.* 2005: 16.1). Processes that are designed to get a sense of how the customer evaluates organisational products and processes become an integral part of the organisational culture based on three fundamental ideas of continuous improvement, ongoing staff training and customer satisfaction. This further relates to another key idea of service quality. Customers in the HE sense experience product and service elements and the quality associated with these often determine the levels of customer satisfaction and re-patronage intentions (Fen and Lian 2006). The relationship between service quality, customer satisfaction and repeat purchase behaviours has been the subject of much research and the general consensus of findings from such research suggests a direct relationship between these concepts (Yi and La 2004). In general, service quality is the difference between quality expectations and performance (Zeithaml *et al.* 1996). When performance exceeds expectation, service quality is said to be high. Conversely, when performance has a lower index than expectation, then quality is poor. The impact on customer satisfaction of these two scenarios is thus fairly straightforward to determine. As such the customer becomes the centre of the business operation. In HE, as in business generally, the relationship between customer satisfaction and student retention, progression and graduation has been established (see for example Kara and de Shields 2004). However, the growing focus on student satisfaction promoted by National Student Satisfaction Surveys and used as basis for ranking universities on league tables has had its critics too. Students are asked to complete a questionnaire in which they rate the quality of teaching and experience in their university. Scores are standardised out of a maximum possible of five. Critics suggest that scores do not reflect the direct quality of teaching but provide a picture of sampled opinion of this quality which may be influenced by a whole range of possible biases such as prior expectation. If, for example, students in an excellent university had very high expectations of the quality of teaching which are not overtly demonstrated during the course of the year, then they may rate their university lowly in terms of teaching quality.

On the other hand, students in a less strong university with low expectations may be surprised by the good teaching they experience, which may not be of the same standard as in the excellent university. Consequently the universities receive different ratings, with the excellent university being ranked lower than the mediocre institution. Other studies have also questioned the validity of student ratings per se (Greenwald 1997).

Models of quality developing in HE which are based on student ratings reflect a growing importance of student as customer in the sector. However, it can also be argued that the growing focus on students could marginalise the role of the staff in exploring the quality of what they do. Peer reviews are generally not taken seriously and are often conducted for administrative rather than for quality improvement purposes (see for example Topping 2004).

The increase in student complaints of university teaching and services over the last years has been attributed in part to the growing customer culture in HE. It is currently speculated that because students feel more directly responsible for payment of fees, that they have greater say in how they are taught, how they are assessed and the overall quality of the services they are entitled to on campus. Frank Furedi, social commentator and academic at Kent University, noted that students now phone tutors at home over the weekends to get some tips regarding their papers, a service they feel they can purchase with their fees; they are now more career focused, due to a dire need to get out of debt quickly after completion of study, concluding that 'fees give a clear and tangible form to the idea of students as customers' (Coughlan 2009).

The concept of client has not grown significantly in use to the same extent as the other sister concepts of consumer and customer. Its origins seem to be from the health sector and generally from the American lexicon. In terms of power differentials, clients seem to be in a subservient relationship with those who provide the service. Clients in the health sector is a term reserved for patients who need special care arrangements usually outside the hospital premises. This does not however diminish their importance in terms of the role they should have in overall decision making for their well-being. In education, clients can be our students, parents, resource developers, indeed anyone who chooses to have a special relationship with the university for one reason or the other. The three concepts are often used interchangeably but their rather specific usage implies that we need to draw some distinctions between them. Table 12.1 below provides a summary of the similarities and differences (albeit subtle) between these three concepts.

There is a great deal of overlap between the concepts, but perhaps the strongest differences are in the nature of the association between the people involved. Client relationships tend to be long term, emergent, developmental and generally incremental. Customer relationships tend to be transient and short term which is the basis for their wide criticism in education. The fact that the relationship is based on exchange usually of money and the goods or service makes them instrumental and manipulative, another reason for its wide criticism in education.

Table 12.1 Differences between client, customer and consumer

	Client	Customer	Consumer
Context of use	Establishment of a one-on-one relationship for personal benefit of client and business benefit of service provider	Can be a one-off purchase or exchange context with little scope for personal relationship building	A consumption relationship focus based on product or service utilisation
Nature of people association	Relationship based, incremental and emergent	Transaction based, the relationship tends to be transient	Rather nebulous association, but tends to be based on consumer appraisal of products or services
Length of relationship	Generally long term	Can be both short and long term	Generally long term
Product or service orientations	Tends to be service oriented	Tends to be product oriented	Tends to be both service and product oriented

On the whole though, unless it is for purely academic purposes, the use of these metaphors in education tends to be interchangeable.

Consumerism in a transforming HE sector

Universities have undergone significant transformation over the years. The old medieval universities were relatively small pockets of isolated excellence where a student–master relationship prevailed and where the notion of consumerism had a different meaning from that obtaining in modern universities. The older universities tended to be elitist, selective and exclusive. Students were consumers in the sense of being at the end of the instructional processes, as receptacles, receiving the wisdom of their teachers in a give and take relationship described by Freire as the banking method of education. However, with the Enlightenment and industrialisation grew a need for greater involvement of society in the affairs of the university. More courses were developed and the fundamental equation of life became more education, more life opportunities. Dore (1976) wrote about this time as a period of the diploma disease. The elitist nature of universities was slowly being eroded while the desire for educational credentials grew in society. In the late 1990s, with the globalisation of the world, universities tended to look beyond the national boundaries to become international or global universities. A key development in recent times has been the introduction of fees in HE in many parts of the world accompanying the liberalisation of trade in education. The student has thus become a consumer in the sense of one paying for a service directly or indirectly and the responsibilities, rights and obligations associated with this have become encapsulated in the consumer metaphor.

The consumer metaphor in HE: affordances and constraints

The debate regarding the affordances and constraints of the consumer metaphor need to be preceded by a brief reference to the discourse around the Service Dominant Logic (S-D Logic). Vargo and Lusch (2004) have argued that service is the appropriate logic of marketing and that it is the 'unifying purpose of any business relationship' (Ballantyne and Varey 2008: 11). In the context of HE, however, the application of this idea may have several limitations. First, education is not provided to other people as in the banking concept of learning and teaching. It is fundamentally a conjoint activity between teachers and learners where new knowledge is gained as result of the conjoint effort of both teachers and learners. In that sense, there is a limit to which the service metaphor can be meaningfully transported into the HE sector. Having said that, it is important to note that there are many aspects which relate to learning, such as the quality of service a student may get in the library, the quality of service in the students' union, bars and cafeterias, service in the clinic and hostels all of which may have a bearing on how customers evaluate the overall experience of HE in a given learning environment.

The most damning indictment of the consumer metaphor in HE is the assumption that the customer is always right. What is right for example about a student who fails to submit an assignment in good time for no apparent reason? Should the student's central thesis or argument in an assignment/term paper not be questioned because they are always right? How far do we apply this metaphor in the HE context if at all? It is argued that by adopting this attitude, staff are likely to be pressured to award better grades in order to satisfy the customers. The notion of customer satisfaction itself is also highly contestable in HE. The question asked is whether guaranteeing and delivering customer satisfaction should be a goal unto itself in HE. In any case, the idea of guaranteeing satisfaction suggests that students and staff need to enter into a written contract before the start of instruction. Satisfaction with instruction and its outcomes should be the primary focus of such guarantees. But as we know, students have varying learning styles and will respond differently to similar types of instruction. Some students will be quite happy with lecture delivery modes while others will be more comfortable with instructional techniques that reflect a more classroom-based ethos. Therefore expecting that students will respond uniformly and positively to the outcomes of instruction despite the best efforts of the lecturer is somewhat myopic. In a case study of the impact of customer guarantees on their satisfaction following a course of instruction, half the students were issued with a written guarantee while the other half were not (McCollough and Gremler 1999). Students who did not receive the guarantee reported higher satisfaction scores than those who had written guarantees. This may have been because those who received guarantees had higher expectations of the course than those who did not receive any written guarantees. In addition, both groups reported that high quality instruction was the most important expectation for a productive HE experience. There is thus a sense in which contracts in their known right do not deliver quality per se. Baldwin (1994) for example argues that peer reviews of instruction are a better guarantee for quality instruction than written guarantees handed to students at the start of courses.

Placing the student at the centre of decision making in HE is a strong argument for the democratisation of HE, for greater accountability and for enhancing quality. However, this should not be done blindly and in a wholesale manner which marginalises the expertise of staff and dis-empowers them in the educative processes of their roles (Delmonico 2000). There are aspects of HE that lend themselves to a polling culture in order to have a good sense of students' response to their experience. For example, students can provide valid data about the availability of resources in the library; about the quality of service in the students' canteen; and about the best starting time for evening lecturers. Polling students' opinions about these matters may provide a reasonably accurate picture of the quality of students' experience. However, they tend to know much less about good instructional techniques; about the resources that can be used to raise course grades; and about how to assess and grade assignments. Basing instructional practice on student views alone about these aspects is unlikely to deliver the quality that students yearn for from their courses. At the end of the day, a university learning experience is not an excursion or a time away on sandy beaches. The satisfaction one derives from a HE experience is often delayed and comes from the pain of a sometimes tortuous journey which takes the student through a vast array of experiences, difficult reading and hard assignments. It is an experience whose quality, relevance and usefulness cannot be guaranteed, assessed and measured by students alone, but in conjunction with their lecturers, parents, employers, government and other interested parties. Some argue that a good education does not offer immediate gratification. Once I asked pupils to indicate two things they hated in life and the majority of them wrote learning and teachers. Taken on face value, teachers and, by deduction, education is the least relevant experience for pupils. But as adults, we know that these customers are not right at all about this matter, in this case.

It is useful to end this paper by commenting briefly on McMillan and Cheney's three propositions against consumerism in HE.

Reviewing propositions against the consumer metaphor in HE

McMillan and Cheney (1996) have provided a robust and widely used set of propositions against the student as consumer metaphor in HE. What follows is a brief discussion of each of these propositions in the context of new research and understanding.

1   *The metaphor distances students from the educational process:* the argument here is that by viewing students as consumers, their role as co-producers of knowledge and understanding is minimised while their role as passive consumers is given greater prominence. Cases that have been highlighted in the press about students' dissatisfaction with their HE experience suggest that students see academics as providers on one hand and not as co-producers with them of their experience (see for example Gajda 2009). This certainly seems to be heightened by the introduction of fees in HE, which endorse the notions of supply and purchase as underlying metaphors in the consumer discourse. Yet students in HE are not supposed to be passive recipients of knowledge and information, but active producers in the creation and co-creation of shared understanding and ideas.

2   *The focus on customer satisfaction in HE is misplaced:* while customer satisfaction is important, it should not be the overall goal of the educative process. There are two problems with the notion of customer satisfaction in HE. The first is that the educative process itself is not an entirely painless experience. Reading, writing and doing assignments are difficult experiences which require discipline, effort and sacrifice on the part of students. The process of learning is not a pleasure-filled experience; it has its own pains and groans. Second, the rewards of an educational process take long to be realised and it can reasonably be surmised that the satisfaction of having achieved some learning is not immediately obvious for students but may become apparent in the very long term. Indeed, if we base our judgements about the quality of instruction on what students say following a course of instruction, we are likely to get a very partial view at best and a potentially quite inaccurate view at worst. While we should aim for customer satisfaction, we should still be wary about its usefulness in the context of HE and it should not be the omnipotent goal of the educative process.

3   *The data processes trivialise the educative intention:* the majority of the data gathering for customer experience and customer satisfaction in education as in other fields of endeavour is achieved through the self-completion questionnaires based on Likert-style questions through which students are asked to agree or disagree with a set of questions. The mean score for each question is taken to represent the overall view of students about the item. While the processes give an impression of a democratic procedure in that every student is polled, it discourages students from reflective evaluation of their experience while promoting what McMillan and Cheney describe as 'push button democracy' lacking in-depth analysis and through which momentary and passing thoughts are granted real legitimacy. In my own teaching, I have found that when students are asked to discuss the outcomes of a unit of instruction and to come up with suggestions for improvement as a group, they tend to provide more thoughtful suggestions than I usually get from them when they are asked to fill in questionnaires. Students also generally do not provide responses to open-ended questions and thus deprive the evaluative process with potentially useful thought-driven ideas.

4   *Meanings are lost in translation*: there is always a danger when we use
    concepts that are imported or borrowed from other areas of practice, in this
    case from the business sector. There is so much that has different meanings
    to how we use the same concepts in education. For example, in education
    a product can be a very difficult concept to pin down. In a commercial sense,
    a loaf of bread or bar of soap may be an easily identifiable product for which
    customers can express opinions regarding its performance. In education the
    product of an educational experience may be a text book, a lecture, the
    written assignment and the student too. So it may be difficult to talk about
    product quality in the same way as we would in a commercial way. Similarly
    the idea that the customer is always right cannot have the same meaning in
    an education context. To begin with students undertake a course of study
    because they want to know more about the subject and the lecturer helps
    with this transformative process. Wholesale application of concepts and ideas
    from the commercial sector does little to promote the real values of HE.
    We need to develop our own language. In my early research, I have argued
    that a proper marketing concept of HE should be based on the idea of
    creating and co-creating the curriculum experience with the student rather
    than delivering value to students as would be assumed in a commercial or
    business sense.

Summary and conclusions

The chapter provides both an appraisal and critique of the consumer metaphor
in HE. It traces its emergence from the TQM movement advocated by Edward
Deming (2000) whose fundamental argument was that the only view of quality
which is important in an industrial or commercial setting is that of the customer.
The chapter then looks at the increasing significance of the customer orientation
through the periods of marketisation, internationalisation and more recently
globalisation. In each of these epochs, the significance and implications of a
consumer orientation is discussed. The chapter also provides a discussion around
competitor concepts such as customer, consumer and client as applied to
education concluding that while there is much overlap in the meanings of these
ideas, their specific usage in the education context provides subtle but important
distinctions. Towards the end of the chapter, the affordances and constraints
of the consumer metaphor are summarised. It is argued in the chapter that placing
the consumer at the heart of decision making in HE helps to democratise the
HE experience, increase accountability and contribute to enhanced quality of
the HE experience. However, the chapter stops short of dismissing Deming's
contribution that the only view of quality that matters in education is that of
students. Rather it calls for a position which argues for a multiple view of quality
as seen by a range of constituents including parents, the students, the staff,
government and other interested parties. There is a sense in which the consumer
metaphor if used without due regard to the specific context of HE might alienate

the students from the learning process leading them to believe that they are on the receiving end of educational instruction rather than at the centre of it; detract from a more discursive and reflective review of quality in favour of a mechanistic 'push button approach' to educational evaluation and ultimately limit our view of the educative process to one that can be evaluated by estimating the satisfaction of students rather than the ultimate transformation they undergo through an often painful and hard process.

References

AimHigher (2006) *Learn Now, Pay Later Student Loans.* Available from http://www.aimhigher.ac.uk/sites/bedfordshire/resources/On_Target_Summer05.pdf (accessed 26 October 2009).

Ayal, E. B. and Karras, G. (1998) 'Components of economic freedom and growth', *Journal of Developing Areas*, 32(3): 327–38.

Ballantyne, D. and Varey, R. (2008) 'The service dominant logic and the future of marketing', *Journal of the Academy of Marketing Science*, 36: 11–14.

Baldwin, G. (1994) 'The student as customer: the discourse of quality in HE', *Journal of Higher Education Management*, 9: 131–9.

Bassett, R. M. (2006) *The WTO and the University: Globalisation GATS and the American Higher Education.* London: Routledge.

Becker, G. S. (1964) *Human Capital* (2nd edn). New York, NY: National Bureau of Economic Research.

Boselie, P., Hesselink, M. and der Wiele, T. (2008) 'Empirical evidence for the relationship between customer satisfaction and business performance', *Erasmus Research Institute of Management – ERIM*, Rotterdam.

Bowden, R. (2000) 'Fantasy higher education: university and college league tables', *Quality in Higher Education*, 6(1): 41–60.

Carnoy, M. and Dieter M. (1975) 'The returns to schooling in the United States, 1939–69', *Journal of Human Resources*, 10(3): 312–31.

Chaffee, E. E. and Lawrence, A. S. (1992) *Transforming Post Secondary Education, ASHE-Eric HE Report No 3.* Washington DC: The George Washington University School of Education and Human Development.

Coughlan, S. (2009) 'Fees fuel campus consumer culture', *BBC News (online).* Available from http://news.bbc.co.uk/1/hi/education/7938455.stm (accessed 26 October 2009).

Cremonini, L. Westerheijden, D. and Enders, J. (2007) 'Disseminating the right information to the right audience: cultural determinants in the use (and misuse) of rankings', *Higher Education Journal*, 55: 373–85.

Delmonico, M. J. (2000) *Is treating students as customers the right move for community colleges?* St Petersburg FL: St Petersburg Junior College.

Deming, E.W. (2000). *The New Economics for Industry, Government, Education* (2nd edn). Massachusetts: MIT Press.

Denham, J. (2008) *Widening Adult Participation in Higher Education*, speech delivered at University of Southampton, 22nd May. Available from http://www.dius.gov.uk/news_and_speeches/speeches/past_ministers/john_denham/adult (accessed 26 October 2009).

Dore, R. (1976) *The Diploma Disease.* Berkeley: University of California Press.

Dyke, M., Foskett, N. and Maringe, F. (2008) 'Risk and trust: the impact of information and experience on the decision to participate in post-16 education', *Education, Knowledge and Economy*, 2(2): 99–110

Fen, Yap Sheau and Lian, Kew Mei (2006) *Service Quality and Customer Satisfaction: Antecedents of Customer's Re-patronage intentions.* Available from http://www.sunway.edu.my/others/vol4/service_quality.pdf (accessed 18 January 2010).

Foskett, N., Dyke, M. and Maringe, F. (2008) 'The influence of the school in the decision to participate in learning post 16', *British Educational Research Journal*, 34(1): 37–61.

Gajda, A. (2009) *The Trials of Academe The New Era of Campus Litigation.* New York: Harvard University Press.

Gibbs, P. (2008) *Marketers and Educationalists: Two Communities Divided by Time?* London: MCB Press.

Gerson, R. (1993) *Measuring Customer Satisfaction.* London: Kogan Page.

Greenwald, A. (1997) 'Validity concerns and usefulness of student ratings of instruction', *American Psychologist*, 52(11): 1182–6.

Guardian, The (2009) 'Keeping fair access to higher education', *The Guardian Online.* Available from http://www.guardian.co.uk/education/2009/may/25/nus-university-fees-fair-access (accessed 26 October 2009).

Janpen, P., Palaprom, K. and Horadal, P. (2005) 'An application of TQM for Thai communities knowledge management systems', *Proceedings of the Fourth Conference on E-business*, November 19–20, Bangkok, Thailand.

Kara, A. and de Shields, O. W. (2004) 'Business student satisfaction, intentions and retention in higher education: an empirical investigation', *MEQ* (Fall 2004), 3. Available from http://www.marketingpower.com/Community/ARC/gated/Documents/Teaching/MEO/student_satisfaction.pdf (accessed 26 October 2009).

Kumar, P. S. M. (2003) 'Total Quality Management (TQM) in HE and the relevance of accreditation', *ICWAI.* Available from http://www.icwai.org/icwai/knowledgebank/ma38.pdf (accessed 26 October 2009).

McMillan, J. and Cheney, G. (1996) 'The student as consumer: the implications and limitations of a metaphor', *Communication Education*, 45: 1–15.

McCollough, M. A. and Gremler, D. D. (1999) 'Guaranteeing student satisfaction: an exercise in treating students as customers', *Journal of Marketing Education*, 21: 118–30.

McEwan, A. (2007) 'Do metaphors matter in education?' *Journal of College & Character*, 8(2). Available from http://www.collegevalues.org/pdfs/Metaphors.pdf (accessed 18 January 2010).

OECD (2006) *Education at a Glance.* Available from http://www.oecd.org/dataoecd/32/50/37392956.pdf (accessed 26 October 2009).

Psacharopoulos, G. (1994) 'Returns to investment in education: a global update', *World Development*, 22(9): 1325–43.

Saxton, J. (2000) 'Investment in education: private and public returns', *Joint Economic Committee Study.* Available from http://www.house.gov/jec/educ.pdf (accessed 25 February 2010).

Schultz, T. W. (1961) 'Investment in human capital', *The American Economic Review*, 51(1): 1–17.

Smith, A. (1776) *The Wealth of Nations.* Reprint, Chicago, IL: University of Chicago Press (1976).

Topping, K. J. (2004) 'The effectiveness of peer tutoring in further and higher education: a typology and review of the literature', *Higher Education*, 32(3): 321–45.

Vargo, S. and Lusch, R. F. (2004) 'Evolving to a new dominant logic for marketing', *Journal of Marketing*, 68(1): 1–17.

Yi, Y. J. and La, S. N. (2004) 'What influences the relationship between customer satisfaction and repurchase intentions? Investigating the effect of adjusted expectations and customer loyalty', *Psychology and Marketing*, 21(5): 351–73.

Zeithaml, V. A., Berry, L .L. and Parasuraman, A. (1996). 'The behavioral consequences of service quality', *Journal of Marketing*, 60: 31–46.

Section 3

Students, consumers and citizens

Chapter 13

The consumer metaphor versus the citizen metaphor: different sets of roles for students

Johan Nordensvärd

Introduction

The dominant metaphor for the student has lately been that of the consumer. This implies that higher education should be considered in market terms, that lecturers provide products comparable to the pizzas of Pizza Hut or the haircut by the hairdresser. Wieleman indicates that 'the metaphor of "the free market", implying competition and the freedom of choice for consumers, has a strong normative impact' on schools and curricula and that 'economic considerations in particular are taking the lead, both in policy objectives (such as expenditure cuts and efficiency) and in the concepts adopted (such as management, productivity, etc.)' (2000: 33). This is not an exclusive development for schools, but can also be observed within higher education institutions.

This chapter argues that the consumer metaphor for students prescribes a singular and seemingly uncomplicated role that students can assume. Here I attempt to unpack the consumer metaphor for students to show how this metaphor does not only emancipate students by allowing them to choose, but at the same time such a neo-liberal approach could reconfigure the students as commodities to consume and to invest in. I argue that a citizenship perspective is far more compelling than a consumer perspective since it can open another set of roles which can give us a better understanding of the complexity of education. The chapter is divided into three parts: the first part will describe and explain the usage of neo-liberal metaphors; the second part will elaborate on this to define the roles of students within a consumer framework; the third part of the chapter will discuss how citizenship contrasts with a neo-liberal consumer framework and open a new understanding for the roles of students and the potential for a radical democratic higher education.

Neo-liberal metaphors

When we describe students as consumers or citizens we are using metaphors to create understanding of a certain phenomena. Metaphors could in this sense be considered as 'a way of comparing two different concepts' (Jones and Peccei

2004: 46) helping in our creation of social reality. Both the strength and the weakness of metaphors are that they attempt to understand one experience in terms of another experience. In one sense all theories and models are metaphorical in their nature (Morgan 1999: 10) and since every metaphor is at its core normative, it promotes one point of view over another. Often metaphors are hard to avoid and become a sort of 'prison of mind'. Still by seeing theories and models as metaphors, we become aware that one theory is not enough to describe reality (Morgan 1999:11–12).

The neo-liberal framework could be seen as rooted in liberalism which puts faith in individuals and the economy over the community and the state. Liberalism 'puts a strong emphasis on the individual, and most rights involve liberties that adhere to each and every person' (Isin and Turner 2002: 3) A liberal governance and rationality implies a certain order of organisation. Such governance is focused around terms like competition, market, freedom, choice, customer orientation, efficiency and flexibility and the market is seen as ideal for governance orientation (Fougner 2006: 175). It is assumed that markets can only exist and prosper under specific political, legal and institutional conditions. These have to be actively established by authorities (Fougner 2006: 176).

Harvey sees neo-liberalism as a political project, a process of neo-liberalisation that aims to 're-establish the conditions for capital accumulation and . . . restore the power of economic elites' (Harvey 2005: 19), and specifically to disembed capital from the constraints of the 'embedded liberalism' of social democracy and the Keynesian welfare state (Harvey 2005: 11). Davies and Bransel mention that neo-liberalism emphasises the choice of individuals to 'further their own interests and those of their family' (2007: 249–50) where the welfare state is often seen as an obstacle for economical growth.

When the market is playing a larger role in our social life, a consequence is that the citizen becomes understood, even by her or himself, through market logic as an individual ability to maximise lifestyle through choice (Stevenson 2006: 485–500). As such, the neo-liberal state should then empower the 'entrepreneurial subjects in their quest for self-expression, freedom and prosperity' (Davies and Bransel 2007: 249–250).

There is no denying that there are some convergences between being a consumer and being a neo-liberal citizen. Neo-liberal citizenship is a very narrow aspect of citizenship theory; it does not take into account other ideological understandings of being a citizen. A more expansive and multiple understanding of citizenship will be discussed below and used to compare with the consumer framework of students.

Neo-liberal consumer framework

A neo-liberal consumer framework could mean two different alternatives for higher education: first, the education system would be transformed into a Higher Education Corporation on a free market basis where students would consume

Table 13.1 Different sets of roles for students

Role	Students
Consumer	1 The student consumes educational services for her/his own pleasure and interest. 2 The student buys educational diplomas for improving her/his position on the labour market (boosting the CV). 3 The student buys techniques, skills and knowledge for becoming a knowledge worker and a self-regulated learner.
Manager	1 The student invests into her/his own human capital through education as her/his body and mind will be like a company supplying services to the market. 2 To increase her/his value the student updates her/his 'software' according to the principles of demand and supply. 3 The student uses education to achieve an employable and reasonable CV and hereby conduct studies and life in an accountable way.
Commodity	1 The Social Investment State ensures that education is wisely invested into human capital and that the educational outputs produce real economical growth. 2 The state manages its human capital in an accountable, transparent, competitive and efficient way. 3 The state has to provide corporations with highly skilled human capital for being able to compete with other countries in the knowledge economy.

to their ability and purse. This would mean a university funded by the logic of the market and run by the market. Alternatively, the higher education system would be run *like* a Higher Education Corporation where students would be regarded as consumers but could be completely or partly funded by the state. This could fit into New Public Management reforms. In this part of the chapter, I will try to discern the diverging roles of students within a neo-liberal consumer framework. For clarity, I have divided this framework for students into three different sets of roles: students as consumers, students as managers and students as commodities.

The student as a consumer

The first metaphor seems to be the most unproblematic one since it starts with the student and seems to expand the possibilities and the position of the student. Here, universities could be seen as providers of products (programmes of study and support in participating in those programmes). The student takes on the role as a consumer when she or he consumes educational products and services connected to these products (compare McCulloch 2009: 171). Such a perspective opens up the question of the consumer motive. Such a motive could be to further the students' own human capital in the form of degree programmes that boost their CV and/or give them skills to make them more employable on the market. Wellen discusses how this consumer perspective is becoming more inherent in the relationship between academia and the student body:

> More students view themselves as active purchasers of academic services, and are calling for stronger quality assurance standards and 'valued' credentials. Institutions are faced with more market pressures to differentiate/specialize in order to succeed as competition for students and faculty grows.
>
> (Wellen 2005: 25)

When we look at employability as the main consumer motive we can have two different approaches: students buy skills or students buy degrees. The first motive focuses more on what students can do with their knowledge; it is a form of employability of knowledge. Heyneman illustrates this perspective with clarity: an 'economistic' standpoint could mean that an educational system in a market economy should 'prepare students for changing careers and flexibility in the labour market' and an excellent school system 'emphasizes those skills which maximize adaptability' (Heyneman 2004: 447). Similarly, others say education needs to be more fitted to the needs of the students in preparing them to succeed in a culturally diverse and globally interdependent world. The goal would be to help the students to develop knowledge, awareness and skills to be effective in society. Education has to supply students with transferable skills (Carroll and Reichelt 2008: 391–2). Skills are seen as something that the universities are supposed to supply to students. This line of argument sees the main goal of education as making students more able to compete with other educated people from other countries. Leithwood, Edge and Jantzi mention that globalisation 'has given rise to the fear that students may not be getting the foundation they need to be competitive in the international markets' (Leithwood et al. 1999: 162).

A more cynical view would be that the students just desire the degree itself and not the skills. The students then have a rather instrumental relationship to joining the university and this leads to a commodification of education where plagiarism, apathy and customer orientation takes place (compare with Wellen 2005: 25). In many ways the education produces a degree which often gets confused with the academic service of teaching. The students aspire for what Molesworth et al. discuss as a mode of existence where students seek to 'have a degree' rather than 'be learners' (2009: 278). This would mean that students buy a fetish form of education where the degree itself is a strong signifier or commodity that can be owned but not traded or shared. The sales of degree qualifications on the internet have driven this aspect of consumerism to perfection.

The third form of consumer considers education more as fun and does not have to have any economic interest other than enjoyment: having a nice phase of life with interesting subjects, friends and some partying. The student buys an educational service just as she or he buys a DVD or a CD. These students buy education for their own pleasure. Such a perspective would foster an education that caters to what a large or small group of paying students find amusing or scientifically interesting. Blake *et al.* argue that education has been degraded to any kind of commodity available for consumption claiming, 'the triumph of the market has declared individual subjective choice sovereign and deliberation, by corollary pointless' (Blake *et al.* 2000: xi). Furthermore, Blake *et al.* argue that 'educational values are simply what the consumer happens to want, and it makes no more sense to undertake any great inquiry into those values than into preferences in the matter of cars or brands of chicken tikka' (2000: xi). This part of the chapter made a distinction between three different consumer attitudes to education. In reality these boundaries are often blurred and all three types of consumer attitudes at the same time can be reasons for pursuing HE.

The student as a manager

The first metaphor focuses on the consumption act of the students; the second metaphor elaborates on the utility of education. When the purchase of education is not just for fun or leisure the first metaphor cannot really explain the roles of the students. The consumption of skills and degrees are not just consumer goods but one could argue that from a neo-liberal perspective education is an investment into the career of the students. The students are therefore not just consumers, but also managers of their life, future and their CV. Education could therefore be seen as an investment in students' personal and individualised capital (compare Robertson (2000) in Wellen 2005: 27). Simons and Masschelein consider this as a transformation where learners should become managers of their own learning. They should develop their own learning strategy, monitor the process and evaluate the result. 'Thus what is at stake is the emergence of a kind of "managerial" attitude toward learning: learning appears as a process of construction that could and should be managed and this first and foremost by learners themselves' (Simons and Masschelein 2008: 401).

Employability is important as part of active labour policies where competencies and competence management become important. 'Policy is no longer about "functions" but about "competencies", that is, knowledge, capacities and attitudes that are employable with regard to an efficient, flexible (and learning-based) adaptation to changing conditions' (Simons and Masschelein, 2008: 401). From this view, the student needs to consider higher education as a way to increase his/her employability.

As mentioned in the last metaphor there has been a focus on skills and one of those skills that students should learn is self-management. An example is the skill to learn. One learns the skill to learn instead of learning a certain knowledge that would become easily outdated in the knowledge economy. Learning is therefore neither limited to schools nor other institutions of education nor to a particular time in people's lives (compare Simons and Masschelein 2008: 397–8). The main aspect of life-long learning is its expansive scope: one could consider every person as a learner who participates not just by classes of learning but also by informally and self-directed learning.

Since the stability of knowledge itself has been undermined, the knowledge and skills learned can easily become outdated. OECD indicates that students need to re-think the value of knowledge rather as skills than as a collection of knowledge. OECD argues that the modern world does not need people that know something; it needs people that have acquired 'prerequisites for successful learning in future life' (OECD 1999: 9). The student manager must therefore be able to manage the skills that she or he learns and value skills and knowledge that are employable in the student's career and in the global economy. In this perspective the student needs to offer products and services that corporations can consume. In this sense; the student does not achieve these goals due to personal interest, but rather as a way to offer something that the market needs and can consume.

The student as a commodity

The second metaphor touched upon the self-management of learning, in order to participate in and to become viable on the market. As such, discussion focuses on the direct strategies to create knowledge and skills that are consumable on the market. One aspect of the knowledge economy is not just the interest of the students to fit the market but also the interest of the state and the market. When the students become reconfigured as consumers and managers the same thing could be said about the state. The state could be seen first and foremost as a manager (of human capital) and as an investor (into human capital) and consumer (of educational investments in Higher Education and research). This metaphor turns the table and dis-empowers the students: the students go from being consumer queens to investment pawns.

One could see a relationship with Paul Romer's analysis of education in the New Growth Theory (Romer 1986), where the importance of education is to produce tacit knowledge. Tacit knowledge is then defined as the technical knowledge that people obtain by experience and by applying scientific theories in real life. This represents the knowledge manifested in a human body which turns the body into human capital. These bodies are a knowledge economy's greatest assets. When a country wants to be successful, it will need to invest in technology (applied science) and human capital (the bodies that carry the applied science). According to the OECD, it is the purpose of education in post-modern time to generate prosperity: 'The prosperity of countries now derives to a large extent from their human capital, and to succeed in a rapidly changing world, individuals need to advance their knowledge and skills throughout their lives' (2004: 3).

Students are no longer subjects under coercive and cohesive powers of the state – they do not have to be forced to become citizens or workers – they are now products of the global market. The renewal itself is a way to renew the human capital within the human body. The learning process and the result of learning (knowledge) could be seen as capital where learning produces added value. Fromm would put it this way: 'Modern man is alienated from himself, from his fellow men, and from nature. He has been transformed into a commodity, experiences his life forces as an investment which must bring him the maximum profit obtainable under existing market conditions' (1957: 67). When the state invests in students, it also expects that these investments will be fruitful. When the state strives for solving social problems it will measure whether social problems are diminishing. When the state strives for economic growth and employability it will measure these in economic terms. The state could be seen as a Social Investment State which invests into its country's human capital, the universities become both service providers for the consumers but also for the state as a risk manager. These service providers need to audit the human capital and assure that they live up to the achieved degrees.

Roles of students from a citizenship perspective

The chosen metaphors are examples to illustrate how a neo-liberal framework of students can be complex and contradictory. Being a consumer, manager and commodity at the same time casts some doubt that consumer frameworks could really empower students. It is therefore hard to consider the neo-liberal framework of consuming as a magical trick of turning a pawn into a queen. I would argue that a citizenship perspective will be able to connect the roles of students to a larger perspective. A broad citizenship perspective could therefore include a neo-liberal definition but it could also include other ideological starting points for understanding the roles of the students. This chapter will focus on two main aspects of citizenship:

1   Citizenship as a set of political rights granted to citizens which means rights to participate in political processes of self-governance. 'These includes rights to vote; to hold elective and appointive governmental offices; to serve on various sorts of juries; and generally to participate in political debates as Equal community members' (Smith 2002: 105).
2   Citizenship as a 'full membership in society' (Holston and Appadurai 1996: 187). Citizenship could be defined as a legal status in a political community connected with rights (political, civil and social) and to some degree duties (pay taxes and obey the law) (Smith 2002: 105).

On one hand, one could understand citizenship as the rights and duties to participate actively in a political community and on the other, the membership to a political community. To use citizenship as a contrasting set of roles we need to use the different ideological interpretations of the concept. *The Handbook of Citizenship Studies* edited by Isin and Turner uses four different ideological starting points: liberalism, communitarianism, radical-democratic theory and republicanism (see Isin and Turner 2002). I would argue that citizenship is always linked with membership on one side depending on the level and nature of participation that is expected from its members and non-members. The first starting point would fittingly be a communitarian citizenship.

A *communitarian* view focuses on 'the community (or the society or the nation), whose primary concern is the cohesive and just functioning of society' (Isin and Turner 2002: 4). The communitarian individual is an individual who emerges from a historical and dense social context. A community defines who belongs and who does not belong to it and suggests a 'strong sense of place, proximity and totality', while society could be said to symbolise 'fragmentation, alienation and distance' (Delanty 2002: 161).

Such a view of education would fit more with the traditional view of education or science where being a student or graduate would mean to enter into an elite community. Education could be seen as a rite of passage more than just gaining knowledge and skills. Another interpretation could consider students as entering a scientific and scholar community and therefore a pledge towards certain values to knowledge and the pursuit of knowledge. In the first example the students go through a rite of passage to become a member of an elite where HE could be seen as a way to reproduce ruling values. The same could happen for a scientific elite community where the students should be at the top of the educational ladder. Education has not just reproduced elite communities; education has also been a source for creating communities.

An example is the role of education within nation states. The modern Western city is defined by Thompson as a 'representative democracy, institutionalized primarily at the level of the nation-state and coupled with a relatively autonomous market economy over which democracy has assumed some degree of regulatory control' (1995: 251). The earlier function of education was according to Green, to be a 'valuable source of national cohesion and a key tool for economic development' (1997: 1). National education was a tool in 'the formation of ideologies and collective beliefs which legitimate state power and underpin concepts of nationhood and national "character"' (Green 1990: 77). MacLaren analyses schooling as ritual performances and highlights two important phases of identities: rituals of becoming a citizen (1986: 226) and the rituals of becoming a good worker (1986: 135). Education could in the case of the state be considered to create members of what Benedict Andersen (1991) would call an imagined community but also to foster people to be useful and obedient in an economic system. For most people this would mean an equal membership and limited participation within the nation state and an extensive participation and unequal membership within the market. From this perspective students could be seen as nation state citizens on one side but also as future members of the economy. There is here a dual role of the students that is also reflected within education.

Liberalism provides a different perspective. Liberalism 'puts a strong emphasis on the individual, and most rights involve liberties that adhere to each and every person' (Isin and Turner 2002: 3). This liberalism does not just have to mean the neo-liberal notion of self-relying actors that have much in common with classical liberalism. The first part of this chapter elaborated in detail what the role of students would be within a framework where 'education is linked with economic productivity and growth in personal income' (Heyneman 2004: 441) and where students are members and participants within a global economy. Within liberalism there could also be a social liberalism much closer to Marshall and Keynes rather than Milton Friedman and John Stuart Mill. Such a social liberal citizenship would focus on positive rights which could mean that the state needs the welfare state to live a dignified life (Schuck 2002: 131–2). Marshall considered the social rights such as the freedom to participate in society as the right to education and health care (Matten and Crane 2005: 170). A social liberal citizenship could therefore argue as a contrast to neo-liberal citizenship: it is the right for the students as citizens to enjoy education and therefore such service should be provided to some degree by the state. To diminish the harmful effects of human competition at the free market, social welfare states have, according to Esping-Andersen, tried to de-commodify work and workers, opening up options for the labour forces to chose between different jobs, to get educated, and to decrease the negative effects of losing employment (Esping-Andersen 1990: 36–7). Education could therefore be seen as one of the foundations of citizenship that empowers the citizen vis-à-vis the market. This does once again highlight the dual and unequal relationship between membership in the state and the market. From such a perspective education is considered to increase the capabilities of students to participate in social and economic communities.

A *radical democratic* citizenship perspective would be to 'generate an anti-essentialist politics that continually attempts to redefine itself in order to resist the exclusion of individuals and groups in the formation of social order' (Rasmussen and Brown 2000: 176–7). The theory hails democracy and a commitment to equality and participation. The radical aspect is the focus on social change and the political struggle by marginalised groups. It is mainly seen as a post-Marxist perspective that tries to redefine politics and the activity of political subjects. It stresses the link between practice and theory as the motor for social change and empowerment. Isin regards citizenship as a generalised problem of otherness, especially concerning the formation of groups of otherness. The formation of groups is a fundamental and dynamic process that is being oriented towards taking positions. Citizenship is responding to positions rather than to identities where one could be a stranger, a citizen and an alien and it is therefore important to see citizenship as a 'specific figuration of orientations, strategies and technologies that are available for deployment in producing solidarity, agonistic and alienating multiplicities' (Isin 2005: 374 –5).

One could see that an alternative goal of education should not just be to create citizens and workers but it should enable the emancipation of the citizens. Among some scholars there is the perception that education should make it possible for the individual learner to work independently on the political dimension of society. This would mean a democratic education that acknowledges the freedom of the citizen and that promotes individual political judgments and evaluation (compare Sander 2005: 15–17). A critical aspect could therefore be to create a critical awareness among students which 'make evident the multiplicity and complexity of history, as a narrative to enter into critical dialogue with rather than accept unquestioningly' and that this pedagogy should 'cultivate a healthy scepticism about power and a willingness to temper any reverence for authority with a sense of critical awareness' (Said 2001: 501, in Giroux 2006: 32). In this sense there is a challenging aspect to being a student. Students should learn how to challenge both the relative position of themselves and challenge the structures of scholarship, science, education, history and other aspects of the self and society.

The fourth ideological perspective is the *republican* perspective where there is an emphasis 'on both individual and group rights' (Isin and Turner 2002: 4). A republican belief is that public life enriches people's life since it draws people out of privacy and draws them together. It also extracts the talents and capacities of the citizen. It creates a community with connection and solidarity, but also conflicts between the citizens. For a republican, individualism or family will not be enough (Dagger 2002: 146–8). Two aspects that come from publicity are the rule of law and civic virtue. Politics should be public to avoid corruption or nepotism. As a member of a community, people must be prepared to set aside their private interests to do what is the best for the public as a whole. The one who does this displays civic virtues. The rule of law is the frame and rules of the practical politics: it sets the limits of with whom and when debates take place and how decisions are made. Publicity needs rule of law for being a practical solution. 'Citizenship has an ethical dimension, in short, because there are standards built into the concept of citizenship, just as there are standards built into the concepts of mayor, teacher, plumber and physician' (Dagger 2002: 146–8).

From such a perspective a student is positioned with values for the common good of society. This perspective is therefore rather far away from being a consumer isolated within a gigantic market for the economy. In the republican perspective, a student could be seen as someone abiding to democracy and its struggle; abide to a common good beyond the individual pursuit for profit. In this way, education should create citizens who set their own interests aside for the greater good and who are willing to offer their knowledge and minds in the service of others. This is the opposite to the neo-liberal perspective of students and citizens pursuing their own self-interest.

Conclusions

The linkage of citizenship and the role of students is not that far-fetched when we consider that education has played a large role in creating citizens of imagined communities such as nation states and a prepared work force. Education has always been seen as a political tool to shape its subjects and solve societal problems. Simons and Masschelein mention that the shared 'horizon for this governmental reflection was the relation between "education" and "society"' (2008: 394). According to Simons and Masschelein, there was the assumption that education has a 'social' dimension and that national government has the responsibility to intervene in education to solve social, cultural and economical problems. The state would therefore consider education as a tool of government or as Simons and Masschelein would call it the 'governmentalization of education' (2008: 394–5). The state translated societal problems like inequality and workforce needs into educational solutions within school reform and curriculum reform. In a neo-liberal world order where the state becomes a corporation and the society is a market, education itself becomes more centered around solving economic problems than social problems. At the same time there remains a belief that education could solve both economic and social problems.

Alvesson discusses these beliefs as the 'the fundamentalism of education' which means a naive trust in education where:

> Education is something inherently good, education has no end, the ideal human being is thoroughly shaped by education, work skills are only fostered in education; low education is a individual deficit, education is a general problem solver and education should be redesignated in terms of higher education.
>
> (Alvesson 2006: 50–1)

Alvesson indicates that the values and expectations of education are one of our most predominant myths with an almost fetishised notion of competence and knowledge.

At the same time one could argue that neo-liberal education draws us closer to a commercial and destructive nihilism since it undermines many normative debates. Blake *et al.* highlight the problems of considering education policy as evidence-based activity in search for 'what works' as the main goal. The means becomes an end in itself where there are 'short-term solutions for problems which may not be problems at all' (Blake *et al.* 2000: xiii–xiv). A neo-liberal definition of education seems to strip education of its political, ideological and normative aspects. To put this bluntly, higher education could be seen as a power tool that is not perceived as one. In neo-liberal theory education is technical and it is good. This means that 'what needs to be managed, the purposes to be and the management process are clear, fixed and unproblematic' (Wearmouth 2003: 255).

Using a citizenship metaphor opens up more roles that a student could take on within society. It was therefore the main aim of this chapter to enlarge the common understanding of citizenship and being a student. As such I have highlighted that education has normative, political, ideological goals that should be reconsidered. We might also hope that education becomes more radical democratic, as proposed by Neary and Hagyard in Chapter 16, and students should not just question the limits of politics but also the limits of education. There is nothing that says that higher education should not be seen as a way to challenge the foundation of knowledge and society and that science should not serve this purpose in addition to the economy and the social investment state.

References

Alvesson, M. (2006) *Tomhetens triumf. Om grandiositet, illusionsnummer och nollsummesspel.* Stockholm: Atlas.

Anderson, B. (1991 [1983]) *Imagined Communities: Reflections on the Origin and Spread of Nationalism.* London: Verso.

Blake, N., Smeyers, P., Smith, R. and Standish, P. (2000) *Education in an Age of Nihilism.* London: Routledge Falmer.

Carroll, E. B and Reichelt, S. A. (2008) 'Using current consumer issues to involve students in research', *International Journal of Consumer Studies* 32: 391–3.

Dagger, R. (2002) 'Republican citizenship', in E. F. Isin and B. S. Turner (eds) *Handbook of Citizenship Studies,* London/Thousands Oaks/New Delhi: Sage Publications.

Davies, B and Bransel, P (2007) 'Neoliberalism and education', *International Journal of Qualitative Studies in Education,* 20(3): 247–59.

Delanty, G (2002) 'Communitarianism and citizenship', in E. F. Isin and B. S. Turner (eds) *Handbook of Citizenship Studies.* London/Thousands Oaks/New Dehli: Sage Publications.

Esping-Andersen, G. (1990) *The Three Worlds of Welfare Capitalism.* Cambridge: Cambridge Polity.

Fougner, T. (2006) 'The state, international competitiveness and neo-liberal globalisation: is there a future beyond "the competition state"?', *Review of International Studies,* 32(1): 165–85.

Fromm, E. (1957) *The Art of Loving.* London: Thorsons.

Giroux, H. A. (2006) 'Academic freedom under fire: the case for critical pedagogy', *College Literature,* 33(4): 1–42.

Green, A. (1990) *Education and State Formation: The Rise of Education Systems in England, France and the USA.* London: Palgrave Macmillan.

Green, A. (1997) *Education, Globalization and the Nation State.* London: Palgrave Macmillan.

Harvey, D. (2005) *A Brief History of Neo-liberalism.* Oxford, Oxford University Press.

Heyneman, S.(2004) 'International education quality', *Economics of Education Review,* 23(44): 441–52.

Holston, J and Appadurai, A. (1996) 'Cities and citizenship', *Public Culture,* 8(2): 187–204.

Isin, E. F (2005) 'Engaging, being, political', *Political Geography,* 24 (3): 373–87.

Isin, E. F. and Turner, B. S. (2002) 'Citizenship studies: an introduction', in E. F. Isin and B. S. Turner (eds) *Handbook of Citizenship Studies.* London/Thousands Oaks/New Dehli: Sage Publications.

Jones, J. and Peccei, J. (2004) 'Language and politics', in L. Thomas, S. Wareing, I. Singh, J. Peccei, J. Thornborrow and J.Jones (eds) *Language, Society and Power.* London: Routledge.

Leithwood, K., Edge, K. and Jantzi, D. (1999) *Educational Accountability: The State of the Art.* Gütersloh: Bertelsmann Foundation Publishers.

MacLaren, P (1986) *Schooling as a Ritual Performance: Towards a Political Economy of Educational Symbols and Gestures.* London: Routledge and Kegan Paul.

Matten, D. and Crane, A. (2005) 'Corporate citizenship: toward an extended theoretical conceptualization', *Academy of Management Review*, 30(1): 166–79.

McCulloch, A. (2009) 'The student as co-producer: learning from public administration about the student-university relationship', *Studies in Higher Education*, 34(2): 171–83.

Molesworth, M., Nixon, E. and Scullion, R. (2009) 'Having, being and higher education: the marketisation of the university and the transformation of the student into consumer', *Teaching in Higher Education*, 14(3): 277–87.

Morgan, G (1999) *Organisationsmetaforer*. Lund: Studentlitterarur.

OECD (1999) *Measuring Student Knowledge and Skills: A New Framework for Assessment*. Paris, OECD.

OECD (2004) *Learning for Tomorrow's World: First Results from PISA 2003*. Paris: OECD.

Rasmussen, C. and Brown, M. (2002) 'Radical democratic citizenship: amidst political theory and geography', in E. F. Isin and B. S. Turner (eds) *Handbook of Citizenship Studies*. London/Thousands Oaks/New Dehli: Sage Publications.

Romer, P. M. (1986) 'Increasing returns and long-run growth', *Journal of Political Economy*, 94(5): 1002–37.

Sander, W. (2005) 'Theorie der Politische Bildung: Geschichte – didaktische Konzeptionen – aktuelle Tendenzen und Probleme', in W. Sanders (ed.) *Handbuch Politische Bildung*. Bonn: Wochenschau Publishers.

Schuck, P.H. (2002) 'Liberal citizenship', in E. F. Isin and B. S. Turner (eds) *Handbook of Citizenship Studies*. London/Thousands Oaks/New Dehli: Sage Publications.

Simons, M. and Masschelein, J. (2008) 'The governmentalization of learning and the assemblage of a learning apparatus', *Educational Theory*, 58(4): 391–415.

Smith, R. M. (2002) 'Modern citizenship', in E. F. Isin and B. S. Turner (eds) *Handbook of Citizenship Studies*. London/Thousands Oaks/New Dehli: Sage Publications.

Stevenson, N. (2006) 'European cosmopolitan solidarity questions of citizenship, difference and post-materialism', *European Journal of Social Theory*, 9(4): 485–500.

Thompson, J. B. (1995) *The Media and Modernity: A Social Theory of the Media*. Cambridge: Polity Press.

Wearmouth, J (2003) 'The use of a narrative approach to illuminate an individual learning need: implications for teachers' professional development', *Journal of In-Service Education*, 29 (2): 255–76.

Wellen, R. (2005) 'The university student in a reflexive society: consequences of consumerism and competition', *Higher Education Perspectives*, 1(2): 23–38.

Wielemans, W. (2000) 'European educational policy on shifting sand?', *European Journal for Education Law and Policy*, 4(1): 21–34.

Chapter 14

Constructing consumption: what media representations reveal about today's students

Joanna Williams

The introduction of tuition fees paid directly by students in 2001 appeared to clarify the position of students as consumers of higher education (HE). However, the construction of the student-consumer was set in place prior to 2001, and does not emerge solely as a result of the payment of fees. The student consumer is also constructed through government policies; the broader marketisation of education at all levels; and broader social and political trends away from a Keynesian welfare state towards a neo-liberal marketised society. This positioning of students is presented in the popular media which (re)constructs the student-consumer for a new generation.

Media representations arguably reveal only journalists' prevailing attitudes towards student-consumers. However, journalists are part of society; their views are subject to many of the same influences as other people and in order to sell articles, pieces must chime with the opinions of at least a section of the population. For this reason, media representations of students are worthy of analysis as they reflect back to society some of the dominant ways in which what it means to be a student is understood today; this may also help reconstruct ways of being a student for new generations. As students are generally young adults preparing to enter the world of careers, politics and culture, the media's opinion of students can reveal much about attitudes and anxieties towards society in the future. I argue that journalists represent (and maybe also construct) the emergence of the student-consumer as a generally positive social development in that such students are increasingly empowered to influence their experience of university. However, a close analysis also reveals that student-consumers may be presented as infantilised through a prolonged period of financial dependency and restricted to influencing only their immediate environment.

This paper focuses solely upon print media, in particular, national newspapers. Other forms of media, such as television and radio, may present a slightly different narrative and portray an alternative version of what it means to be a student. This is most especially the case with forms of media which are controlled by students themselves, in particular; internet blogs and contributions to chat-rooms, or student-run newspapers and radio stations. An analysis of the portrayal and construction of students in such alternative forms of media would provide fertile ground for study but is beyond the remit of this particular chapter. For my purposes here, twenty articles for analysis were selected, particularly from the 'broadsheets' but also *The Daily Mail*, dating from 2000. Articles were chosen that made specific reference to students as consumers of higher education. This represents almost all the articles that have been written on this topic and so sampling was only necessary to avoid repetition. The articles selected were a mixture of opinion pieces and reported news articles. Techniques of critical discourse analysis (Scott 1990; Fairclough 2003) were applied to a close reading of the articles and revealed four main themes, or categories: the role of parents as co-consumers; the importance of consumers gaining value for money from their degree programme; the rise in students complaining about negative experiences of university; and finally, the relationship of student-consumers to broader society.

Constructing consumption

Historically, education has always, perhaps, been 'purchasable' by some in society, with the recent past of free access to a state-funded HE sector and generous student grants a historical anomaly. However, the payment of fees alone does not sufficiently account for the creation of student-consumers. Payment may instead have 'the effect not of commodifying their learning, but galvanising their endeavours on their own behalf' (Grayling 2002). Other trends have enhanced the development of the student-consumer model. The past decade has witnessed an acceleration of changes in relation to both the perceived purpose of HE and the composition of the student body.

Newman confidently described the purpose of the university as 'the cultivation of the intellect, as an end which may reasonably be pursued for its own sake' (1852 (1959): 170; see also Potts 2005). Yet in the intervening years the instrumental purpose of economic utility (be it for individual or national gain) has come to dominate HE. Civic universities, founded with a practical aim of developing science and technology for local industries, served to open up the opportunities for social mobility associated with HE to a slightly broader section of the population. Although the roots of instrumentalism and widening-participation can be traced back over many decades, it is important not to lose sight of the historical specificity of the current period. Charles Clarke (writing in *The Future of Higher Education*) urges universities 'to make better progress in harnessing knowledge to wealth creation' (DfES 2003: 2). In June 2009 the government's view on the relationship between universities and the economy was clarified when a Cabinet reshuffle saw Prime Minister Gordon Brown place HE under the remit of Lord Mandelson's Department for Business, Innovation and Skills. In his speech, *Higher Education and Modern Life*, given at Birkbeck College, Mandelson describes universities as 'engines of social mobility' and HE as an 'entry ticket to the best paid employment' and 'a ticket to higher lifetime earnings' (2009). This presentation of HE as a 'ticket' creates the sense that in attending university, students are accessing (perhaps purchasing) the 'graduate premium' (Smithers 2007) irrespective of the extent of their engagement with the learning process.

Such explicit instrumentalism belies pretension to the pursuit of knowledge for its own sake and instead creates students who do what it takes to succeed 'where succeed is defined in terms of graduation' (Potts 2005: 62). As a result, the aim for many students becomes obtaining the outcome, a degree, rather than a full engagement with the learning process. It is important to note that not all students want to consider education in this way and may serve to remind government ministers of alternative models. Gemma Tumelty, president of the NUS asks: 'What about learning for learning's sake? . . . What about expanding your mind? It's not just about looking for a course that will get you on the career ladder' (Wignall 2006). There is perhaps a danger that the insistence of politicians upon a focus on outcomes rather than processes will enhance the creation of a consumer mentality and the belief that students should seek to obtain a degree product rather than participate in lengthy periods of study. This stands in contrast to the idea that HE is perhaps better considered as a 'relationship' between lecturers and students, a relationship which is 'structured by purpose and content' (Biesta 2009). This kind of relationship clearly cannot be given or 'done' to someone. It needs effort and collaboration between student and lecturer. At most it may be considered that people have a right of access to facilities and resources (both human and material): in other words, to the 'products' or commodities of a university. To term HE a 'right' risks denying the responsibility upon individuals to intellectually engage with subject content through education and, in effect, create the processes and relationships for their own learning.

It has been suggested that today's students seek to *have* a degree rather than to *be* learners (Molesworth *et al.* 2009). This move from 'being' to 'having' represents an intellectual shift from engagement to passivity with some students seeking satisfaction in the fulfilment of their rights as opposed to a struggle with theoretical content. This is represented in newspapers:

> The problem with treating students as consumers, many observed, was that it gave them the impression they had rights but no responsibilities. 'They think that because they are paying they should be awarded a 2:1 without making any effort,' was a repeated complaint.
>
> (Clare 2006)

Rather than challenging such ideas, universities often encourage students to act as consumers by making demands and have their voices heard. Students are expected to complete course evaluation forms and are recruited onto staff-student liaison committees. By institutions placing attention so firmly upon the student experience enhances the idea that the purpose of HE is the creation of satisfied consumers.

This focus upon creating satisfied consumers emerges from the USA and has come to influence HE policy in the UK. Dill (2003) and Singh (2002) note that historically, due to funding following individual students rather than institutions, the USA has always operated as a market in which universities compete to attract students. However, genuine competition between institutions only emerged after the Second World War with cheaper and faster transport links between states and more standardised admissions tests. In order to compete in the HE market place, US universities have long since published data concerning student satisfaction. Singh notes that Harvard University first collected and published student ratings of teaching in the mid 1920s and that this was followed by other institutions in the 1960s and 1970s as a 'student empowerment mechanism' (2002: 687). In the early 1990s the World Bank suggested that a US-style market-driven model of HE be replicated internationally and this coincided with a period of growth in the popularity of human capital theories (knowledge economy) and global trends towards reducing public sector expenditure. Since the early 1990s there has been a similar international increase in monitoring student satisfaction.

In the UK, institutions and lecturers are held to account for student satisfaction through structures such as the National Student Survey and course evaluation forms. The demand to produce satisfied consumers potentially has an impact upon pedagogy as it may lead some lecturers to avoid making intellectual demands of their students and provide 'entertainment rather than education' (Morley 2003: 90). Newman indicated the dangers of using the word 'educated' when in actual fact what is meant is 'amused, refreshed, soothed, put into good spirits and good humour, or kept from vicious excess' (1852 (1959): 164). An irony is that whilst the promotion of satisfaction may appear to be a response to students perceiving themselves as consumers it also enhances trends towards the construction of the consumption model. The more universities present themselves as responding to student demands, the more students are encouraged to see themselves as behaving correctly (doing what is expected) in demanding satisfaction.

The empowered consumer

Newspapers frequently represent student-consumers as empowered by their consumer status. One way in which this manifests itself is that students are able to make demands of the institutions they attend; in particular they are able to demand 'value for money' on their degree purchase. We are told: 'It is a hardly surprising consequence of the introduction of fees that students . . . increasingly see themselves as consumers. And like all consumers they want value for money' (Wignall 2007) and 'Universities hate being ranked – they spend increasing amounts on marketing to an increasingly money-fixated market of students who want value-for-money for their £3,000 per year' (Leach 2006). What is apparent in this discourse is the assumption of common sense over the issue of students seeking value for money. There is not felt to be any need for evidence to corroborate representations of students as people who 'see themselves as consumers' and are 'increasingly money-fixated'. Similarly, the connection, between paying fees and seeking 'value for money' is presented here as logical and obvious: 'hardly surprising' and not in need of substantiating. There is, perhaps, a risk that the assumption of common sense becomes based solely upon the frequency of repetition: and that future students may adopt these attitudes as expected norms of behaviour. As suggested in the previous section, paying fees does not automatically lead to a consumer mentality. It may be the case that the importance of gaining value for money represents the concerns of parents (see below) or the generation and social class most dominated by journalists. It may be the case that today's students accept accruing quite high levels of debt as a normal part of life and the quality of education received bears only a tangential relationship to debt occurred.

Newspaper reports often promote the idea of the student-complainant to the extent of crusading on their behalf: 'There have . . . been well-publicised cases recently about students complaining about the amount of "contact" with teachers, and the more publicity there is about this, the better' writes Bahram Bekhradnia, Director of the Higher Education Policy Institute in *The Times* (2009). Yet there is little to suggest that students have a clear idea of exactly what they consider to be value-for-money higher education. To suggest they have implies students are capable of making judgements on what is a good standard of education, the financial worth of such an education and the actual value of the education they do receive. As students are not, by definition, in possession of all the specific content to be covered they are perhaps not best placed to pass pedagogical judgement. Instead, many students equate value for money with contact time with teaching staff (more being necessarily better – although this may run contrary to the promotion of more independent learners). Value for money may also be equated with success: if students are rated highly by their lecturers they are gaining value for money, if they receive low marks, they are not. 'The majority of complaints were about academic status, i.e. students' degree passes' (Garner 2009).

One reported effect upon students of the desire to gain value for money is an increasingly instrumental emphasis upon gaining skills for employability that can be traded in the post-graduation labour market:

> Could it be that for this year's generation of freshers – already no strangers to the pressures and demands of target-led, performance obsessed education – university isn't an adventure playground for learning or licentiousness, but a business transaction, an exchange of money for a guaranteed leg-up in the post-graduation 'real-world'.
>
> (Wignall 2006)

This quotation describes the author's perception of the changes in student mentality, away from, a perhaps mythical 'golden age' of learning and licentiousness which could be enjoyed more securely in the knowledge of assumed social mobility, towards a focus upon employment prospects. However, it links this shift not just to the payment of fees but also to broader policy changes that have occurred in the education system. The use of 'real world' reinforces the idea that time spent at university is a break from normality; that the process of learning is less important than the outcome of a degree. The sense of university as a 'business transaction' is reflected in other articles, for example:

> The survey of 20,000 full time undergraduates found that three quarters view university as a way of improving their career potential. Money is also increasingly important to today's career minded students, with 60% saying they are motivated to study by a desire to achieve higher salaries, compared to just 36% in 2004.
>
> (Frean 2008)

This quotation reinforces the perceived instrumentalism of student-consumers in 'buying' a degree which can then be traded for future employability. This idea is promoted by Higher Education Minister David Lammy: 'The overwhelming majority of students from all backgrounds still consider the benefits of higher education to outweigh the costs. In an increasingly competitive world, we also know that employers are aware of the range of skills that graduates can bring to their businesses' (Clark 2009). The focus upon outcomes rather than processes is not limited to studying (having a degree is more important than being a learner) but also to future employment (having a high salary is more important than the nature of the work). This may represent a broader change in generational attitudes beyond the commodification of HE.

The frequent media representation of value for money as an important quality in a university degree programme perhaps serves to legitimise the process of students complaining if they consider themselves to be in receipt of a service which does not fulfil such expectations. One newspaper reports: 'Disgruntled historian, Lizzie Edwards declared: "I thought I was paying to be educated by leading academics, not for library membership and a reading list"' (Smallman 2006) thus clearly setting out both the student's expectation and how this had not been met. The perception from the media is of a huge increase in complaints: 'big growth in the numbers of students complaining' (Garner 2009) although reading beyond the headlines suggests this may be exaggerated: 'the number of justifiable complaints . . . has fallen from 11 per cent in 2008 to just 7 per cent in 2008. . . . while there were 900 complaints – there are 1.9 million students at higher education institutions' (Garner 2009). The article points out that most complaints were from UK-based students (despite overseas students paying much larger fees) and that the majority of complaints concerned the awarding of degree passes rather than educational opportunities. Both these points reinforce the arguments that consumer status does not simply emerge from the payment of fees but from other trends which also push students into a pre-occupation with learning outcomes rather than processes.

Despite acknowledging that the number of students who complain is a tiny proportion of the overall student population, newspapers appear to be very keen on stories of complainants, often focusing upon cases of students seeking legal redress for breach of contract in articles headlined: 'Students win their fight for damages' (Lightfoot 2003) or 'Universities pay £15m a year to students when courses go wrong' (Henry 2004). Such articles tend to champion the cause of the student-complainant:

> 'I think students do complain more,' says Professor Howard Newby, the President of the Committee of Vice-Chancellors and Principals and the Vice-chancellor of Southampton University. 'They are adults, and we're not in loco parentis. It is good for the system that students exert their consumer rights.' Ian Pearson, the Labour MP for Dudley South and author of a new pamphlet on Higher Education from the Social Market Foundation, agrees. 'I hope we will get more of these complaints,' he says. 'I want to see students empowered as customers. I think more students should complain if they feel they're not getting the quality of teaching and other services that they deserve.'
>
> (*The Independent* 2000)

Arguments that it is 'good for the system' for students to be 'empowered as consumers', enable students to hold academics to account for the service they provide. Complainants, it has been suggested, may be 'represented as the personification of civic virtue' (Furedi 2009) and the act of complaining, 'an inherent virtue' (Furedi 2009). A possible pedagogical risk of encouraging students to hold lecturers to account in this way is that it may have the perverse consequence of undermining the trust necessary for truly educational collaborative or mentoring relationships.

Deconstructing subjectivity: parents as co-consumers

Although newspapers are eager to portray students as empowered by their consumer status, a close reading reveals a number of potential problems inherent in this assumption. The first is the issue of who are the real consumers of HE: it is often parents who are presented as consumers: 'It might be their show but – surprise, surprise, we're still paying for our ringside seats' (Moorhead 2009) and *The Daily Mail* points out that: 'Parents, particularly those from middle-class backgrounds, are behaving more and more like consumers: they pay the money, they expect to see results' (Smith-Squire 2008). The reference to parents from 'middle class backgrounds' is interesting because it chimes with this particular paper's complaint that whilst upper-class parents can afford to pay for university and working-class parents get government support in the form of grants and bursaries, it is the middle-class families who are left to carry the burden of fees. It is also interesting to note that the product sought is not attendance at a particular university or to a certain type of experience; rather, it is to 'results'.

Middle-class parent-consumers expect to see results in exchange for their money. At very least, parents become co-consumers in what is considered to be a family purchase. Again, this is most often linked to demands for value for money: 'The findings, taken from a survey of 15,000 students, also raises questions over the value that they and their families are getting for top-up tuition fees of £3,000 a year' (Doughty 2007).

As with student-consumers, the construction of parents as co-consumers may be based upon broader social trends than the payment of fees. It is not the case that parents have to write cheques directly to particular universities. It could be argued that the fully independent university student was also a historical anomaly and current changes merely return society back to a long-standing status quo. Prior to the Family Law Reform Act of 1969, universities were in loco parentis to students below the age of 21. The introduction of means-tested maintenance grants did not allow financial independence to youngsters from wealthier families. Yet prior to 1970, there is little to suggest that parents considered themselves to have a specifically consumer status. It may be the case that the current generation of students' parents experienced HE for free and now resent implications they must finance their offspring without any power to influence decision-making. It is also the case that since the Conservative government's 1980 Education Act, parents have been encouraged to exercise consumer choice when actively selecting primary and secondary schools for their children from the educational market place and are now reluctant to see the process of choosing a university as any different. Universities reinforce this notion by marketing themselves to both students and their parents. As is noted in *The Guardian*, this may cause problems:

> To operate as a market, as university education now does, that market needs the flexibility of its consumers to go beyond long-held vision of prestige created by a parent's idea of a 'proper' university.
>
> (Leach 2006)

Taken together, these trends encourage both children and parents to consider childhood as a prolonged period extending into the university years, with parents entitled to be involved in decision-making and checking progress. This trend is sometimes treated with derision in a particularly gender biased way: 'The curse of the helicopter mothers who hover over their grown-up children' (Smith-Squire 2008) is one headline. However, such 'interference' is also represented as a benevolent act of parental duty: 'to find out when the UCAS deadlines were, to prompt and to listen' (Moorhead 2009) but for others: 'Letting parents loose on UCAS though, is taking things to the next level' (Johnson 2008). Even critical representations of some of the consequences serve to entrench the general idea that parents are indeed co-consumers of their child's education and thereby reinforce the creation of students who are emotionally, as well as financially, dependent upon their parents. Such infantilisation may be experienced as disempowering by students.

This process of infantilisation may contribute to the 'diminished subjectivity' (Furedi 2001) of many of today's students. In order to exercise subjectivity, students must have some sense of themselves as actors or 'agents' in the world: resilient in the face of change, capable of influencing their environment and contributing to the society they inhabit. With a diminished sense of their subjectivity, students may not have such a firm belief in themselves as resilient, capable actors and instead might see themselves as vulnerable, fragile and in need of support. Individual subjectivity is eroded by the status of students as consumers, as Morley notes: 'Whereas in the 1960s students were seen as change agents, radicals and transgressives, their identity at the beginning of the twenty-first century is described in the language of the market' (2003: 83). Hayes also notes a change in how students are seen: 'The changed conception of a student is not as an autonomous person embarking on the pursuit of knowledge, but as a vulnerable learner' (2009: 127). The experience of attending university is presented to students as 'stressful' and it is the consumption model that is blamed by some for causing this stress. Gemma Tumelty, speaking as president of the NUS (2006) declared: 'Students see themselves as consumers and vice-chancellors see them as consumers. It isn't the experience it once was, it's far more stressful' (Wignall 2006). Telling potential students the university experience is stressful may encourage them to interpret their feelings in this way.

Diminishing subjectivity is a complex social and cultural phenomenon and it is important to recognise that the marketisation of HE and the emergence of the student consumer provide only a small explanation as to why these trends occur. As already discussed, parents are encouraged to consider themselves as co-consumers, pushing some students into relationships of dependency for longer than would have been the case a generation ago. However, few students appear to rebel against such parental interference: in a previous generation the student with wealthy parents who was denied a maintenance grant may have railed against the inequity of prolonged dependence. Instead, it appears that many students today are keen to be accompanied by their parents onto campus for introductory visits: 'Open days at university are increasingly catering not just for potential students, but for their parents too' (Moorhead 2009). Parents are not left behind after the visit day but increasingly drawn upon to make appointments on their child's behalf or to accompany their children to meetings with tutors. Although some students no doubt wish to be left alone, for others having their parents around is clearly a welcome source of support.

The presentation of university as stressful and students being in need of support is clearly something new. Some students may enter university with a sense of confronting a daunting and threatening experience and one that they may not be able to cope with (Ecclestone and Hayes 2009). It may be the case that marketisation and the construction of students as consumers unintentionally contribute to promoting the perceived need amongst students for support with their studies. The President of Universities UK, Professor Rick Trainor, notes that: 'Universities have a duty of care to our consumers, our students, and it's in our interest that we tend to their concerns' (Lipsett 2008).

Instead of universities challenging the idea that new (particularly intellectual) experiences are stressful and daunting, they often reinforce these notions through the proliferation of institutional mechanisms for providing emotional, practical and academic support. The intention seems to be that through such support services, students can access a tangible product and emerge satisfied from their experience of university. The message to students is that they are justified in feeling daunted because they are vulnerable and in need of protection. There is perhaps a degree of irony in the increase in support services at a time when institutions are no longer formally in loco parentis. Students who believe themselves to be vulnerable may not be best placed to exercise individual subjectivity.

Deconstructing subjectivity: restricted sphere of influence

A further disempowering consequence of the student-consumer model is the more restricted sphere of influence it permits. As already discussed, student-consumers are permitted (perhaps even encouraged) to complain when the service they receive does not meet their expectations:

> There are reports of students' unions planning to draw up charters detailing what they expect from their universities in return for their fees, and complaints from students at a diverse range of institutions about inadequate teaching time or facilities. Students at the University of Sussex are running a campaign to address areas of their education they don't feel represent good value for money.
>
> (Wignall 2007)

Such campaigns can rouse a great deal of passion: 'Angry students demand value for fee money' (Asthana 2008) and 'Students win their fight for damages' (Lightfoot 2003). Portraying students as 'angry' and involved in a 'fight' against the academy risks pitching student against lecturer to the detriment of the pedagogic relationship. However, there is also a tendency for student complaints to be presented as fairly trivial: 'Moan, moan, moan. Students are not as easygoing as they might be, it seems, and are complaining about everything from exam papers to the price of a college cappuccino' (*The Times* 2005) and may not rouse passion so much as internet flaming: 'Pelted with cyber-tomatoes' (Smith 2008).

These quotations reveal how the construction of consumer status may serve to impose limits, if not upon the topics students want to protest about, then to the media interest in such protests. Just as it would be inappropriate to go into a shoe shop and complain about global warming, for example, so student-consumers can become restricted to matters of immediate interest. Whilst this is by no means a formal imposition, or a legal requirement, it appears as a natural consequence of the consumer status. Students are not commonly presented in the media as agents of change except within their own university and can therefore appear to be quite passive in relation to broader society wide issues. Whilst students may be able to express their (dis)satisfaction with their course or their lecturers, they find it more difficult to get their voices heard in relation to broader issues. There are relatively few references in the press to students (as an identifiable group) protesting about more general political issues. This lack of protest is presented as resulting from an unintended consequence of the fee imposition: 'students now can't afford lengthy protests. Unlike students in the 60s, most of them have part-time jobs to go to' (Redmond 2009). Lack of collective action is also linked to the inherent instrumentalism of today's students: 'The parents of the current generation of undergraduates could use their university years – assuming they had them – for experimentation, for politicisation, for a sense of collective purpose' (Wignall 2006).

However, tuition fees may provide an overly simplistic explanation here; in previous generations even full-time employment failed to prevent people protesting over issues about which they felt passionately. It may well be the case that in an increasingly a-political culture, students have little motivation to re-enact the political battles of their parents' generation. President of the University of Liverpool's Guild of Students (2009), Danielle Grufferty suggests an alternative reason for a lack of protest:

> Two million marched in February 2003 calling for no war in Iraq, and what became of it? . . . When students campaigned to keep the cap on university tuition fees, we drew out huge numbers. Nevertheless, the vote was lost. People keep targeting students for their apathy, but when nothing we say or do seems to affect government policy, what is our alternative?
>
> (Redmond 2009)

The model of the student-consumer may provide radical commentators with a more palatable explanation for a lack of protest than a broader disillusionment with politics.

Conclusions

Neither the payment of fees nor newspaper representations of students alone account for the construction of the student-consumer. Yet both of these serve to cohere broader social and political trends into an identifiable phenomenon. Newspaper reports present a generation of student-consumers demanding value for money on their educational investment in return for a graduate-premium in their future employment. They are keen to champion the moral cause of the student-crusader's quest for satisfaction over the reserve of the academy. Whilst this can construct consumer status as empowering to future generations, newspaper reports also promote the idea that parents are co-consumers and that students should restrict complaints to the limited arena of immediate concerns. These factors can serve to infantilise students at the moment they seek independence and limit their horizons when they seek to find their place within the world and thereby deconstruct their individual subjectivity. Furthermore, the consumption model, in shifting the focus so successfully away from learning processes and onto educational outcomes, denies students the transformative potential of higher level study in exchange for satisfactory experience and a suitable product (degree attainment).

Recommendations for practice focus around the need for lecturers to maintain a critical vigilance about their own role in promoting the idea that students are passive consumers of an intellectual product they are purchasing as a 'ticket' to safeguard future employability opportunities. Lectures need to question students about why they are attending university and what they hope to gain from higher level study. Furthermore, lecturers could communicate to students the expectation that studying for a degree will be challenging, require considerable effort and may (indeed should) lead to a questioning of assumptions and prior knowledge – rather than immediate satisfaction.

References

Asthana, A. (2008) 'Angry students demand value for fee money', *The Observer* (19 November).

Bekhradnia, B. (2009) 'Good University Guide 2010: counting the hours to graduation', *The Times* (3 June).

Biesta, G. (2009) *Good Education: What It Is and Why We Need It.* Inaugural lecture at The Stirling Institute of Education: University of Stirling (4 March).

Clare, J. (2006) 'Lecturers unite in their refusal to dumb down', *The Telegraph* (12 April).

Clark, L. (2009) 'Average student debts will hit more than £10,000 by the end of the decade', *The Daily Mail*, (21 April).

DfES (2003) *The Future of Higher Education*. London: The Stationery Office.

Dill, D. (2003) 'Allowing the market to rule: the case of the United States', *Higher Education Quarterly*, 57(2): 136–57.

Doughty, S. (2007) 'UK students are "least hard-working in Europe"', *The Daily Mail* (24 September).

Ecclestone, K. and Hayes, D. (2009) *The Dangerous Rise of Therapeutic Education*. London: Routledge.

Fairclough, N. (2003) *Analysing Discourse: Textual Analysis for Social Research*. London: Routledge.

Frean, A. (2008) 'Students prefer studying to socialising, says survey', *The Times* (11 September).

Furedi, F. (2001) *Paranoid Parenting*. London: Allen Lane.

Furedi, F. (2009) 'Now is the age of the discontented', *Times Higher Education Supplement* (4 June).

Garner, R. (2009) 'Why are students complaining so much, and do they have a case?', *The Independent* (20 May).

Grayling, A. C. (2002) 'I'm not a commodity', *The Independent on Sunday* (3 November).

Hayes, D. (2009) 'Academic freedom and the diminished subject', *British Journal of Educational Studies*, (57)2: 127–45.

Henry, J. (2004) 'Universities pay £15m a year to students when courses go wrong', *The Telegraph* (14 March).

Independent, The (2000) 'The rise and rise of the student as a consumer' (11 May).

Johnson, R. (2008) 'It's their life not yours', *The Sunday Times* (24 August).

Leach, J. (2006) 'The informed choice', *The Guardian* (2 May).

Lightfoot, L. (2003) 'Students win their fight for damages', *The Telegraph* (4 March).

Lipsett, A. (2008) 'Let's deal with complaints quickly, says Denham', *The Guardian* (11 September).

Mandelson (2009) *Higher Education and Modern Life*. Department for Business, Innovation & Skills. Available from http://www.bis.gov.uk/higher-education-and-modern-life (accessed 22 February 2010).

Molesworth, M., Nixon, E. and Scullion, R. (2009) 'Having, being and higher education: the marketisation of the university and the transformation of the student into consumer', *Teaching in Higher Education*, 14(3): 277–87.

Moorhead, J. (2009) 'Ready for the empty nest?: open days at university are increasingly catering not just for potential students, but for their parents, too' in *The Guardian* (30 June).

Morley, L. (2003) 'Reconstructing students as consumers: power and assimilation?', in M. Slowey and D. Watson, *Higher Education and The Lifecourse*. London: SRHE and Open University Press.

Newman, J. H., Cardinal ([1852] 1959) *The Idea of a University*. New York: Image Books.

Potts, M. (2005) 'The consumerist subversion of education', *Academic Questions*, 18(3): 54–64.

Redmond, P. (2009) 'Power struggle: who said students today were apathetic? They have simply found new ways to protest and new targets', in *The Guardian* (6 January).

Scott, J. (1990) *A Matter of Record*. Cambridge: Polity Press.

Singh, G. (2002) 'Educational consumers or educational partners: a critical theory analysis', *Critical Perspectives on Accounting*, (13): 681–700.

Smallman, E. (2006) 'Please sir, can we have some more?', in *The Times* (18 November).

Smith, K. (2008) 'Pelted with cyber-tomatoes', in *The Guardian* (15 July).

Smithers, R. (2007) 'Degrees continue to pay off for graduates', in *The Guardian* (7 February).

Smith-Squire, A. (2008) 'The curse of the helicopter mothers who hover over their grown-up children', in *The Daily Mail* (17 January).

Times, The (2005) 'Student moans adding up' (23 August).

Wignall, A. (2006) 'You have passed Go. Pay £3,000', in *The Guardian* (26 September).

Wignall, A. (2007) 'How to fulfil those great expectations', in *The Guardian* (20 February).

Chapter 15

A degree will make all your dreams come true: higher education as the management of consumer desires

Helen Haywood, Rebecca Jenkins and Mike Molesworth

Introduction

One compelling story of post-Fordist, experiential consumption sees the contemporary consumer as a Romantic daydreamer using the resources of the market to imagine the 'good life' (see Campbell 1987; McCracken 1988). This is quite different from the rational, utility-maximising consumer who ensures that markets meet society's needs, so the implication is that markets actually respond to elaborate and individualised fantasies. In this chapter we consider how marketised higher education (HE) may operate as a resource for students' daydreams, and in doing so may facilitate, or support socialisation into contemporary 'work and spend' culture. We do this by reflecting on the stories students tell about their experiences of university and their dreams for the future.

We do not intend to argue that desire for future 'success' is a bad thing, or that it is not an important role of a university to help expand young peoples' hopes for life, but rather that an irony of some of the daydreams constructed by students is that they are unrelated to education, or even to the skills required in a specific career, but are instead focused on consumer lifestyles supported by 'well-paid' jobs. Consequently, we are concerned that Higher Education Institutions (HEI) may fail to successfully guide students to ambitious intellectual or even civic dreams and may instead be content to pander to fantasies of a leisure-based 'good life' whilst actually preparing students for more mundane career outcomes.

Although this focus may not be explicitly stated, it is evident in marketing materials, in courses offered and in curriculum and assessment design. For example HE is now sold on the premise that it will 'help make your dreams a reality ... and help you find your dream job' (Goodlad and Thompson 2007: 2). We note how promotional materials instil desire in students by encouraging a focus on ideal futures. In selling their courses and institutions, prospectuses and websites are 'filled with the prose of temptation and persuasion, also known as advertising' (Jack 2009: 25) and have been criticised for their tone and content by a variety of individuals including government-run student juries (Fearn and Marcus 2008; Attwood 2008). Specifically, they often feature information about the student lifestyle (Molesworth and Scullion 2005) and location. For example, one website claims: 'You can enjoy a breath of fresh air and fantastic sea views on [location] seafront. Four miles of beach are backed by green spaces of [location], great for meeting friends, picnics in the summer as well as running, cycling and football'. Another offers, '[the institution] is located in the heart of the city, which has grown dramatically into a busy, cosmopolitan centre of culture, entertainment, nightlife and shopping'. These are the words of a holiday brochure (Jack 2009). HEIs also use 'marketing puffery and opaque jargon' (Reisz 2009) but often lack specific details of their courses. One HEI proclaims 'Our ethos is dream, plan, achieve and we aim to nurture the dreams of every single student'. This language extends to course descriptions where there may be little to inform potential students of the realities of the courses or industries in which they may work. For example we read of 'Degrees with the WOW factor: It is a unique programme available to all students that brings them closer to the World of Work and which can help them to develop the skills to succeed in their career' and 'The course can be tailored to suit the interests and aspirations of individual students, and is especially suited to students wishing to apply their learning in the work place'. These idealistic work-based daydreams may be further emphasised by reference to graduate destinations, employability and links with industry such as a claim that 'Many of our graduates have quickly achieved varied and senior positions within television, eg.: Commissioning Editor, Channel 4; Director, Casualty; Head of Technical Development, BBC; Director, GMTV; Producer/ Director, Top Gear'. Linked with this we note how HEIs often emphasise exceptional success stories, associating themselves with people in the public eye, famous alumni or honorary graduates, particularly pop stars and TV personalities (Jack 2009). One website lists 'Our alumni include: Zoe Ball, Neil Tennant, Vic Reeves, Jamie Theakston, Zandra Rhodes, Charlie Wheelan . . . Alison Moyet and Viscount Linley'. Finally, enthusiastic student testimonials are commonplace – 'This is a dream job for me as I am getting well paid to travel the world but I doubt I would have been considered for this position without my degree from [institution]'. Together these techniques reinforce the notion that university can make your dreams come true.

That many prospectuses and websites prefer emotional sales appeals to factual information about courses is perhaps not surprising considering that HEIs see themselves as operating in a competitive market. Whether they instil desire or fuel a pre-existing desire, the examples here demonstrate that the marketing of HEIs plays on and panders to student fantasies; encouraging high hopes and 'selling the dream', but placing very little emphasis on academic development, or even the realities of working life. As we shall see, this is mirrored in students' daydreams that are structured around celebrity lifestyles, travel and portrayals of jobs in films and television, which play a large role in creating and sustaining desire (see Belk *et al.* 2003). Essentially, it seems that students may indulge in what might be typical of teenage daydreams and 'bolt' HE onto these, and that HEIs may be complicit in such activity as they turn to marketing techniques to acquire 'customers'.

So we may locate students' experience of HE in consumer behaviour literature and draw parallels between consumer desire and students' daydreams. Yet there are limits to the metaphor of 'consumer' when applied to the transformational experience of HE; in this case a clear problem is that any initial fantasy that is used to sell must be sustained for several years of study. Through the stories students tell, we want to explore the implications of that effort.

Method

Drawing from a phenomenological study of 60 predominately white, middle-class students studying at a post-1992 vocational university, we consider the stories provided about their dreams for the future at different stages of their university experience; from their decision to study for a degree to their experiences leading up to graduation and looking for a first job.

Consistent with Thompson *et al.* (1990) questions were based on actual lived-experiences and interviews averaged approximately one hour each. Data analysis was undertaken separately by two researchers based on a detailed reading of the transcripts to first produce an idiographic analysis of each narrative and then an identification of global themes (Thompson *et al.* 1990).

Through our discussions we noted three 'stages' that students' daydreams seemed to go through as they moved from creating an initial daydream, to sustaining and protecting it and then, in some cases, to modifying it as reality intervenes. It is not our intention to 'model' a process here, but rather to provide a loose structure through which we can explore the themes that emerged.

The construction of student fantasies

The hope of future consumer pleasures may already frame the 'purchase' of education where a degree is seen as providing a way to actualise a fantasy of a material 'good life'. In this sense, the process of undertaking a degree acts as what McCracken (1988) calls a bridge to displaced meanings; a satisfying future lifestyle is both distanced from the here and now and maintained as something made possible by obtaining a degree. The students we spoke to could provide clear narratives for these exciting futures, echoing McCracken's (1988) and Campbell's (1987) views that consumers enjoy daydreaming and are in fact complicit in creating a 'perfected vision of life' (Campbell 1987: 84). We note how the richness of imaginings relating to these idealised lifestyles contrasts with a lack of detail expressed about any actual career or skills required. For example Nicola, a final year PR student, describes her ideal future:

> [In the future I'll be] living in [my] barn conversion, working 9–5.30 and being successful and not being stressed because PR's quite stressful, it's synonymous with that and I don't want that . . . I've got my kitchen sorted and everything. Whether I would get 'Grand Designs' in or something and do it from scratch I don't know . . .

Similarly Anton, studying for an MA in Business Finance, describes how he has planned the purchase of a boat in which he'll be sailing to the Caribbean once he has succeeded in his chosen career as Senior Consultant: 'Last week ... I was down at the biggest lake in Hungary where they had a boat show. So I went to see exactly the boat which I'm going to purchase.'

We see how their imagination is structured through goods and services so that they take pleasure from consumer desires (Belk *et al.* 2003); by attending a boat show Anton intentionally indulges in and deepens his desire, while watching *Grand Designs* has helped to shape Nicola's ideas of her dream home. Here we see media representations entwined with expectations of the future. Nicola's dream is of the *lifestyle* of someone who works in PR, rather than of the work itself. Such idealised lifestyles foreground consumption and 'other' professional work, so hopes for the future are consumer hopes and a career is understood in terms of providing access to desirable consumption activity. This introduces a wider debate about the role work now plays in society. Bauman (1988; 1992) and Campbell (1987) are among many sociologists of consumption who note that the work ethic has been dislodged by the consumer ethic where we derive our sense of self from consumption not production. Gabriel and Lang (1995: 87) add that 'Consumption, not only expands to fill the identity vacuum left by the decline of the work ethic, but it assumes the same structural significance that work enjoyed', hence life is about a consumer lifestyle that work affords even for those undertaking study that might relate to professional identities.

A further illustration of this is the way these students imagine workplace culture and perks. For example Natalie, a final year Communication student, reflects on her placement experience assuming that it reflects everyday working practices:

> I don't know what type of job I'll be going into yet, so I can't quite see what I'm doing but I'm doing something very fun, well paid and exciting. Like when I worked for [placement company], they haven't even launched yet but the company just was amazing, like they went on weekends to Amsterdam and they all went out for drinks every Thursday and they had company lunches ... and it just, it was a really nice place to be and I could see myself doing something that's enjoyable like that.

Also displaying a lack of knowledge of any particular career, Katie another final year Communication student, tells us of her hopes for the future that are built around success, fun and exciting travel:

> I imagine myself being successful, just because it's something I've always obviously wanted to be. And I probably imagine myself working [...] somewhere where I can really have fun. Like I wouldn't want to work some- where where it's numbers, I'd like kill myself, I wouldn't because I wouldn't end up in that kind of job, but definitely somewhere where I can be creative. And I would quite like to travel as well ... I definitely will look into moving abroad and working.

Such reasoning is consistent with Campbell's (2004) analysis of the 'wannabe' where it is the (consumer-like) desire for success alone (rather than an associated determination to acquire a skill) that is thought to lead to success, i.e., there is a belief that wanting something is sufficient for it to happen. What is absent from these accounts is any detail of actual work, instead the emphasis is on the lifestyle that a successful job might bring. Further, it seems that Katie has internalised the message that doing a degree enhances job prospects, but has done less work to consider the requirements in any particular job. She actually seems to rule out what might be one important requirement: mathematics.

This issue merits further discussion. Students frequently use ambiguous terms, unrelated to subject-based knowledge, to describe what they 'want' in a job; these included being 'creative', as expressed by Katie. Similarly, 'being innovative' is appealing, whilst dismissing the possibility of technical skills; a desire to work with people is declared, but not associated with an understanding of, say, psychology, and the desire to travel or live abroad is popular, but without recognition of a need to learn other languages. Such constructions are reflective of a consumer response, a focus on 'what I desire' and students may apply this 'picking and choosing' attitude to HE and their careers without consideration of what achievement of such hopes may entail. Fantasy is of course pleasurable (see Campbell 1987) and anything capable of undermining such feelings needs to be dismissed; hence we see little evidence of information search that might reveal the necessary, but more mundane aspects of work.

It was equally evident that students have a strong sense of what they *don't* want to do. For example, there was a desire to avoid ordinary 'desk' jobs and routine: 'I didn't want to go into a boring job like being an accountant, I just didn't want to follow a mundane, everyday, filling out your reports kind of thing' says Tom, a final year Business student, who despite being good at finance thinks that working with numbers would be too boring.

Perhaps the vagueness over the details of specific jobs is partially a result of some of these careers being poorly defined and consequently poorly understood. While students may know 'traditional' humanities, science and social science subjects from school, and perhaps have an understanding of what careers like teaching or nursing entail for example, there may be a less clear picture of what it means to work 'in advertising' or 'in the media'. This vagueness may allow for greater freedom to create pleasurable daydreams, untarnished by mundane or unpleasant realities. Here we are confronted with a potential problem as students may be choosing these narrow, yet rather vague vocational courses based on misguided perceptions which are likely to have been influenced by media representations.

The media can provide stimulation for the imagination by enhancing the symbolic meaning of consumption (McCracken 1988). These can include media such as TV, film and magazines (Belk 2001, Belk *et al.* 2003, Stevens and Maclaran 2005, Friedberg 1993). The media also takes a prevalent role in young people's construction of imagined futures, making new identities and aspirations possible (Wildermuth and Dalsgaard 2006). This is exemplified by Lucy, a first year Advertising student, who tells us how her choice of subject was partly inspired by a film:

> Another really slightly stupid reason, is like seeing films and what they do for their job, I'm always like 'That's what I want to do', Because I remember I think a couple of films I was like 'That's what I want to do' and they worked in like advertising . . . the films? There was 'What Women Want'. . . .

And Lauren, a first year Media Production student, evokes a TV programme as influential in her choice of course:

> Well if I enjoy the media, there's no reason why I can't have a career in it. I think my dream job is to have a job on 'Wish you Were Here' because I love travelling and I'm pretty passionate about travelling, I'd love to travel and I'm quite talkative as well, and I actually thought I could get paid to do both.

Television and films may be a significant resource as young people consider what they want for their future. Media representations are especially important where intangible services and experiences are the object of desire. Urry (2001), who applies a hedonic experiential approach to the consumption of tourism, recognises for example that tourists rely on non-tourist practices, such as film, television, literature and magazines, to construct and sustain daydreams about future holidays. HE may be aligned with this notion; a (future) career is intangible, therefore various imaginative resources are required to create images and impressions of it. Moreover, popular media are likely to feature glamorous and fun lifestyles; think here of US television series like *Ally McBeal*, where associates in a 'quirky' law firm spend more time discussing their personal lives in the office and dancing in a bar than practising law.

Beyond being stimulated by unrealistic media representations, for this group of students there was an apparent lack of real desire to find out about the jobs that specific degrees may lead to. For example Emily, a first year International Marketing student, describes how she decided not to talk to a friend who works in marketing about her decision to study this subject:

> [I didn't talk to her about it] in depth because obviously I haven't done marketing so I don't know at the moment what it . . . well I do know some of it, but I don't know, because she does it everyday, I couldn't have a conversation with her about it . . . no we didn't really talk in depth.

As Emily struggles to explain why she avoided discussing marketing with her friend it becomes clear that she didn't want to hear 'real stories' as this could result in mundane aspects of work undermining her pleasurable daydream. Initially this seems peculiar, as in many consumption situations the 'real' experiences of significant others tend to be more influential than the media because they signal an ability to actualise daydreams (Belk *et al.* 2003; Rojek and Urry 1997), but here we note that Emily prefers not to allow 'reality' to force her to modify the dream. We might explain this by considering that a service like HE takes place over several years and therefore the initial construction of reality may be distanced from knowledge that might normally be sought when making an immediate decision. In this respect it is simply 'too soon' to worry about reality. In any case what students told us was that it wasn't really the elements of a job that were the basis for any fantasy of the future, but rather the lifestyle that a job might allow.

Sustaining daydreams whilst studying

It seems that students may need to take actions to protect the dreams they have constructed when they conflict with aspects of their course. One key way that these students sustained their daydreams was to avoid aspects of the course that were thought to be difficult (and therefore likely to result in failure) instead focusing on options or subjects which they like and/or that 'speak' to what they hope will be useful in the workplace. Again they work on idealised images of jobs and dismiss ideas that may contradict them. Thus they become resentful of any subjects which are not relevant to the imagined career.

For example, Hannah, a Communication student, tells us of her dislike at being taught something she doesn't feel is necessary for her vision of working in politics:

> But I just don't want to do things that I don't want to do obviously. And there were certain things like journalism and PR that really did not interest me . . . And I don't see why I should do something that really is not my thing . . . I don't want to be trained for that, because I know I'm not going to use it . . . so why would I be trained for something that I'm not going to use?

Hannah works from a clear idea of what is 'her thing' and what is useful to her and is not interested in anything else. This rejection of certain activities seems consistent with a demand for activities that reflect current preoccupations or those which students see fitting with an idealised view of a career. For example, many students discussed their enjoyment in working on 'real' briefs as a way of experiencing what their ideal career would be like. They particularly liked practical work which allows role-play and therefore an aesthetic actualisation of a dream job. David, a second year Public Relations student, describes his enjoyment in doing an assignment where he can choose a brand and focus on a 'real' campaign:

> We had to work on real PR campaigns. So like an agency and we got a real client. We had to pitch to the client about our ideas and stuff, so quite real life . . . So that was really fun. We had about a month to develop the pitch and then we had to propose it to people, [. . .] I know it sounds sad but it was fun in a way because it was more live . . . It felt like we were an actual agency.

He then contrasts this experience with the 'boring side' of his degree where the focus is on business (finance and law): 'I know why you have to do it, but it's just not fun. It's just sitting there learning all the laws. So that side of it I guess is not that great.'

Such feelings seem irrational on the face of it. Clearly PR cannot be just about pitches and elements such as law and business are compulsory precisely because of their importance to this industry. However the enjoyment gained through role play may be likened to research by d'Astous and Deschênes (2005) that reveals that consumers focus on those activities that bring their dreams closer. Such activities act as surrogate experiences for the 'real thing', which cannot yet (if ever) be realised (Fournier and Guiry 1993; MacInnis and Price 1987). Hence the HE curriculum may also be framed in these terms and rejected when it does not meet these expectations.

Similarly, for these students, guest lecturers seemed to embody their fantasy by acting as a stimulus that inflames desire in much the same way that a specialist car magazine may sustain a desire to own a sports car (Belk 2001). For example Bethany, a second year Media Production student, explains how a guest speaker motivates her and how this is better than reading about a subject:

> We had a lecturer who came in to talk to us, who did production management, and she works on 'Casualty', and feature films and 'Pride and Prejudice' and all that and she really inspired me. She was so honest and upfront about it, she didn't sugar coat it, that I thought, 'This could be really for me'. I mean when I was researching like sound . . . and lighting, the text didn't stand out to me. It wasn't involving me . . . I was switching off . . . It was too technical. It was too wordy. Whereas when she spoke . . . she was really enthusiastic . . . and made it a bit more animated and personal . . . that was probably a big part of it, that it was a person talking to me rather than me researching it and getting facts and figures off the internet and reading books on it . . .

In offering 'real briefs', role play and guest speakers, a curriculum sustains desire for an idealised job. However, by actively encouraging students to focus on the most exciting parts of industry, such approaches also pander to unrealistic fantasies. Although it is understandable that students have a preference for aspects of the course that sustain pleasurable, if improbable, daydreams, HEIs have to balance this with their responsibility to ensure the achievement of professional and academic skills. Where HEIs encourage pleasurable dreams, academic work and theory may be reduced to and regarded by some students, as something that must be endured, as illustrated by Ross (TV production final year):

> I didn't go to that many of the very theoretical lectures . . . some of them were very good, it wasn't that, but I just struggled to see the relevance of them for me . . . it was something that I wasn't very interested in and there was something that I couldn't see myself ever . . . like using for anything practical.

In rejecting certain aspects of the experience students protect their daydreams – what they see themselves doing – by removing aspects of the course they dislike or think irrelevant, and focusing on the most exciting or interesting parts, honing the dream accordingly, to keep it alive and pleasurable in the hope of actualising it in the future. In line with Campbell (1987), who asserts that in order to increase pleasure the inconveniences of everyday life are removed so that daydreams come to represent films, we see how students remove the more mundane or even realistic aspects of work and study to construct daydreams that are more like the media images they see and desire.

The need to modify dreams in light of experience

Earlier we referred to the notion of 'bolting' HE onto a more general kind of consumer fantasy reflecting Campbell's (1987) claim that consumers hook their daydreams onto various goods and services as and when they need to. When a good is attained and the imagined lifestyle it promised is not realised, the daydreamer can simply 'unhook' the dream and attach it to a new good. From our discussions with students, it would seem that when disillusionment sets in – either because aspects of a course or the reality of working in certain careers disappoint, or students realise the limits of their own talents – they cannot so easily find new objects of desire – they are, after all, signed up for three years – and instead must modify, or 'correct' their daydream to 'construct a more 'realistic' anticipation of those events to come' (Campbell 1987: 87).

For example, postgraduate students James (Computer Animation) and Nadia (Sound Production) explained how they came to realise that in the industries they have chosen, they will go in at the bottom and ultimately therefore just hope to get 'a' job in the industry – a 'foot in the door'. To be working, and hopefully on a permanent basis, becomes the dream now and extravagant lifestyles no longer come into it. A result is that thoughts about the future become less pleasurable:

> I'd be happy just having a reasonably good entry job into some company (James).

To get an in-house position is ideally what I'd like, but they're quite rare and hard to get, most of the work is freelance and you have to have space and equipment of your own to do the work and that's very expensive (Nadia).

Second year Bethany also describes how she has come to realise that she doesn't have the skills for any of the other specialisms within her degree programme (TV Production) and so hopes for a job in production management:

> I didn't realise how technical it was going to be . . . stuff about science that I wasn't good at it at secondary school . . . and wasn't going to be good at it at university . . . you did need to sit down and study and read through the books . . . so that for me I was like, 'OK, I'm not going to do camera because it's too technical . . . I'm going to make mistakes and break the equipment . . . Sound, I didn't have a chance to be soundman on any of the pieces. So, without even realising it, that made the decision that I'm not going to do that because I'm not confident in using the equipment . . . And then the director was, is very, very creative, and I think . . . there's a lot of pressure on a director . . . I didn't think I was creative enough . . .

And Kelly, a final year Management student, describes disappointment amongst her cohort following the realisation that fashion buying involves a lot of maths and paperwork:

> all the girls on my course wanted to be buyers but having done this [course] we realised that it involves a lot of calculations . . . and it's obviously put a lot of people off . . . They liked the idea of going abroad to buy but they didn't actually like the idea of there's actually quite a lot of paperwork to do.

Some students seem to maintain idealised daydreams right to the end of their course, for others however there is the gradual realisation that the much desired career may not be for them after all. For example, final year Archaeology student Oliver describes how after three years of study he has now decided not to go into a career in this area:

> I don't want to go into [. . .] archaeology . . . [because of] the money if I'm honest, because it's so bad . . . It's just not worth it. I just can't take that. I couldn't live like that really it's too low [. . .] I think it's the lifestyle, the fact that it's a lot of outdoor work and you have to be just a digger for quite a few years before you can actually manage anyone. And even then you're not really doing much.

Such a rejection is all the more problematic where the course has been reduced only to idealised aspects of a now unwanted job and the opportunity to develop intellectually and attain a wide set of skills may have been lost.

Conclusions

We have described a desire for a consumer lifestyle, where goods represent success and happiness, as the overarching hope for students as they study. Initially, daydreams specifically related to a job may be rather fanciful, where students pick and choose elements that they enjoy and discard any they dislike. Rather than being based on subject/industry specific research, dreams may be informed by glamorous media representations. But when we reflect on the promotional approaches described in our introduction we may have angst that some HEIs are complicit in projecting idealised images through marketing that tends to pander to such student fantasies. HEIs may find it easier to sell a lifestyle that students desire than to promote a desire to study a complex subject in depth or to undertake the sort of intellectual challenge that we might hope a degree represents.

Of course such approaches to marketing are consistent with the ways other markets attempt to manage and exploit desire: a tendency to over-promise, a focus on ideal visions of things, but with an awareness that what is actually being offered is far more mundane. We might even call this 'good' marketing practice. Beyond prompting the initial purchase it is also evident that some HEIs continue to pander to student fantasies throughout the sustained period of 'consumption', by enabling them to aesthetically actualise the dream in the form of role play and industry speakers that embody fantastic jobs. Whilst we recognise that it is important to inspire and motivate students, the problem here is the possibility that there is too little reflection on these aspects of courses such that the differences between 'fantasy work' and critical education are not well understood by those involved. When reflecting on what happens in a university, we cannot avoid questions about what degrees are for, and we are faced with the tantalising possibility that course and curriculum design are informed as much by the need to satisfy student daydreams as they are by the needs of society, whether for an intellectualised population, or a skilled workforce.

This tension between hedonism and utility is prevalent in our understanding of contemporary consumption practice where, for example, everything from food to cars is marketed on the basis of desire even when this is in conflict with broader social concerns. We could therefore simply accept that the marketisation of HE is just part of the broader consumer culture that ironically drives the economy that HE is now being re-focused to support. We could acknowledge that the fee system has contributed to the creation of a consumer-outlook in students and a business approach to HE recruitment which leads to students shopping around to match courses and institutions with daydreams for the future. Glossy prospectuses and websites naturally respond to this.

Alternatively we could argue that the experiences we have described, and the consumer sociology that informs our analysis of them, raise issues with regard to assumptions that underpin the idea of markets self-regulating through supply and demand. For example the perception might be that demand-side control would regulate what universities offer to ensure the rigour of degrees that prepare students for the workplace. However, this may not be working effectively, as some students may be unable to make informed decisions about the likelihood of employment in certain sectors or make a realistic appraisal of the skills needed to succeed in these careers (or even to study effectively for them). Instead, we would argue that some are simply selecting courses based on pleasurable daydreams, choosing hedonically rather than rationally. Unless we wish to interfere with the supply side of education through, for example, such measures as controls on the numbers of university courses in certain areas, more stringent requirements on what must be taught, or more drastically the removal of financial incentives that require institutions to compete for students, then it is the demand-side controls which may need to be strengthened. This could be done through helping students to make more informed choices. The information currently provided by universities may need to be strengthened to assist with this. The irony of the current excess of information available to prospective students (through websites, open days, league tables and university guides), is that it may not be of the right sort to enable responsible decisions. What we might need is rather less 'good' marketing material and a little more good advice from universities themselves even if this means they don't maximise the effectiveness of the recruitment campaigns. This may also mean that universities may need to be encouraged to retreat from recruiting students and trying to persuade them to study particular courses, and instead return to a system where students are selected by universities based on their suitability for the course and understanding of it, as well as their ambitions, so that there can be a better match between students and courses.

References

Attwood, R. (2008) ' "Holiday brochure" prospectuses can create unrealistic picture', *Times Higher Education*, 17 April. Available from http://www.timeshighereducation.co.uk/story.asp?storycode=401509 (accessed 22 September 2009).

Bauman, Z. (1988) *Freedom*. Milton Keynes: Open University Press.

Bauman, Z. (1992) *Intimations of Postmodernity*. London: Routledge.

Belk, R. (2001) 'Speciality magazines and flights of fancy: feeding the desire to desire', *European Advances in Consumer Research*, (5): 197–202.

Belk, R., Ger, G. and Askergaard, S. (2003) 'The fire of desire: a multisited inquiry into consumer passion', *Journal of Consumer Research*, 30 (3): 326–51.

Campbell, C. (1987) *The Romantic Ethic and the Spirit of Modern Consumerism*. Oxford: Blackwell.

Campbell, C. (2004) 'I shop therefore I know that I am: the metaphysical basis of modern consumerism', in K. M. Ekström and H. Brembeck (eds) *Elusive Consumption*. Oxford: Berg, 27–44.

d'Astous, A. and Deschênes, J. (2005) 'Consuming in one's mind: an exploration', *Psychology and Marketing*, 2 (1): 1–30.

Fearn, H. and Marcus, J. (2008) 'Living the dream', *Times Higher Education*, 1 September. Available from http://www.timeshighereducation.co.uk/story.asp?storycode=403454 (accessed 1 September 2009).

Fournier, S and Guiry, M. (1993) 'An emerald green Jaguar, a house on Nantucket and an African safari: wish lists and consumption dreams in materialist society', *Advances in Consumer Research*, 20: 352–8.

Friedberg, A. (1993) *Window Shopping: Cinema and the Postmodern*. Berkeley: University of California Press.

Gabriel, Y. and Lang, T. (1995) *The Unmanageable Consumer*. London: Sage.

Goodlad, C and Thompson, V. (2007) *Dream Weavers and Dream Catchers: Exploring the Aspirations and Imagined Futures of Students in Transition from Further Education to Higher Education*, paper presented at *International Conference on Researching Transitions in Lifelong Learning*, University of Stirling 22–4 June 2007. Available from www.shef.ac.uk/.../Goodlad_and_Thompson_-_dream_weavers_and_dream_catchers%5B2%5D%5B1%5D.doc (accessed 22 September 2009).

Jack, I. (2009) 'The subtext of the university brochure', *The Guardian*, 11 July, p. 25.

MacInnis, D. and Price, L. (1987) 'The role of imagery in information processing: review and extensions', *Journal of Consumer Research*, 13 (4): 473–91.

McCracken, G. (1988). *Culture and Consumption: New Approaches to the Symbolic Character of Consumer Goods and Activities*. Bloomington: Indiana University Press.

Molesworth, M. and Scullion, R. (2005) 'The impact of commercially promoted vocational degrees on the students' experience', *Journal of Higher Education Policy and Management*, 27(2): 209–25.

Reisz, M. (2009) 'This involves what exactly?' *Times Higher Education*, 26 February. Available from http://www.timeshighereducation.co.uk/story.asp?storyCode=405470&sectioncode=26 (accessed 22 September 2009).

Rojek C. and Urry, J. (eds) (1997) *Touring Cultures: Transformations of Travel and Theory*. London: Routledge.

Stevens, L. and Maclaran, P. (2005) 'Exploring the "shopping imaginary". The dreamworld of women's magazines', *Journal of Consumer Behaviour*, 4(4): 282–92.

Thompson, C. J., Locander, W. B. and Pollio, H. R. (1990) 'The lived meaning of free choice: an existential-phenomenological description of everyday consumer experiences of contemporary married women', *Journal of Consumer Research*, 17 (December): 346–61.

Urry, J. (2001) *The Tourist Gaze* (2nd edn). London: Sage.

Wildermuth, N. and Dalsgaard, A. (2006) 'Imagined futures, present lives: youth, media and modernity in the changing economy of northeast Brazil', *Young*, 14(1): 9–31.

Chapter 16

How choice in higher education can create conservative learners

Elizabeth Nixon, Richard Scullion and Mike Molesworth

> I do like having choice but it's the deciding that's not good. It's the pressure I guess. I think it's the idea of blame . . . when you're choosing things, when it's your decision you can't blame anybody else for the outcome, that's what I don't like about it, that I'm to blame. But not having choice would be restrictive.
>
> Caroline

Introduction

In this chapter we focus on students' experiences of choice within HE, particularly noting the consequences and contradictions of consumerist choice-making for educational environments. The assumption that 'choice is good' is largely unquestioned in our consumer society. It is indeed at the heart of a system that is assumed to ensure quality, diversity and individual freedom. Furthermore, since traditional sources of identity are 'lost' in contemporary society, it is often through the choices we make in the marketplace that we now come to understand who we are. We must each now create a story of self, 'amid a puzzling diversity of options and possibilities' (Giddens 1991: 3). The marketplace has become both the prime provider of a multiplicity of choice, and therefore also a key location for a solution to the requirement that we 'choose who we are'.

Higher education now exists *within* this 'consumer-chooser' socio-cultural context where individuals have learnt to demand their rights as choice-makers. However, even without market demands, extending student choice is considered to be sound pedagogy. Yet detailed accounts of the nature of choice experiences that students face are missing from this literature and we might recognise that the learning-related choices that lead to complex individual transformations are not the same as the often fickle and short-term consumer-related choices that seem to dominate in the market.

The HE environment and choice

Offering students choice has largely been promoted as pedagogically effective. According to Ramsden (1992), the opportunity for independence offered by choice leads to high-quality outcomes by encouraging deep approaches to learning. Since students who adopt a deep approach to their studies tend to generate complex, well-structured understanding, as opposed to memorisation of often fragmented content, offering choice is framed as a key mechanism for enhancing cognitive development. Pedagogic texts such as Biggs and Tang (2007) and Fry, Ketteridge and Marshall (2009) assert that offering choice to students leads to increased motivation and interest in the task, and intuitively we may tend to agree with research that suggests that choice of content will enhance students' engagement, motivation to learn and feelings of ownership of their work (Barnett and Hallam 1999). Ramsden (1992) and Biggs (2003) separately declare that choice, in terms of how students learn and which aspects they may focus on, is not only related to learning at a higher cognitive level but is also crucial in helping students become independent lifelong learners.

Ramsden (1992) also explains that greater opportunities for student choice in HE allow for the accommodation of students' individual differences rather than enforcing a 'one size fits all' approach to mass education. Similarly, Biggs (2003) advises that freedom to make learning-related choices such as basing work on students' interests encourages wider reading and therefore greater autonomy. Having some control over the method of assessment is also believed to encourage greater responsibility for self-directed learning (Barnett 2000). Perhaps unsurprisingly, choice is repeatedly rated as favourable by students when evaluating their academic environments (Ramsden 1992; Biggs 2003). Currently then, offering choice in degree programmes is proclaimed to be both pedagogically effective and popular with learners.

However not all academics share this enthusiasm. Writing more than ten years ago, Robertson recognised that British academics were largely dismissive of such 'cafeteria curricula' since students were considered poorly informed and thus likely to make 'haphazard and fanciful selection[s] of questionable quality' (1999: 88). Similarly, Knight and Yorke (2004: 95) warn of the coherence that may be lost in modularised degree programmes as students tread a pathway through the 'thickets of choice' on offer. So there is at least some uncertainty as to the overall benefit of offering choices when students may not be sufficiently informed to choose 'responsibly'.

Despite these concerns many HEIs have committed themselves to increasing flexibility and student choice within their programmes (Fry et al. 2009), often on the basis of modularised and/or part-time study. The financial benefits of doing so, in terms of maximising fee income and increasing efficiency of teaching, have also not gone unnoticed (Rothblatt 1999), and satisfying student-customer demand may be as important to a university's success as robust pedagogy. For example, student evaluations of their experience (for example via formal surveys) are argued to function in the interests of informed consumer choice for others considering HE study. The notion of the student as a consumer reveals the increasing dominance of the market discourse in academia that has also positioned tutors as service providers (Molesworth et al. 2009). One result is that we see course and curriculum design operating within a system that offers students choice in their education on the premise that doing so allows students to 'personalise' their learning experience and therefore 'do *only* what they really want to do'. Whilst the development of autonomy and independent learning may have climbed the ranks towards that of critical thinking in the hierarchy of core purposes of HE, if they are to be operationalised through increasing student choice, as asserted by D'Andrea and Gosling (2005), they are also consistent with an ideology that privileges individual 'wants' as the basis for a market structure.

Where knowledge has become a commodity to be traded by a variety of providers, student choice in curriculum design becomes an important promotional imperative for universities that need to retain a competitive advantage. Universities may now legitimately claim to 'give customers the choices they desire', otherwise understood as 'what the market demands', in preference to what subject specialists may intuitively feel that students need, or the subject demands. This position has to be understood in relation to the broader marketised environment in which HEIs exist, and it is to this that we now turn.

Consumer identity and choice

Western neo-liberalism places a high value on individuals' freedom to satisfy their desires through consumption (Bauman 2001). A consumer society privileges the individual with free choice that allows the determination of lifestyle through interaction with the marketplace. As such, the concept of personal choice itself forms the foundation of a mechanism that forces competition between service providers to drive better 'quality' offerings (in terms of satisfying consumer wants) and a wider variety of options. This then empowers the consumer with the 'freedom' to choose between them. The market apparently offers a non-discriminatory structure, offering the opportunity to express one's agency (Edwards 2000). Contemporary life is thus guided by a consumer ethic where the market can satisfy *all* life spheres so that our experiences as consumers permeates *all* that we do and are (Bauman 2001). Not only is our identity now based on being consumers, but consumption has come to embrace all concerns, such as health, transport and education, that would once have been considered, if not exclusively, then largely in the political domain and therefore for us to ponder as citizens. In short, we cannot help but experience the world as consumers.

The rise of individualism as the consequence of consumer choice inevitably has ramifications for spheres outside consumption, including education. The loss of a strong sense of common good, common experience and common troubles limits the value of co-operative and collaborative spaces and systems (Bauman 2002). In such a context, institutions must either (and ideally) adapt to be supportive of a dominant notion of autonomous self-identity, or become 'zombie-like', unable to cope with and serve the consumerist 'self' that has emerged (Beck and Beck-Gernsheim 2002). This, then, is the context in which HEIs are embedded, where consumer-oriented choices are taken for granted. As Campbell

(2004) argues, in contemporary culture consumer choice becomes a ubiquitous necessity.

However Bauman (2001; 2007) raises doubts about our ability to gain meaningful identity as consumers in a multitude of marketplaces by drawing our attention to the fluidity, or 'liquid nature' of contemporary consumer culture. Since there is no sustaining meaning but to carry on the shopping spree, Bauman suggests there is now only durability through transience, and this allows only temporary self-identity in consumption. To Bauman the 'glory and the blight of consumer society' (2007: 28) are rooted in the same condition – *enforced* individualism. Here choice may then become a burden, or obligation rather than an expression of freedom. Others go further in noting the 'joylessness' of endless, meaningless choice (Mick 2004) or in noting the angst excessive choice may cause (Swartz 2004).

For students making choices as consumers in an educational marketplace there may be other specific problems. Consumer choice privileges instant gratification, allowing us a sense that we can establish our identity *without* recourse to lengthy and complicated procedures or activities, but rather through purchasing something; for example, Gabriel and Lang (1995: 162) note how consumers are 'frequently presented as thirsting for identity and using commodities to quench this thirst'. Worse, as we increasingly define ourselves in terms of *our* tastes – building a personal profile of our wants and desires that we then articulate as needs – the only person who can legitimately know our needs is ourselves. This may potentially reduce the role of tutors to service providers who must meet the instant needs of customers.

Students' experiences of choice in HE

We have two models of choice, but we must ask how students themselves experience choice in higher education: as liberating and transformational, engendering scholarly activity, or as just another transient consumer duty.

We draw from a large phenomenological study concluded in the 2007/2008 academic year involving 60 students at a vocational university on the south coast of England. Our focus here is not how a degree is chosen, but how a degree is experienced through the choices it makes available. The quotes are from a subset of Level I (2nd year) and Level H (3rd year) undergraduates from degree courses that we selected from across one school, all of whom will have had opportunities to exercise choice during their course. The range of choice offered is summarised in Table 16.1. We may see this as typical of a course structure that is not yet modularised (although a greater move to a modular approach has now been taken), but nevertheless has embraced the idea that choice is desirable, especially in the final two years. Choice is found not just in modules taken, but also in assessment.

The stories about choice that these students told indicated that at a meta-level many were concerned with maintaining a previously chosen identity through

Table 16.1 Summary of 'structural' choice across the four degree courses selected

	Course A	Course B	Course C	Course D
Unit options	Yr2: None Yr3: 3 from 8	Yr2: 6 from 7 Yr3: 3 from 9	None	Yr2: 2 from 6 Yr3: Free choice of projects
Dissertation/major project topic	Free choice	Free choice	Free choice	Free choice
Group work (selecting members)	Sometimes	Rare	Sometimes	Often
Placement	Limited to associated companies	Wide parameters	Limited to associated companies	Limited to associated companies
Assessment	Choice of case study or question	Choice of case study or question	Choice of solutions to set briefs	Choice of solutions to set briefs

the choices they made – a personal narrative that we argue is largely of a consumerist nature and as such is unable to easily incorporate the potential for the intellectual development initiated through becoming a scholar of their chosen field. The consequence is limited transformation of the self during their studies. For example, many of these students had already established a sense of self through the ubiquity, infectiousness and salience of consumer culture (for example before university and when away from the campus) and had decided upon their future employment in the rather vague sense of having a 'well-paid job' that would provide the finance for *continued* consumption. Having decided that what they want to be is a consumer, they choose to do a degree as a way to ensure this identity.

Although choice, especially HE choice we would hope, provides opportunities for changes to the personal narrative – to expand or revise identity – the students' stories suggested that this was overruled by the enthusiasm students had for avoiding 'difficult' choices in favour of reassurance and familiarity. We want to explore this through two main themes: the way such a position leads to safe academic choice because choosing is 'joyless' and angst-ridden, and the way students seek consumer-like pleasures in HE choices and in student culture away from the campus.

Risk and insecurity in student choice

Students persistently reiterated the discourse that having choice is 'good', as it was associated with notions of freedom, whilst often actually strongly disliking the experience of having to make a decision (as illustrated by our opening quote from a participant). As Katherine also explained to us, the choices offered during a degree were unfamiliar. Her expectation, and that of others, was that choice is simply not associated with learning:

> Going through school and college you're not given choices, this is your assessment, there's an exam and coursework, you've got things to stick to haven't you; now there's nothing . . . It's not what we're used to, we don't know what to suggest and because you could suggest anything . . . people feel a bit . . . we've been given so much free reign people don't know what to do with it.

Here then we see choice as angst-ridden and 'joyless'. Some dealt with this potentially contradictory and anxiety-inducing circumstance by ensuring they used choice to stay within their 'comfort zone' and spoke of being 'relieved' when a decision was made. Others were keen to abdicate the responsibility that came with pedagogic choice which triggered disquiet, or even hostility. This hostility appeared to stem from a perception that such opportunities for higher-order learning threatened students' desire to simply pass so that the 'real' choices of extra-campus activity and post-university life could be kept alive. Choices within a course were considered to put future career choice at risk by creating uncertainty and with it the possibility that errors might be made. For example, Thomas told us of his frustration with one unit that entailed the co-construction of assessment criteria between staff and students. He links this to a risk of getting a low grade, jeopardising his aim of getting a 'good' job and its associated lifestyle. To him the course should make it as straightforward as possible to award a degree so that an employer can use that information to employ him:

> And then they say, well you are taking responsibility for your own learning but . . . that's fine . . . but it's just . . . I guess some think that you are here just to learn but you aren't, you aren't here just to learn, you're here to get a degree, because you're here to get a job at a later point in life. It's not all about learning, it isn't! I mean you would think so to go into a learning institution you know . . . but it's not! It's partly learning, but mostly to get a job and to get good grades and then get a job. That's what it is. And then that gets you money, and then a wife, and house and children . . .

In this context, choice does not encourage learning for its own sake but is perceived as a barrier put in place simply to make it harder for students to achieve the high grades they 'need' for future employment.

Many students talked of favouring 'safe' routes of study, avoiding experimentation where the possibility of failure was felt to be high. As such, students' experiences of choice tended to appraise the risks involved and to avoid them where possible. Where work seemed unimportant, for example, they may choose simply to neglect it. Aidan provided one such confession:

I remember one essay last year where I just decided, because there was so much other stuff going on that I was so much more interested in, I just thought that . . . so I calculated 'alright, this essay is about 2% of my degree, my final degree, I'm not going to put that much work into it. I'm going to focus on the production work which is what I enjoy doing, which is what I really am good at, and then I'm going to let this essay sort of slide'.

Students also mentally judged the options (electives) on the perceived difficulty of the subject or its assessment, and particularly on the 'hard or soft' reputation of the tutor, or on previous experience of them. In this context Natalie explains how she decided on her option choices:

I'd known from the first year that the person who taught it had never given me a particularly strong mark for an essay, whereas with other lecturers, I'd got much stronger marks. We were all, I think all of us, were kind of inclined to go . . . for subjects where we know the lecturer likes our style of writing.

Students' enthusiasm for making evaluations based on the chances of getting a good mark was painfully evident. Just as a known lenient tutor was considered safer than a new tutor in their quest for an upper second (2:1), a subject was more comfortable if studied previously. Akin to Natalie, Paul explained to us how his choice was based on his judgement of how he could achieve the best mark. Like others that we spoke to, he did not seek advice from tutors for fear that they would attempt to persuade him to use different criteria for choice, increasing his angst and the required cognitive effort. He goes on to explain:

I often knew in my own mind what I would be good at, or better at, or less worse at . . . I sometimes worry that if I'd have gone and seen them perhaps they would've suggested I do one that I'm not very good at just for the sake of learning it . . . whereas I'm a bit of a chicken when it comes to that, I'd rather just do something I know I can get a 2:1 in without sort of having to really work as hard as perhaps I should do.

Similarly Vicky explains why she thinks choice of modules is a good thing. Initially she seems to support the idea of choice as motivational, but in the end it comes down to assessment (and we might also note that the staff who advised her appear to pander to a desire for good marks here):

We picked the ones we knew we'd enjoy. Choice allows you to tailor your course to what you want to get from it I think. It allows you to pick units you think you'll enjoy and we were also told to look at how you're going to be assessed as well . . . it allows you to pick the options that'll give you the best chance of a good grade.

The implication here is that students may use choices offered to deliberately *narrow* their learning experience. Choice allows students to negotiate the perceived 'easiest' route through the degree, thus the opportunity for and discomfort of intellectual challenge and personal transformation is minimised. Equally, minimising the risk of intellectually stretching experiences that encourage a critical analysis of industry avoids any potential dissonance over the previous decision to study a vocational subject. Rather than students encountering the potential to expand their self-concept or consider building a new identity, perhaps as a scholar of a particular subject, students recounted more instrumental approaches to study that were subservient to the structures and demands of the employment market that they had previously decided to work towards. The choices these students made were based on choices they had already made. Jessica tried to explain this to us:

> I chose the things that relate to my future choices if you can say it like that ... I tailor what I'm doing to that future profession, it's the same thing with my dissertation, choosing the topic ... It wasn't like, back when I was choosing universities ... I read what the choices were and I immediately knew what I wanted to do, or what I didn't want to do. I didn't have to go home and read the details or anything to think about it because I knew that those were the things that I didn't want to get involved with so I didn't have to think about it.

Hedonism in student choice

Having established a self-identity where learning is probably a chore, students also made pedagogic choices based on what might be described as consumerist criteria. For Katherine this seemed obvious:

> I guess it's quite similar to the way that consumers have now taken over the role from marketers, kind of the power and through word of mouth they can influence how a brand is communicated. In the same way students have now got a say; it's now more kind of balanced. Obviously it's down to the university and the tutor, I think generally the University is listening more to students 'cause we're like the consumers and not the University.

Students often described a 'hedonistic' attitude towards their educational choice using anticipated enjoyment, fun or entertainment value, or how much they liked the tutor, to decide what options to study. Here the opportunity for changing their identity through learning was dismissed in favour of more instant gratification. This focus on hedonism was apparent in the broader descriptions of the lifeworlds provided by students. For example, students would explain that they were careful in choosing the 'right' nightclubs, clothes and mobile phones and that such activity was a much more obvious source of pleasure than their studies. Zoe summed this up for us: 'Yeah, and there is that kind of, you know, you're a student so it's almost expected of you that you're going to go out and blow your student loan on alcohol.'

However some *hoped* that their choices within education could also be a source of pleasure too. The significant thing here is that one criterion applied to choice is 'entertainment'. For example, Hayley explains that she chooses entertaining tutors rather than specific subjects:

> The tutor that does [unit] is a really good tutor and like he makes it interesting. So I'm not going to fall asleep in the lectures, I'll get up for him and make notes . . . I wouldn't want to choose a lecturer who would put me to sleep and who wouldn't interest me, because it wouldn't stimulate me and wouldn't make me want to go lectures. So that was a really big part of me making the decision of choosing the unit because he was the lecturer. I think if he wasn't the lecturer, I probably wouldn't have chosen that subject.

At first Hayley's description seems to be a reasonable account of good lecturing practice that makes a subject accessible and interesting, but as she goes on it is clear that this isn't just a criterion to be applied to any subject, but a preference for a particularly 'laid back' tutor and a possible rejection of the possibility that she must take responsibility for her own engagement in a subject. 'An engaging tutor' is a key criterion for option choice as if the selection was tonight's TV viewing.

Other consumerist thinking was evident in students' descriptions of their experiences. Units where there was an expectation of reading, or seminar preparation were often rejected in favour of those that were perceived as allowing students to do 'fun things', where 'fun' often meant 'things I can do easily', or especially tasks that require little effort.

As already suggested, identity for a student was not developed in isolation from their lives outside of HE. Identity was tightly related to being part of a social group that might strongly influence choices. For example, students explained that they chose units that their friends chose, delegating choice to others and using friendship as a justification for pedagogic decisions. As Warde (2005) suggests of choice in general, many students were simply indifferent to the outcome of their choice-making or attached only fleeting meaning to it. For many students, staying in their social circle was of greater importance than engaging in new identity work through learning. For many, self-esteem was gleaned from these cliques in which students experience university life, choosing the right bars to go to, the right clothes to wear *and* the right people to be seen with for example. Meaningful choice was experienced in this context and maintaining this position appeared to become more important than developing identity through the practice of study.

Such social bonding only sometimes overlaps with learning, often revolving around project work that ran late into the night and here again working with the right people was deemed important. In these cases the powerful element of the experience was the camaraderie and sense that they all had to face the same 'pain' together – spending time with chosen friends was fun, the learning was tedious. Thus their sense of identity in sharing a learning task remained dominated by social aspects rather than intellectual and scholarly ones that were seldom the focus of the experiences recounted. For example, Zoe tells us about what is good about group work:

> I just love the atmosphere . . . I think there's a real kind of camaraderie between everyone, especially last year, late nights up in the edit suite, everyone would bring each other tea to keep each other awake. It was kind of that, that was really nice.

Discussion: consumer and scholarly identities

Overall what we highlight here is the way students experience educational choice. By rejecting educational choice as meaningful, students may understand their studying and assignments to be *for their tutors* rather than for themselves and therefore reject the importance of choice. Such students often complained that they had been asked to choose a topic for an assignment, and declared that they would prefer the tutor to simply tell them 'what they wanted', as Thomas explained earlier. Similarly, they preferred set reading to be clear (and printed out for them) and did not feel the need to read beyond a core text – tutors' minimum requirements were often understood by students to be the sum total of what was required. Supplementary reading presented no meaningful choice and was largely ignored. Put simply, students rejected the idea that university study might allow them meaningful choice in investigating a range of conceptual or theoretical areas such that they might become knowledgeable in these fields.

One consequence of this approach was that students chose to minimise the breadth of their learning by dismissing the theoretical content of their course. They perceived this aspect as largely irrelevant to their future identity. Thus for these students in vocational education we found little evidence of intellectual-isation or even experimentation in their studies. If possible, they chose to avoid experiences considered pointless in their main quest to gain lucrative graduate employment. Opportunities to reflect on their chosen profession or even to trial different roles within the industry sector that might have required a change in focus were relinquished in order to ensure that all of their study was related only to its perceived usefulness in securing particular employment. More than this, engaging in learning that may have disturbed or changed their self-concept was considered dangerous given the 'need' to gain the high marks.

For most of the students we spoke to, the offer of choice therefore largely acted as a conservative force in their educational lives. In looking for clear externally imposed standards, our young students became fixated with the implications of their choice for the mark they might gain. This point has been made previously in educational studies. But here we see that the prior choice of vocationalism and their focus on a future job that will allow them to gain choosing power as a consumer becomes their key reference point for accounting for such a stance. It is like HE has been reduced to a necessary process to gain access to life's 'real' choices in the marketplace – that this is the only possible purpose of education for these students. In such a situation students may suffer angst about educational choice. They may also 'make the most' of what social and entertainment pleasure there may be in such choices, or attempt to reject and narrow their choices often deferring them to others. So it's not so much that educational choices are a 'bad' thing, but more that the way they are experienced by students is distorted by their understanding and preference for consumer choice.

Challenge and risk, and the opportunity for transformation that such things provide, are largely avoided. Other characteristics of a scholarly identity such as curiosity, a willingness to learn for learning's sake, persistence in tackling complexity and the development of critical capacity are nullified through the pervasiveness of consumerist choice that foregrounds a consumer life as the 'real' goal. Consequently the potential for university to help students develop deep reflective abilities may be undermined; offering choice seems, somewhat perversely, to reduce the opportunity for well-rounded intellectual development of the person. Consumerist attitudes may be so deeply engrained that many students believed their instrumental approach to learning to be obvious, 'natural', that it was rational to take the easiest route through the challenges of academia in order to 'get the degree' at the end. Through their choice practices, the students prioritised what contemporary society regards as the most important facets of success in life, material wealth on completion of their studies – and of course many 'practised' this outside of the university and emphasised to us the importance of choices in their social lives. Overall, experiences of educational choice were neither the thrill nor freedom of the market nor the possibility of autonomy and transformation through knowledge. The latter were undermined by the promise of the former on graduation (and by the easy access to the former outside the campus).

Student choice appears logical and attractive in the pedagogic literature but in the marketised HE environment, where a degree may be reduced to a passport to a privileged consumer lifestyle, choice appears to detract from allowing students to become autonomous, critical thinking individuals. There seems to be a disturbing paradox here. If HEIs pander further to consumer choice by allowing students to choose what they find fun, easy, or especially secure and familiar, they risk restricting even further the space where at least the possibility for transformation exists through the complex acquisition of new, especially critical knowledge. However, if they limit choice (as students also claim to want), but in doing so aim for 'compulsory' challenge, complexity and difficulty, they are likely to see increased student dissatisfaction and, within the logic of the marketplace, find their customers going elsewhere. Attractive educational choice for students is choice that makes things easy or pleasant, but attractive choice for education is choice that requires reflection, complexity, challenge and therefore often the sort of dissonance and angst that good marketing usually works hard to eliminate. The market's mantra is often 'give them what they want, and make it as easy to get as possible'. We suspect this is close to the current management approach at many institutions. What then should our response be to these observations?

Conclusions

Despite the consumer identity that students arrive with at the start of their university studies, the context co-created by their tutors and peers still has the *potential* to be used for identity work beyond that promised by a future job. We need to consider whether choices offered to students can and should challenge how they have come to acquire and sustain their existing identity so that the potential for its transformative role remains. Perhaps that might be a good starting point in any debate on curriculum design: a discussion about what a university is, what philosophy or central belief a department holds, and on what it is that a degree should 'do' to students (not what it merely offers them as customers). In other words tutors might ask more often: 'what transformations are we looking for here?'

Hence we might pose questions that aim to encourage readers to reflect on their own practice. How do students gain from the choices offered exactly? How can we frame choice in a way that helps students move away from the dominance of consumerist models of choice? How can choice resist the market?

One way to start this process might be to ensure that students justify their choices, articulate their rationale, and are given space to reflect on them. This might result in a system where students *apply* for options, for example rather than academic staff automatically accepting their choice as sovereign – a system where all choices are difficult and demand responsibility.

More than this though, educational choice can be a much more constructive and meaningful experience in terms of learning and even in terms of how students come to understand choice and identity in their future lives. For example, educational choice could stand as a point of resistance to the individualised consumer choices that otherwise prevail in our society, allowing graduates to reflect on and even dismiss the seduction of market-based consumer identities. By the end of their studies they might come to recognise that identity is gained more through the way one chooses and the responsibility that one takes for choice rather than simply through what is chosen.

References

Barnett, R. (2000) *Realizing the University in an Age of Supercomplexity.* Buckingham: SRHE and OUP.

Barnett, R. and Hallam, S. (1999) 'Teaching for supercomplexity: a pedagogy for higher education', in P. Mortimore (ed.) *Understanding Pedagogy and Its Impact on Learning*. London: Paul Chapman.

Bauman, Z. (2001) *The Individualized Society*. Cambridge, Polity.

Bauman, Z. (2002) 'Foreword', in U. Beck and E. Beck-Gernsheim (2002) *Individualization: Institutionalized Individualism and its Social and Political Consequences*. London: Sage

Bauman, Z. (2007) *Consuming Life*. Cambridge: Polity Press.

Beck, U. and Beck-Gernsheim, E. (2002) *Individualization: Institutionalized Individualism and its Social and Political Consequences*. London: Sage.

Biggs, J. (2003) *Teaching for Quality Learning at University* (2nd edn). Buckingham: SRHE and OUP.

Biggs, J. and Tang, C. (2007) *Teaching for Quality Learning at University* (3rd edn). Buckingham: SRHE and OUP.

Campbell, C. (2004) 'I shop therefore I know that I am: the metaphysical basis of modern consumption', in K. Ekstrom and H. Brembeck (eds) *Elusive Consumption*. Oxford: Berg.

D'Andrea, V. and Gosling, D. (2005) *Improving Teaching and Learning in Higher Education: A Critical Approach*. London: McGraw-Hill.

Edwards, T. (2000) *Contradictions of Consumption. Concepts, Practices and Politics in Consumer Society*. Buckinghamshire: Open University Press.

Fry, H., Ketteridge, S. and Marshall, S. (2009) *A Handbook for Teaching and Learning in Higher Education: Enhancing Academic Practice* (3rd edn). Abingdon: Routledge.

Gabriel, Y. and Lang, T. (1995) *The Unmanageable Consumer: Contemporary Consumption and its Fragmentation*. London: Sage.

Giddens, A. (1991) *Modernity and Self-Identity: Self and Society in the Late Modern Age*. Stanford: Stanford University Press.

Knight, P. and Yorke, M. (2004) *Learning, Curriculum and Employability in Higher Education*. London: Routledge Falmer.

Mick, D. (2004) 'Choose, choose, choose, choose, choose, choose, choose: emerging and prospective research on the deleterious effects of living in consumer hyperchoice', *Journal of Business Ethics*, 52(2): 207–11.

Molesworth, M., Nixon, E. and Scullion, R. (2009) 'Having, being and higher education: the marketisation of the university and the transformation of the student into consumer', *Teaching in Higher Education*, 14(3): 277–87.

Ramsden, P. (1992) *Learning to Teach in Higher Education*. London: Routledge.

Robertson, D. (1999) 'Students as consumers: the individualization of competitive advantage', in P. Scott, *Higher Education Reformed*. London: Falmer, pp. 77–92.

Rothblatt, S. (1999) 'A Connecticut Yankee? An unlikely historical scenario', in P. Scott, *Higher Education Reformed*. London: Falmer, pp. 3–26.

Swartz, B. (2004) *The Paradox of Choice*. New York: Harper Collins.

Warde, A. (2005) 'Consumption and theories of practice', *Journal of Consumer Culture*, 5 (2): 131–54.

Chapter 17

Pedagogy of excess: an alternative political economy of student life

Mike Neary and Andy Hagyard

> 1968 was an explosion, and the sound of the explosion still echoes . . . what interests me is . . . how, in the wake of that explosion, we can think of overcoming the catastrophe that is capitalism.
>
> (Holloway 2009)

> What is revolutionary is excess, overflow and power.
>
> (Negri 2009)

Introduction

The pedagogy of excess is based on the premise that re-engineering the forms in which teaching and research are configured in universities has the potential to transform the nature of higher education in ways that undermine the current consumerist and marketised model.

The mainstream literature on the relationship between teaching and research at the undergraduate level is limited in scope and ambition, restricted to an orthodox pedagogic agenda involving the training of students as researchers or to enhance their enterprise and employability skills (Healey and Jenkins 2007). Where the writing on this subject extends beyond these restrictions it is limited to students solving problems to deal with the complexities of modern life (Brew 2006; Barnett 2000).

In order to fundamentally challenge the concept of student as consumer, the links between teaching and research need to be radicalised to include an alternative political economy of the student experience. This radicalisation can be achieved by connecting academics and students to their own radical political history, and by pointing out ways in which this radical political history can be brought back to life by developing progressive relationships between academics and students inside and outside of the curriculum.

A review of the mainstream literature reveals that where writing on this topic does engage with more radical historical and political issues, for example Elton's engagement with the writings of Wilhelm von Humboldt (1767–1835), the political implications of this engagement are not fully developed. The implications are that the laissez-faire liberalism that underpinned Humboldt's political project to create the University of Berlin in 1810, if carried through by contemporary universities, will make the appearance of the student as consumer more rather than less likely.

Is it possible to create a radical pedagogy based on the links between teaching and research to counteract the identity of the student as consumer? A radical pedagogy can be designed around another version of student life, based on events in Paris, France in 1968. By making connections between the university and its own political history, and by developing a pedagogy that connects teaching and research at the undergraduate level, it is possible that a radical new pedagogy might emerge. It is the possibility of this new radical pedagogy that is described as a pedagogy of excess.

The essential aspects of this pedagogy of excess are that students can be enabled to transcend the constraints of consumerism by overcoming the limits of what it is to be a student in higher education. They can do this through collaborative acts of intellectual enquiry, working with academics and with each other, on subjects that look beyond their own self-interest and identity as students. This academic activity can include exploring the origins of – as well as progressive responses to – the general social crisis out of which the attempt to reduce students to the identity of consumer is derived.

This pedagogy of excess can only be sustained within the moment of a real political history. The pedagogy of excess emerges in a period that has seen strikes by academics and students around the world against the proposed marketisation of their higher education system (Klimke and Scharloth 2008). The pedagogy of excess does not look for a repeat of 1968, but seeks to develop a critical academic project that builds on the radical political history of the university, inside and outside of the curriculum – in and against the current version of higher education.

Literature review

The leading advocate of connecting research and undergraduate teaching was Boyer (1990) who conceptualised the relationship between teaching and research in terms of what he referred to as the scholarship of teaching and learning. This concept of scholarship has been taken forward by Griffiths (2004) and Healey and Jenkins (2007), among others, who have designed scholarly-based pedagogic models organised around the teaching-research nexus which they refer to as research-based learning.

Connecting teaching and research at the undergraduate level is now regarded as the essence of student centred-ness (Ramsden 2001), an important strategy in preparing students for the 'knowledge society' (Scott 2002) as well as for developing the qualities of professional expertise among undergraduates (Weiman 2004; Brew 2006). At the same time, linking teaching and research in the undergraduate curriculum is seen to have the potential to promote inter-disciplinarity, and to challenge fundamentally the meaning and nature of research (Brew 2006). Where the evidence for the effectiveness of linking teaching and research stretches beyond the acquisition of academic and professional skills, research-based learning is seen as a way of providing students with problem solving and coping skills for a complex world (Barnett 2000; Brew 2006).

Evidence for the effectiveness of connecting teaching and research at the undergraduate level continues to emerge in an increasing body of work, e.g. Pascarella and Terenzini (2005), Baxter Magolda *et al.* (1998), Healey (2005) and Healey and Jenkins (2007). However, the potential for further pedagogical advances, grounding research-based learning in the political history of higher education, remains undeveloped.

This lack of engagement with the political history of the modern university is surprising given the prominence in the literature to the work of Wilhelm von Humboldt, the political philosopher and educationalist. Humboldt is widely credited as having established the first modern European university in Berlin in 1810 on the principle of connecting teaching and research.

A notable exception to this lack of political engagement is found in the work of Lewis Elton. Elton's writings and translations have been important in promoting the ideas of Wilhelm von Humboldt in relation to the historical development of university education in Europe. Elton uses Humboldt's work as a way of arguing against the increasing interference in higher education by successive governments. Elton maintains that government interference is likely to endanger the future of universities in the UK and in Europe (Elton 2008a).

For Elton, as for Humboldt, the key to limiting state interference and promoting the interests of universities is the promotion of scholarship, and key to the promotion of scholarship is the way in which research and teaching can be connected in higher education. Following Humboldt, Elton argues that research and teaching are to be joined in a process whereby students work together with academics in the service of scholarship (Elton 2008b).

Elton does not fully develop the political implications of the points he is making, limiting the discussion of Humboldt's notion of scholarship to recent advances in managerial science, and to integrating research-based learning into professional staff development programmes (Elton 2008a and 2008b).

Humboldt's political philosophy

An understanding of the implications of Humboldt's political philosophy requires an engagement with his book *The Limits of State Action* (1852). In this book Humboldt sets out the basis for his commitment to an extreme laissez-faire philosophy (Humboldt 1993 xlix–lvi). For Humboldt political philosophy was based on 'the proclamation of complete self-sovereignty of the individual' or 'extreme individualism' (Knoll and Seibart 1967: 17–19). The state was to have no positive role in the area of social welfare, but was a necessary evil whose role is to protect its members from external threats: every effort by the state to interfere in the private affairs of the citizens is to be 'absolutely condemned' (Humboldt 1993: 16). Neither was the state to have any influence on education, which was to be a private rather than a public affair: public education was to lie wholly outside the limits within which the state should exercise its effectiveness (Humboldt 1993: 52). While working for the Ministry of Education in Prussia Humboldt had to temper his thoughts on public education, but he did not wholly abandon his reservations about the state and, with regard to his university reform, devised a model with considerable autonomy (Knoll and Seibart 1967).

Humboldt's impeccable liberal credentials make him no figure on which to base a critique on the concept of student as consumer. At the core of liberal theory lie the fundamental principles of consumerism: the concept of the individual freedom and pursuit of self interest in a context which promotes the self organising nature of markets and denigrates state intervention. Schemes based on liberal social theory are, therefore more likely to move higher education further in the direction of marketisation (Zizek 2009). In order to develop a critical account of the student as consumer it is necessary to look elsewhere into the historical and political development of the modern university.

1968: the poverty of student life

A more progressive basis for the development of a radical pedagogy that engages critically with the concept of the student as consumer can to be found in the history and politics of the global student protest movement of 1968 and, in particular, in Paris, France in May of that year.

Although the student protest in France began in the universities of Nanterre and the Sorbonne, it quickly spread to include not only students but academics and workers, across the whole of France. The protest by the students and workers was not in response to an economic crisis, but was a reaction to the general crisis in French society as a whole, expressed in a variety of political, economic and cultural forms. These forms included a lack of democratic accountability in the universities and the national political system, an alienating technological and bureaucratic form of capitalism, and a culture of anti-war protest against French colonialism in Algeria and American imperialism in Vietnam (Ross 2002; Gilcher-Holtey 1998; Quattrocchi and Nairn 1998; Seidman 2004; Singer 2002). Within the French universities this was experienced as an abundance of ennui and 'the poverty of student life'.

The protest movement culminated in a general strike, which almost destroyed General De Gaulle's government and very nearly succeeded in creating a new form of society (Ross 2002; Gilcher-Holtey 1998; Quattrocchi and Nairn 1998; Seidman 2004; Singer 2002). The revolt was eventually suppressed but the protest has left a controversial legacy about its nature and significance. This legacy has been the subject of much debate among sociologists, historians, anthropologists, biographers and autobiographers around a series of issues that are pertinent to the pedagogy of excess (Gilcher-Holtey 1998). These issues include the relationships between the student and the teacher, the relationship between intellectual and manual labour, the relationship between the student movement and other social movements and the relationship between the university and its external environment. At the centre of these issues lies the question about the representation and production of knowledge, raising the question about the nature and role of the university, suggesting that a new form of university is possible based on the principles of democracy, self-management and social justice.

A key issue for the protest was the way in which the students engaged with the critical social theory within which the events were conceptualised. In France, and throughout Europe, the protests coincided with the emergence of a radical critique of orthodox Marxism based on previously unpublished versions of Marx's own work and other subversive versions of Marx's social theory that had been suppressed throughout the twentieth century.

Key among these critical theorists was the existential Marxist humanism of Sartre, whose work reinserted human agency (*praxis*) against the crude materialism of structural Marxism (Fox 2003: 19), promoting a 'humanist philosophy of action, of effort, of combat, of solidarity' against 'the quietism of despair' (Sartre 1966, cited in Fox 2003: 16). For Sartre human existence is constituted 'outwardly by its engagement and actions in the concrete world' (Fox 2003: 16).

The students were inspired by the work of Walter Benjamin (1934) who expounded a radical theory of action and engagement based on the radical cultural movements of Dadaism, Surrealism and Russian Constructivism. Key to these critical cultural activities was involving the consumer in the process of production: where the reader becomes the author and the audience becomes the actor, not only as the producers of artistic content, but as collaborators of their own social world, as subjects rather than objects of history.

Henri Lefebvre, a professor in Nanterre during the protests, argued for the recovery of the concept of 'everyday life' as a critical and theoretical category, currently constituted by the 'bureaucratic society of controlled consumption' and experienced as boredom and banality (Lefebvre 1984). For Lefebvre the revolution must transform everyday life as well as the social relations of production. He argued that the irreducibility of human subjectivity is the key to revolutionary action. The impulse for progressive political activity was to be found in the human attributes of creativity and desire, expressed as what he described as 'poesis', i.e. resistance to the alienating consequences of modern consumerism (Hirsch 1982).

In *The Society of the Spectacle* (1970), Debord argued that the social world had been overwhelmed by capitalist relations of production, and that direct experience and the determination of real events had been reduced to the passive contemplation of everyday life (Jappe 1999). Debord and his collaborators in the Situationalist International, of which he was a founding member, argued in favour of direct action through the creation of situations which would reveal the absurdity of everyday life. These spontaneous political protests would be supported by local worker-student councils which would 'transform the totality of existing conditions' so that students and workers could 'recognise themselves in a world of their own design' (Debord 1970: para 179).

What all of these writings have in common is the application of Marxist social theory to a committed and concrete political action, against the condition of consumerism and the commodification of everyday life. What is remarkable about the events of May 1968 is the ways in which this theory was realised in practice.

Action committees: poesis in motion

May 1968 was a moment in which everything happened politically (Ross 2002: 15) – an event that was pregnant with a new sense of 'creative political capacity in France and elsewhere' (Ross 2002: 18). There was a feeling that 'politics is – everywhere and everything' (Quattrocchi and Nairn 1998: 123), especially in education. Within the universities self-managing, democratic, non-hierarchical groups, known as Action Committees, were established (Posner 1970; Ross 2002; Seale and McConville 1968). These committees comprised of between ten and fifteen members, academics and students, initially for dialogue and discussion, promoting 'constant criticism and self discovery' so that 'the movement was able to constantly radicalize itself' (Posner 1970: 47). The committees went on to occupy campuses across Paris and France. The Action Committees coordinated demonstrations and demands, and made contact with the workers and other grassroot protest movements, dissolving the separation between workers and intellectuals through expressions of solidarity and the provision of information through various forms of creative political art, music and drama (agitprop). The aim of the Action Committees was to abolish the current autocratic, non-democratic, industry-focused structure of universities with a system based on democracy and social justice (Ross 2002).

But, if the movement was defined by its theoretically informed organisational forms, something even more significant was occurring. Ross (2002) points out that the really transforming aspect of the protest was that the participants did not perform the roles that had been accorded to them by sociologists, journalists, historians and politicians, i.e., those who defined the events of May 1968 as a 'student protest'. The significant point, argues Ross, is that the students refused to act as students: 'In the so called "student action" students never acted as students but as revealers of a general crisis, of bearers of a power of rupture putting into question the regime, State, society' (Blanchot 1998, quoted in Ross 2002 p25). This refusal to act as students was compounded by the students' refusal to speak about student issues, choosing only to speak about 'common affairs' (Ross 2002: 118), raising the protest to the level of society. As Badiou describes it, the events of 1968 were 'something that arrives in excess, beyond all calculation ... that proposes an entirely new system of thought' and which 'led infinitely farther than their [the students] education ... would have allowed them to foresee; an event in the sense of real participation ... altering the course of their lives' (Badiou 1998, quoted in Ross 2002: 26). Indeed this appears to contrast sharply with the media representation of students by Williams (Chapter 13) that sees students positioned as largely passive to societal issues.

Key to the notion of revelation was the way in which knowledge about the events of May 1968 was to be produced, reported and recorded. Those involved with the struggle maintained that research should begin from contestation and revolt. In this way they aimed to break with the tradition of academic elitism so as to produce knowledge in a populist and highly accessible style (Ross 2002: 117). This radical way of producing knowledge and presenting information was to be a form of 'direct communication' providing 'a new means of comprehension between different groups' (Ross 2002: 114) so as 'to give a voice to those without voices' and to contest 'the domain of the experts' (Ross 2002: 116).

In this way those engaged in the struggle sought to demystify the process of research. For the students and the workers 'We are in our way researchers, but this is work that anyone can do' (Ross 2002: 118). A key means of dissemination of critical ideas was through graffiti art:

Plagiarism is progress, history demands it
Boredom is counterrevolutionary
Be realistic, demand the impossible
We work, but we produce nothing.

A pedagogy of excess

The events of 1968 have had a profound effect on the development of higher education in France and around the world. The post-1968 period saw the emergence of a new form of university: democratic (Scott 1995), postmodern (Lyotard 1979) and multiverse (Kerr 1963). The key feature of this new type of university was that universities had now become sites of contested space, not only for the control and management of the higher education, but in relation to the meaning and purpose of knowledge itself (Delanty 2001).

A central facet of the post-1968 period was the development of progressive pedagogies in higher education based on 'left wing ideas', reflecting the radical political agenda that had been established by the students in Paris. Key to these developments was the engagement of students in the design of curricula, including deciding on the content of courses as well as forms of assessment; and, through the proliferation of independent study programmes, a recognition that undergraduate students were capable of creating knowledge of real academic content and value (Pratt 1997).

In the period since then university administrators and politicians have struggled to de-politicise the radical substance of these pedagogical initiatives, while at the same time contain and pacify students and academics through the imposition of increasingly managerial and bureaucratic strategies (Zizek 2009). Readings (1996) maintains that the concept of 'excellence' is the revenge of the university bureaucrat for 1968.

The events of 1968 provide a powerful historical and political framework within which to re-conceptualise the relationship between teaching and research in higher education in a way that offers a challenge to the notion of student as consumer and the politics of marketisation. The problem is how to recover the radicality of the 1968 agenda in the current contemporary crisis. A progressive way forward is to connect current pedagogies that link teaching and research with their own radical academic history, and to develop them in a form that is appropriate for the contemporary situation. Key to this issue of connectivity is the relationship between action and progressive political theory. It is the relationship between theory and action, linked to contemporary struggles within higher education, that provides a framework for the emergence of a pedagogy of excess.

Action

Key to the development of a pedagogy of excess is that during the struggles of May 1968 the students exceeded their role as students – they became the revealers of a general crisis in society, and the personification of the ways in which that crisis might be interrupted and reconsidered, calling into question the principles and protocols through which the social was organised and controlled. In the process the students moved beyond the limits of where they might have expected their experience of university education to have taken them, exceeding their expectations about the potentials and possibilities of student life.

Through the reengineering of research and teaching at the undergraduate level, considerable advances have been made in developing a progressive agenda for students in ways that take them beyond the mainstream student experience. Through the process of real collaboration with academics the role of student as consumer is challenged, reinventing the student as the producer of knowledge of real academic content and value (Neary and Winn 2009). The strength of this approach is that the student becomes the student as producer rather than student as consumer, but in the mainstream model the student is still confirmed as a student.

The extent to which these collaborations move beyond the mainstream teaching and learning agenda depends on the extent to which the politicised nature of higher education is made explicit, and the ways in which the knowledge that is produced is contextualised politically, as well as theorised critically. Teaching and learning is made political when it is based on an agenda of contestation and struggle rather than the managed consensus of university bureaucracies, calling into question not just particular aspects of teaching and learning in higher education, but the nature and purpose of higher education itself. For a pedagogy of excess these contestations and struggles might include course content, assessment strategies and student fees, but a fully developed pedagogy of excess would look beyond student issues, to matters of more general social concern, 'common affairs', in which the interests of students are not the main issue.

The extent to which these forms of collaboration extend into projects that attempt to reveal the origins for the general capitalist crisis is a matter of negotiation between the students and their teachers, but clearly a framework can be established within which these revelations can occur. This framework might be extended to become the organising principle for the institutions of higher education as a whole.

Theory: alternative political economy

What was learnt from 1968 is that practical action is made dynamic when it connects to social theory. In this context the theory of excess becomes an antidote to the concept of consumerism and a guide to social action.

The concept of excess as critical political intervention has its roots in sociology (Bataille), anthropology (Mauss), and Marxist social theory (Debord). If consumerism is based on the economic theory which demands that individuals act rationally and in their own self-interest (Fine and Milonakis 2009), the category of excess is offered 'as an alternative to the rationalist calculation of capitalist exchange' (Kosalka 1999).

The concept of excess was most developed in the work of Bataille (1991), who offered the notion of excess as an alternative framework to the capitalist basis of exchange, replacing what he regarded as a 'restrictive economy', with a 'general economy'. For Bataille this more general economy would provide a humanistic and non-utilitarian basis for the organisation of modern society. For Bataille the key to the organisation of any society was the way in which it dealt with the surplus that had been produced. Anthropology (Mauss 1922) had revealed the ways in which non-capitalistic societies distributed their surplus on the basis of generosity and abundance, as gifts, promoting a sense of social solidarity through sharing, with an emphasis on collaboration and consensus. Acts of extravagant generosity afforded status and respect to the person who was doing the giving; and, as the gifts that were being distributed were often intimately connected to the person who was doing the giving, generating feelings of personal satisfaction and self worth. These acts of extravagant giving created a sense of obligation on the part of the recipient, leading to bonding between individuals and groups. This process of excessive distribution is contrasted with the consumerist exchange process of capitalist society which is characterised by dissatisfaction and alienation.

This promotion of acts of extravagant generosity might seem somewhat utopian in the context of the modern social world. However, this process of exchange described by the concept of excess is instantly recognisable as being at the core of the academic enterprise (Fuller 2002). The practice of academic excess has been given further impetus by online computing through, for example, the free distribution of teaching and learning materials on the World Wide Web, defined as Open Educational Resources (Iiyoshi and Kumar 2008). A pedagogy of excess would seek to promote and develop these activities as a counter to the economistic and market-driven restrictive practices that increasingly dominate the activity of scientific enquiry.

However, what the politics of student protest has taught us, during and post 1968, is that radical consumption is not enough: the transformation of capitalist social relations lies not simply in the politics of consumption, but the politics of production, which, as the revolutionary social theory of the period demonstrated, can be found in the theory against capitalist work elaborated by Marx in *Capital* and the *Grundrisse* (Debord 1970).

The essence of Marx's revolutionary theory of production lies in his theory of surplus value (excess) which provides the conditions through which the social world can be progressively transformed. According to Marx's theory of surplus value, labour is the source and substance of all value in a society dominated, uniquely, by the production of excess (surplus value). In capitalist society, surplus value (excess) is produced by the quantitative expansion of human energy in the process of industrial production. While the value of labour (human energy) is the value of all things (commodities), the value which labour produces is not fully recognised in the financial reward paid to workers (wages). The difference between the value of the reward and the value that is produced by workers constitutes the excess or surplus value. In the world of capitalist work excess equals exploitation.

The physical limitations of human labour, and the continuing resistance of workers to the imperatives of waged work, mean that human labour is removed by the representatives of capital from the process of production and replaced by technology and science. For the labour that remains, work is intensified physically and enhanced intellectually – with a clear distinction between mental and manual workers. As labour is the source and substance of all value, this joint process of the expulsion and enhancement of labour is profound. On one side, the expulsion of labour from the process of production means that the production of surplus value (excess) breaks down, resulting in dramatic declines in profitability. On the other side, the release of labour from the production process provides the opportunity for labour – and, therefore, for society as a whole – to develop its full creative capacity, in ways that are antithetical to the logic of capitalist production. Both scenarios, singularly and together, spell crisis and catastrophe for capitalism (Marx 1993: 706–8).

In practice, capital has sought to restrict the development of discarded labour through the politics of oppression and the imposition of scarcity, poverty and violence. Yet the creative capacity of labour remains undiminished, as seen in May 1968 and by the continuing movement of protest against the law of surplus value in all its manifestations. These struggles against capitalist oppression make up the substantive history of modern political protest (Hardt and Negri 2001).

Higher education is directly involved in the development of technology, science and the production of knowledge. The student-academic is both the producer and personification of this form of knowledge, and, therefore, has a key role to play in re-engineering the politics of production. Since 1968, and before, student-academics have played a key role in the worldwide protest movements against the social relations of capitalist production. These protests might form the core curriculum for the pedagogy of excess.

The curriculum which informs the pedagogy of excess cannot get ahead of the protests out of which it has been constituted, nor seek to ground a new movement of academic struggle in the events of the past. The pedagogy of excess requires that the radical history of 1968 is connected to the contemporary situation by recovering the subversive inspirations around which a more radical form of progressive pedagogy might be invented. Such a pedagogy would involve inventing a curriculum that includes grounding the concept of excess in an alternative political economy, involving a critique not simply of the politics of consumption but the politics of production. This critical political economy would provide a theoretical framework within which to conceptualise the ideology of protest, but no blueprint for action. Direct action should be informed in this curriculum by the lessons learned from the history of struggle inside and outside of the academy. This connection with the history of academic struggle should include an engagement with other critical pedagogical discourses, including critical pedagogy and popular education (Freire 2007; McLaren 2000; Amsler and Canaan 2009), as well as ideas that have sought to connect academic struggles with the worldwide movement of protest: 'public sociology' (Burawoy 2005), 'participative pedagogy' (Lambert 2009), 'mass intellectuality' (Hardt and Negri 2001) and 'academic activism' (Castree 2000).

Working within this curriculum academics and students can develop networks of alternative research projects. A list for such projects has already been provided by Dyer-Witheford and includes: the establishment of new indices of well-being beyond monetised measures; the new capacities for democratic planning afforded by new technology; systems of income allocation outside of wage-labour; the development of peer-to-peer open source communications networks; research projects that seek to enrich critical political economy with ecological and feminist knowledges, and the formation of aesthetics and imaginaries adequate to the scope of what a progressive and sustainable humanity might become (2004: 90–1). In this way the pedagogy of excess becomes a learning process which promotes the creative capacity of people in accordance with their needs as social individuals (Kay and Mott 1982).

These models of progressive curriculum restructuring can become frameworks on which to design a progressive model for higher education. In the recent period French academics and their students have protested against proposed market-based reforms, although with a much more pragmatic agenda than in 1968. There is a growing body of literature that is recording the worldwide intensification of academic labour as well as struggles to subvert capitalist work (Nelson and Watt 2004; Bousquet 2008; De Angelis and Harvie 2009), while at the same time provide alternative models to the neo-liberal university (Muhr and Verger 2006; Santos 2003; Emery 2009; Ainley 2005; Berry *et al.* 2002; Rogoff 2005).

Higher education at the level of society

The pedagogy of excess suggests that 1968 offers a much better model around which to organise resistance to consumerism and marketisation than Humboldt's liberal vision for the University of Berlin.

The pedagogy of excess requires that the radical history of 1968 is connected to the contemporary situation by recovering the subversive inspirations around which new forms of pedagogies were invented. In 1968 the idea that research was something that students can do was a revolutionary political statement. The fact that by the beginning of the twenty first century these subversive motivations have been reduced to the technical imperatives of research-based learning should not conceal the intellectual power that is generated when academics connect with undergraduate students through their own research activities, nor the importance for the future of the academic project that these connections are made, and raised to the level of society.

References

Ainley. P. (2005) 'For free universities', *Journal of Further and Higher Education*, 29(3): 277–85.

Amsler, S. and Canaan J. (2009) 'Whither critical pedagogy in the neoliberal university today? Two UK practitioners' reflections on constraints and possibilities', ELiSS – *Enhancing Learning in the Social Sciences*, 1(2).

Barnett, R. (2000) *Realising the University in an Age of Supercomplexity*. Society for Research into Higher Education and Open University Press: Buckingham.

Bataille, G. (1991) *The Accursed Share*, volume 1: *Consumption*. New York: Zone Books.

Baxter Magolda, M., Boes, L., Hollis, M. L. and Jaramillo, D. L. (1998) *Impact of the Undergraduate Summer Scholar Experience on Epistemological Development*. Miami: University of Miami.

Benjamin, W. (1934) 'The author as producer' in M. W. Jennings, H. Eiland and G. Smith (eds) (2004) *Walter Benjamin: Selected Writings, Volume 2, 1927–1934*. Harvard: Harvard University Press.

Berry, J., Heise, H., Jackobsen, J., Slater, H. (2002) *On Knowledge Production: Copenhagen Free University*. Available from www.copenhagenfreeuniversity.dk/exchange.html (accessed 23rd February 2010).

Bousquet, M. (2008) *How the University Works*. New York: New York University Press.

Boyer, E. L. (1990) *Scholarship Reconsidered: Priorities of the Professoriate*. New Jersey: The Carnegie Foundation for the Advancement of Teaching.

Brew, A. (2006) *Research and Teaching: Beyond the Divide*. London: Palgrave Macmillan.

Burawoy, M. (2005) 'For public sociology', *American Sociological Review*, 70: 4–28.

Castree, N. (2000) 'Professionalization, activism and the university: whither critical geography?', *Environment and Planning A*, 32(6): 955–70.

De Angelis, M. and Harvie, D. (2009) 'Cognitive capitalism and the rat race: how capitalism measures immaterial labour in British universities', *Historical Materialism*, 17(3): 3–30.

Debord, G. (1970) *The Society of the Spectacle*. Boston: Red and Black.

Delanty, G. (2001) *Challenging Knowledge: The University in the Knowledge Society.* Buckingham: Society for Research into Higher Education and Open University Press.

Dyer-Witheford, N. (2004) *Cognitive Capitalism and the Contested Campus.* Available from http://www.data-browser.net/02/DB02/DyerWitheford.pdf (accessed 25 February 2010).

Elton, L. (2008a) 'Collegiality and complexity: Humboldt's relevance to British universities today', *Higher Education Quarterly*, 62(3): 224–36.

Elton, L. (2008b) 'Continuing professional development in higher education – the role of the scholarship of teaching and learning', *Practice and Evidence of Scholarship of Teaching and Learning in Higher Education*, 3: 193–208.

Emery, E. (2009) *The Free University.* Available from http://thefreeuniversity.net/ (accessed 23 February 2010).

Fine, B. and Milonakis, D. (2009) *From Economics Imperialism to Freakonomics: The Shifting Boundaries between Economics and Other Social Sciences.* London: Routledge.

Fox, N. (2003) *New Sartre: Explorations in Postmodernism.* London: Continuum.

Freire, P. (2007) *Pedagogy of the Oppressed.* New York: Continuum.

Fuller, S. (2002) *Knowledge Management Foundations.* Boston: Butterworth Heinemann.

Griffiths, R. (2004) 'Knowledge production and the research-teaching nexus: the case of the built environment disciplines', *Studies in Higher Education*, 29(6): 709–26.

Gilcher-Holtey (1998) 'May 1968 in France: the rise and fall of a new social movement', in C. Fink, P. Gasert and D. Junker (eds) *1968 The World Transformed.* Cambridge: Cambridge University Press, pp. 253–76.

Hardt, M. and Negri, A. (2001) *Empire.* Harvard: Harvard University Press.

Healey, M. (2005) 'Linking research and teaching exploring disciplinary spaces and the role of inquiry-based learning', in R. Barnett (ed.) *Reshaping the University: New Relationships between Research, Scholarship and Teaching.* Maidenhead: McGraw-Hill/Open University Press, pp. 30–42.

Healey, M. and Jenkins, A. (2007) 'Linking teaching and research in national systems', paper prepared for *International Policies and Practices for Academic Enquiry: An International Colloquium*, Marwell, Winchester, UK, 19–21 April. Available from portal-live.solent.ac.uk/university/rtconference/rtcolloquium_home.aspx (accessed 23 February 2010).

Hirsch, A. (1982) *The French Left: A History and Overview.* Montreal: Black Rose Books.

Holloway, J. (2009) '1968 and doors to new worlds', in *Turbulence, Ideas for Movement Magazine.* Available from http://turbulence.org.uk/turbulence-4/1968-and-doors-to-new-worlds/ (accessed 23 February 2010).

Humboldt, W. von (1993 [1852]) *The Limits of State Action* (ed. J.W. Burrow). Indianapolis: Liberty Fund.

Iiyoshi, T. and Vijay Kumar, M. S. (eds) (2008) *Opening Up Education: The Collective Advancement of Education through Open Technology, Open Content, and Open Knowledge.* Massachusetts: MIT Press. Available from http://mitpress.mit.edu/catalog/item/default.asp?ttype=2&tid=11309&mode=toc (accessed 23 February 2010).

Jappe, A. (1999) *Guy Debord.* Berkeley and Los Angeles: University of California Press.

Kay, G. & Mott, J. (1982) *Political Order and the Law of Labour.* Basingstoke: Macmillan.

Kerr, C. (1963) *The Uses of the University.* Cambridge, MA: Harvard University Press.

Klimke, M. and Scharloth, J. (2008) *1968 in Europe: A History of Protest and Activism, 1965–1977.* Basingstoke and New York: Palgrave Macmillan Transnational History Series.

Knoll, J. H. and Siebert, H. (1967) *Humboldt: Politician and Educationalist*. Bad Godesberg: Internationes.

Kosalka, D. (1999) 'Georges Bataille and the notion of the gift' in *Historian Underground: Making History Relevant for Life*. Available from http://www.sauer-thompson.com/essays/Bataille%20and%20the%20Notion%20of%20Gift.doc (accessed 23 February 2010).

Lambert, C. (2009) 'Pedagogies of participation in higher education: a case for research-based learning', *Pedagogy, Culture and Society*, 17(3): 295–309.

Lefebvre, H. (1984) *The Revolution of Everyday Life*. New Brunswick: Transaction Books.

Lyotard, F. (1979) *The Postmodern Condition*. Manchester: Manchester University Press.

Mauss, M. (1990 [1922]) *The Gift: Forms and Functions of Exchange in Archaic Societies*. London: Routledge.

McLaren, P. (2000) *Che Guevara, Paulo Freire and the Pedagogy of Revolution*. Maryland: Rowan and Littlefield.

Marx, K. (1990) *Capital Volume 1*. London: Penguin.

Marx, K. (1993) *Grundrisse*. London: Penguin.

Muhr, T. and Verger, A. (2006) 'Venezuela higher education for all', *Journal for Critical Education Policy Studies*, 4(4). Available from http://www.jcep.com/?pageID=article&articleID=63 (accessed 20 February 2010).

Neary, M. and Winn, J. (2009) 'Student as producer: reinventing the undergraduate curriculum', in L. Bell, H. Stevenson and M. Neary (eds) *The Future of Higher Education: Policy, Pedagogy and the Student Experience*. London: Continuum.

Negri, A. (2009) 'On Rem Koolhaas', *Radical Philosophy*, 154, March/April: 48–50.

Nelson, C. and Watt, S. (2004) *Office Hours: Activism and Change in the Academy*. Abingdon and New York: Routledge.

Pascarella, E. T. and Terenzini, P. T. (2005) *How College Affects Students (Vol 2): A Third Decade of Research*. San Francisco: Jossey-Bass.

Posner, C. (ed.) (1970) *Reflections on the Revolution in France*. Harmondsworth: Penguin.

Pratt, J. (1997) *The Polytechnic Experiment*. Buckingham: The Society for Research into Higher Education and the Open University Press.

Quattrocchi, A. and Nairn, T. (1998) *The Beginning of the End*. London: Verso.

Ramsden, P (2001) 'Strategic Management of Teaching and Learning', in C. Rust (ed.) *Improving Student Learning Strategically*. Oxford: Oxford Centre for Staff and Learning Development, pp. 1–10.

Readings, B. (1996) *The University in Ruins*. Cambridge, MA and London: Harvard University Press.

Rogoff, I. (2005) *The Academy as Potentiality*, lecture given at *MODE05 Conference*, available as video recording http://mode05.org/node/152 or text available from http://summit.kein.org/node/191 (accessed 14 January 2010).

Ross, K. (2002) *May '68 and Its Afterlives*. Chicago and London: The University of Chicago Press.

Santos, Boaventura De Sousa (2003) *The Popular University of Social Movements*, available from http://www.ces.fe.uc.pt/universidadepopular/indexen.php (accessed 14 January 2010).

Scott, P. (2002) 'A lot to learn: we are all researchers now', *Education Guardian* (8 January). Available from http://www.guardian.co.uk/education/2002/jan/08/highereducation.uk1 (accessed 23 February 2010).

Scott, P. (1995) *The Meanings of Mass Higher Education*. Buckingham: Open University Press.

Seale, P. and McConville, M. (1968) *Red flag/Black flag: French Revolution*, 1968. London: Heinemann.

Seidman, M. (2004) *The Imaginary Revolution – Parisian Students and Workers in 1968*. Oxford and New York: Berghahn Books.

Singer, D. (2002) *Prelude to Revolution: France in May 1968*. Cambridge, MA: South End Press.

Wieman, C. (2004) 'Professors who are scholars: bringing the act of discovery to the classroom', presentation at *The Reinvention Center Conference*, November 2004, 'Integrating research into undergraduate education: the value added'. Available from http://www.reinventioncenter.miami.edu/conference_05/wieman/presentation.htm (accessed 23rd February 2010).

Zizek S. (2009) *First as Tragedy then as Farce*. London: Verso.

Conclusion

Chapter 18

Arguments, responsibility and what is to be done about marketisation

Richard Scullion, Mike Molesworth and Elizabeth Nixon

We could, with justification, conclude this edited collection by pulling the various themes of the chapters together to illustrate the complexity of the investigation of market-orientation in higher education (HE). We could then simply point out the many contradictions apparent when reading the contributions and then leave them to 'hang in the air' by drawing the attention of the reader to the inevitable tensions that arise when asking the types of questions this book does. However we want to try to move beyond a concluding statement that merely re-states that the higher education sector – with its multitude of stakeholders and missions – is bound to have conflicting expectations placed on it, including in terms of how students should be perceived.

What we don't see in this book are nostalgic calls for a return to a more elitist system, and equally there is no sweeping rejection of the idea that the student should have a say in the type of education they receive. Instead, participation in a university sector that is receptive to contemporary culture is acknowledged as having merit. However there is a difference between being receptive and an un-reflective acceptance of the hegemony of the dominant cultural discourse regardless of context. So we may still gain something valuable by recalling traditional con-ceptualisations of the purposes of universities and their distinctive role.

We might also be careful not to reject the concerns expressed in these pages as simply being the 'vested interests' of the academy who see its roles changing, and recognise that marketisation might make it accountable in new ways. If we accept that one of the core roles of a university is to investigate phenomena in order to broaden our understanding of them, that universities are valuable to society because they may independently reflect on things, it is appropriate that critique of marketised HE comes from *within* – indeed it can only come from the academy. It is unrealistic and problematic to envisage that government would itself look to critique its own policy direction. Neither might we expect industry or students to undertake the detailed and systematic reflections contained in this book and elsewhere.

Against this background we first review what we believe to be key arguments underpinning the various contributions. This serves as a way of mapping out the common ground that emerges when reflecting on a marketised HE sector and its implications for student identities. Second, we ask, in a deliberately contentious manner, who and what are responsible (to blame or praise) for the context, the practices and the overall purpose of contemporary, marketised universities. This question is not presented for some self-serving cathartic purpose, but rather because the very process of addressing it informs the third and final part of the conclusion: what might now be done, and by whom? The book is written by academics (some of whom have been or still are also institutional managers) but it is not only for the academy to read, but for policy makers, sector managers, students, potential students and other interested stakeholders (parents, employees, taxpayers, etc.). The third part of the conclusion therefore offers tentative thoughts on how each of these groups might respond to the issues this book has raised.

Key arguments in the marketisation of higher education

The book starts by setting out global and historical perspectives to contextualise the emergence of a 'market-orientation' in the relationship between university and government, and more implicitly the relationship between university and society. What we find is that both global economic forces and historical precedent point to an inevitability of marketisation that seems hard, or even pointless to resist. Instead, 'we' must simply react as best we can. Another core theme is a reflection on the motivations for a critique of marketisation in HE. We must be careful to understand the ideological nature of some complaints, where HE is a 'stand in' for a more general resistance to neo-liberalism. Yet this does not mean that marketisation is beyond critique. Other themes include a mapping-out of what the terms relating to marketisation and consumption might mean when applied to the HE sector, and in relation to this, a consideration of some consequences of a market-orientation for universities.

This first section illustrates that a major reason that government and institutional management turned to markets as an organising principle was because they seem to hold, as an assumed fact, that expansion of the sector, particularly at the speed policy-makers required, could *only* be achieved in this way. To governments, such expansion seems like a requirement if the economy is to remain globally competitive. Hence fees help fund expansion so that students feel they are paying for a service, league tables (appear to) make the product offering transparent to consumers (or customers), performance-related pay ensures staff deliver the required service, and so on.

These early chapters also start to interrogate the nature and meaning of a marketised HE sector, invariably using the label of 'quasi-market' or similar to denote the limits of its transferability from a market to a still largely non-market context (see chapter 2 for a fuller explanation of this distinction). Higher education is yet to be a free market of course (but then such things are elusive even in advanced capitalist economies), rather a certain type of market-orientation has been added to the mix of what now constitutes 'being' a university. Even so, it is also clear that with this introduction HE is transforming. In the consumer sphere where a market-orientation has been prevalent for several generations, it is widely held that the purpose of consuming is to *be* a consumer; the market has the ability to appropriate even anti-consumer practices by developing them as segments within. So the problem is that a market-orientation in the HE context has the potency to quash spaces for reflection about the market – to inhibit thinking that can be located outside of itself.

This leads to the first key point that we want to make in this concluding chapter, that the very process of becoming marketised in order to achieve specific objectives is likely to significantly shape not just the 'how' but also the 'what' of higher education expansion. Hence we have reflections on how marketisation commodifies time, looks to use economic criteria such as 'added value' to judge worthiness, creates environments where growth for growth's sake perpetuates the need for ever more marketisation, and where the idea that students consume a service offering is widely accepted.

Section two of the book focuses specifically on some of the manifestations of a marketised HE in practice. These often lead to systemic tensions. Market-driven initiatives and a modus operandi familiar to the private commercial sector may collide with an entrenched public service ethos and wary – sometimes hostile – academics and other staff. At a macro-level these tensions may indicate a lack of reflection by those (managers) implementing market-oriented practices, coupled with an unwillingness on the part of many academics to embrace such changes in anything more than a perfunctory manner or to engage in a serious critique of them. There are many specific tensions emerging from the chapters in this section of the book. There is a desire to offer greater access that raises concerns about the 'quality' of provision. The development of mission statements in an attempt to mark out a distinctive space for a university sees almost all universities attempting to occupy similar spaces of 'excellence' as a result. Tensions are also caused when institutional managers embrace the idea that a university is a brand, and yet many stakeholders act 'off brand'. As with most systems that are operationalised by targets, the establishment of league tables to incentivise staff, make comparison transparent and informed choice possible are also open to manipulation, distortion and used to serve 'other' agendas. This section also starts to signpost the inevitable tensions in expectations of the student role that marketisation creates.

It is not simply that the complex introduction of market-oriented practices inevitably leads to short-term tensions, but that much of this sense of conflict and contradiction is the result of *unintended* consequences that have yet to be fully realised. This leads to another key point – the irony of the situation. Perhaps this is illustrated most powerfully by reading chapter 8 which outlines a fictitious view of a university based on a future where marketisation continues to shape the definition of a university *and then* reading chapter 7 that discusses some *current* university mission statements. It is harder to spot differences than might be hoped.

The notion of irony continues when we consider widening participation, an initiative that might be widely viewed as socially, ethically and pedagogically worthy Yet because of the way competing universities have incorporated this social equity initiative into their own promotional agenda, we see little change in access to and participation in HE.

Collectively the implications from the first two sections suggest that marketisation of higher education also asks us to deal with students who are now de facto more like consumers (even if as Ronald Barnett suggests we may hope that a transformation into 'customers' may be a more positive thing). This is the focus of the third section.

This last section shows how a marketised HE environment may create certain dominant student identities, and then, in the way they respond to the idea of student as customer/consumer serves to perpetuate such a discourse. Much of this may well be further unintended consequences of the macro decisions being made about the structure and management of the HE sector filtered through a more general shift to a consumer-orientated society (where work and education-for-work are subservient to the potential delights of consumption). What may seem a positive move to 'put the student at the centre' may have been appropriated within a market-oriented context to mean accepting and even pandering to consumerist attitudes and behaviour of students who increasingly see it as their right to get what they want from a HE sector as if it is like any other service industry (a holiday, bank account or restaurant, for example). Whilst offering insights into what this means in the everyday lives of contemporary students (particularly in relation to their expectations and choice practices), this section of the book also offers alternative metaphors for conceptualising roles available for students to 'play'.

We might see ongoing reflection on these metaphors as a positive thing. Perhaps if students realise the narrowness of allowing one discourse to dominate, and if they can comprehend what they are missing by accepting the current vogue to be a consumerist student, some of the more seemingly radical options become more attainable than they currently appear to be. This implies that it is for the student body to take the lead in responding to the marketised environment they encounter. Indeed that would be the point of a market where the consumer not only has a choice, but must also take responsibility for those choices. However, as the following paragraphs will make clear, this is only part of the argument with which we want to conclude.

Who is responsible for the marketisation of higher education?

We now respond to the question that became apparent to us whilst reading each chapter – who or what is responsible (to blame or praise) for our marketised HE sector and thus for its consequences?

Our answer is not unexpected given our own disciplinary backgrounds in consumer culture. We argue that it is all agents who seek, allow or simply passively accept as normal the view that public concerns or issues with a deeply civic quality are, as Canclini puts it, now 'best answered in the private realm of commodity consumption' (2001: 15). The contributors to this volume have highlighted in various forms and to varying degrees an encroachment of market machinations, coupled with a decline in the value attributed to public voice, common interest and the civic character and role of HE institutions.

These somewhat abstract notions become tangible when they are rooted in everyday practices and when individual agents (including academics and institutional managers) seek (or not), through their actions, to bring about such a civic society. Reading the book in light of broader societal concerns, the ready acceptance of the sector to take a subservient position *within* a consumer culture has reduced the space for emancipatory narratives. This seems particularly ironic to us given the tradition of emancipatory discourses in consumer research. Researching consumers often uncovers attempts to resist or escape the limitations of the market. Thus higher education may have the potential to stand proud as spatially temporally 'outside' consumer culture, as one of a shrinking number of institutions that don't enact market exchanges, or resign to being just one more place for market performances.

At one level, all stakeholders, from government ministers through to 17-year-old 'would-be' students, appear to 'take-for-granted' the cultural shifts briefly referred to here. When reading these chapters the force of marketisation seems unstoppable, like an outside agent acting on 'powerless' individuals. So the first site of accountability is the amorphous dominance of a consumerist culture, which amongst other things, crushes the critical faculties of individuals as citizens in favour of individuals as shoppers (Bauman 2008). But of course it is agents in the form of organisations and structures, and as individuals, who enact such a discourse thus establishing and perpetuating its cultural dominance.

Prime amongst these agents in the context of HE is Government who continue to shape the underlying institutional arrangements through finance, policy directives and the language used to describe the purposes of modern universities. However, where governments are elected democratically they inevitably seek to maintain sufficient public support to retain power, and thus it follows that the general public through their expressed political will (or lack of it) are also responsible for a market-oriented HE sector. Superficially, top-up fees and other private sector initiatives in HE can seem to reduce the burden of public spending and so forms part of a larger discourse advocating lower tax and less direct government involvement. Society gets the higher education it deserves. What this book illustrates is that this focus on resource can only be one part of a broader discussion that includes both what the core purpose of the sector should be and takes account of the many unintended (many negative) consequences of making the sector more responsive to market drivers. As we have also seen here that discussion – about what a university is, or at least what students are – takes place in public and through the media. Here it seems the neo-liberal message is largely supported and presented back to stakeholders.

Managers of the individual institutions also seem surprisingly willing to accept the roles and policies that Government thrusts their way. One reading of this group, especially evident in section two of the book, is that they seem to be following each other by introducing market-oriented practices – in part because they believe their institution simply has no choice but to compete with other universities in ways similar to commercial brands. The lack of reflexivity in their decisions is as striking as their willingness to accept – even embrace – the inevitability of the market logic of growth, internal markets to improve efficiency and to compete for funds, external competition through often superficial branding devices, the use of commercial promotional techniques and the role of academic as entrepreneur and service provider. Almost inevitably this approach assumes the belief that students must be treated as paying customers. Ripe for further investigation are more specific studies about how and why these senior managers – many, but not all, academics – appear to be so accepting of the current dominant discourse of consumption in a sphere normally suspicious of any meta-ideology.

In the spirit of reflection we must acknowledge that academics are also culpable for the market orientation this volume elucidates. For a number of reasons academics have allowed their universities to become market spaces. Perhaps academics feel weak and passive through general neglect, through poor collective instincts and even through management coercion. Perhaps it could be that (some or many) academics are themselves seduced by the consumerist culture all about them and so are less willing to stand aside from it (or to see any reason why it might be desirable to do so). Indeed, many seek career advancement and so buy into the internal power structures put in place by institutional managers; this is perhaps especially true at newer universities where the idea of genuine collaborative structures and work practices never had time to take hold. Some academics positively embrace the changes to the sector brought about by marketisation. As witnessed in other professions from nursing to politics, many who teach in HE do so now as 'pseudo-academics' who, like the students described in our studies in chapters 15 and 16, accept a work and spend culture where the 'job' of an academic is to maximise efficiency and wait for the rewarding weekend shopping trip. But that clearly is an insufficient answer. This book, in part a critique of current practices of the HE sector, has been created within that very system and its editors and contributors are certainly not martyrs to the cause.

This is not elitism but merely accounting for an academic body that may be less attuned to the 'uniqueness of being wedded to a scholarly discipline' and thus more amenable to market influences. It may also be that many academics have little interest in the discipline of learning itself, a point elaborated by Lewis Elton. One consequence of this may be a less developed ability to understand the sometimes subtle and nuanced impact of markets and consumption on pedagogy. Academics may be so wedded to their discipline through grant applications, research, conferences, journal and book publishing to notice or care about changes to how institutions are managed or to the student experience.

And so to the part students themselves play in performing marketised HE. However much we might want to 'blame' students for changing the nature of work as an academic, we should mostly resist this. It is tempting – especially if you are reading this as you mark a pile of student assignments that you have been instructed by managers to finish in three weeks in the hope that doing so will favourably impact on student 'satisfaction' scores. But this book has helped to illustrate why attributing responsibility to the student body is also flawed. That is not to say that current and 'would-be' students and their parents are neutral in all of this. They arrive on campus enthused and alive to possibilities. Yet by this point students have become well-tuned consumers, their wealth of experience in commercial markets has shaped much of the way they respond to their desires, to opportunity and to choices they face. In Fromm's words they have adopted a 'marketing personality' (1976) where 'the emphasis is on having the personal attributes that successfully position the individual in a capitalist system' (Molesworth *et al.* 2009: 281).

As part of this baggage, students widely buy into the idea of consumer sovereignty. Often inadvertently, this stance acts to reduce the potential value that studying at degree level can offer; for example, many students will opt to satisfy often whimsical personal tastes and preferences, rather than immerse themselves in the ambiguity and angst of deep learning. But they do this because HE institutions let them and therefore allow them to see their experience of getting a degree in such a limited way as, for example, no more than a necessary hurdle before employment that ensures future consumer pleasures.

Parents of students seem to support their offspring's instrumental approach that, at least superficially, is accommodated in a market-oriented environment. Parents as tax payers and members of the electorate are generally inactive in the debate about the quantity and quality of HE provision. This provides support for the idea that increased quantity without matching resource can somehow take place without any impact of quality of provision. This is fuelled by a wider discourse about 'getting more for less' by redefining what efficiency means, for example through the ideas that public-private partnerships and PFIs somehow square this circle. Inadvertently it also leaves a gap in financial provision of HE that market-oriented actions seek to fulfil. Like managers, parents may also feel that there is no choice – no option other than to hope that their children can do well enough in their studies to get a well-paid career. Again we see that irony in consumer culture more generally – that the way of living that promises freedom through choice can enslave the mind into assuming that only an outright *rejection* of the market is not a choice. As Edwards (2000) explains, people are using market expectations in their appraisals of public service, judging it by the same personal tastes and preferences we come to know as consumers. The market offers the appearance of endless opportunity to express one's agency but that means choice is always contained and constrained within the market.

What is to be done about marketisation of higher education?

Now that we have held everybody except the university mascot liable for the marketisation of HE (although perhaps if mascots are replaced with logos we could even find fault here), we want to finish with some tentative responses to the question 'so what can be done?'.

Stakeholders – all stakeholders – in universities owe it to the importance and longevity of the sector to reflect critically on the issues the contributors to this book have raised as well as other academic and popular discourses on higher education. The first thing we might hope to have more of is reflection on the changes taking place. More specifically we should consider not just what we intend to achieve when introducing or passively accepting market-oriented processes, but also first the possibility that the methods we use to accomplish something might change the nature of what is accomplished, and second the nature of the many unintended consequences of introducing marketing practice and discourse into the HE sector.

From this there are some issues that we feel are critical calls to action. The first is greater transparency. HE remains primarily publicly funded. It belongs to us all as citizens. As such we should tolerate nothing less than a default position of openness about all aspects of its operation; a case should need to be made for any deviations from this principle. This should apply throughout, from how and why individual institutions use funds for widening participation, to appointments and promotions, to criteria being used to assess students' work, through to the commercial agreements entered into for on-campus retail outlets. What would the public make of such information on how their tax money is spent we wonder? How can we do more to highlight the social value of the university and to get society more broadly to take an interest in university affairs?

The second call to action is for academics to restate the intricate relationship that exists between scholarly research and good teaching and learning practice. This might also mean that institutional decisions are made with the same concern and thought that is applied to academic research and careful pedagogy. Quality must not be jettisoned for other institutional priorities – since pedagogically speaking there can be no other greater priority for a university. Put another way, there is no point in growth, or in more 'market share' of applicants, or brighter cafeterias, or higher league table positions, unless such things transparently feed into enhancing this 'Archimedean-like' point.

And the final call we make is for academics and those who 'manage' them to at least leave themselves open to being transformed by their practice. Most ambitiously this could be the radical vision of student and university as painted by Neary and Hagyard in Chapter 17, and we recommend that such visions are given air. Why shouldn't universities routinely consider alternative and radical structures and roles for themselves? There might be other exciting models that emerge if we think and talk and act. This is a reminder that the marketisation of higher education and the transformation of students into consumers is not inevitable. It requires constant (often thoughtless) enactment. This also makes it surprisingly fragile. Through care in everyday practice we can reshape expanded higher education by reimagining the value of independence and critical distance from the concerns of governments and markets.

In February 2010, as we were writing up this conclusion, we were also reviewing comments about HE in the media and online. Here is a selection from the last few days:

> Universities are not factories for workers. *Government website*

> The 'commodification' of higher education is here to stay. *Senior Academic Manager*

> Reject the short-termist slash and burn strategy of Government policy in HE. *UCU*

> Students exchange money for knowledge, it's that simple. *Blog about university life*

> Academics raising ethical concerns about their institution's links to China told to 'get real'; if you don't like it, get out. *Comment responding to article in 'Times Higher Educational Supplement'*

> Professor PB, who had a quarter of a century's experience in teaching and exam marking, was taken to task for failing too many students on his course. Today he won his case against his university who will now have to pay substantial damages. *Telegraph*

> University students should be treated as consumers and given 'value for money' and universities should give them a guide to how much they could earn once they have their qualifications. *Secretary of State responsible for HE*

> See our top tips on how to climb the league tables. *Times Higher Educational Supplement*

> We even have to pay to run the SPSS system for analysing the data we have collected, what next? *Student Facebook entry*

The angst, tensions and unpredictable nature of the outcome of marketisation seem well illustrated here. It's clear that as a result of the marketisation of higher education we are witnessing a period of ambiguity, of marginality and of change, but that nothing is yet fixed. We therefore suggest an alternative way of understanding the situation HE faces, in contrast to the dogma of 'change management' that limits the scope of dialogue by assuming inevitability. These circumstances of uncertainty and readjustment following a 'breach' in normalcy, fit well with Victor Turner's concept of social drama, a space of potential transformation (1983) where actors must work to regain a sense of routine and shared meaning. It is in such temporal conditions that seminal opportunities arise for us all. To paraphrase Kierkegaard (Gardiner 2002), what is so sparkling, so fragrant, so intoxicating, as possibility?

References

Bauman, Z. (2008) 'Exit homo politicus, enter homo consumens', in K. Soper and F. Trentmann (eds) *Citizenship and Consumption*. Basingstoke: Palgrave Macmillan, Chapter 9.

Canclini, G. (2001) *Consumers and Citizens: Globalization and Multicultural Conflicts*. Translated and with an introduction by George Yudice. Minneapolis: University of Minnesota Press.

Edwards, T. (2000) *Contradictions of Consumption. Concepts, Practices and Politics in Consumer Society*. Buckinghamshire: Open University Press.

Fromm, E. (1976) *To Have or To Be?* New York: Harper and Row.

Gardiner, P. (2002) *Kierkegaard. A Very Short Introduction*. Oxford: Oxford University Press.

Molesworth, M., Nixon, E. and Scullion, R. (2009) 'Having, being and higher education: the marketisation of the university and the transformation of the student into consumer', *Teaching in Higher Education*, 14(3): 277–87.

Turner, V. (1983) *Liminal to Liminoid, in Play, Flow, and Ritual: An Essay in Comparative Symbology*. Illinois: Human Kinetics Publishers, Inc.

Chapter 19

A concluding message from the Vice-Chancellor of Poppleton University

Laurie Taylor

I am only too pleased to contribute a few final words to this important new book on (*Mrs Dilworth. Please check title*).

Here at Poppleton University (or The University of Poppleton as it was better known before our recent re-branding exercise) we pride ourselves on leading the field in the marketisation of higher education. Our recent decision to describe all students as 'shoppers' has been broadly welcomed by all our sales staff (formerly the academic community) while my own previous experience in the management of a large biscuit factory has given me unique insights into the art of persuading people to purchase well-wrapped objects of little value.

As evidence of our commitment to the new face of higher education, I am only too pleased to append some examples of how this university is tackling some of the key issues of the day going forward.

New developments in degree classification

In the past the calculation of final degree classifications has involved the manual determination of averages by long-winded examiners' meetings. Our Head of Curriculum Development, Janet Fluellen, has now unveiled a new system of degree assessment which she describes as 'more consonant with the vision of student as shopper'.

In future all essays and projects submitted by students will be stamped with a barcode representing their assessment value. This allows the final calculation of degree class to be made automatically. In future years, therefore, graduating students will simply be required to carry a basket containing their bar-coded achievements to a checkout point in the administration block which will electronically compute their class of degree and issue an appropriately embossed degree certificate.

Ms Fluellen claims that this new system will do away with the present 'over-personalised' system in which academics are able to engage in 'special pleading' for students whose work had been affected by such 'extraneous factors' as nervous breakdowns, post-traumatic stress disorder and attempted suicide. However, she firmly denied the 'scurrilous' rumour that students who submit their work in advance of the university deadlines will be awarded extra Nectar points.

Marketing disciplines

'We are bringing religion into the twenty-first century'. That was the controversial claim made by our deputy head of Marketing, Mike 'Discount' Summerby, as he revealed his intention to increase the marketisation of our Department of Theology. In a paper presented to the university's Asset Realisation Committee, Summerby pointed out that other departments in the university had already successfully capitalised upon their specialist knowledge by concluding deals with a variety of commercial interests. He instanced the Biology Department's active role in approving dubious new pharmaceutical products, the successful manufacture of boxed fireworks by the Chemistry Department and the financial benefits which had accrued to the Psychology Department through the sale of mature experimental rats to the local branch of Pets 'U' Like.

Although the plans for the Theology Department were 'still at an early stage', Mr Summerby said that active consideration was currently being given to the possibility of the department retailing approved saints' relics and a variety of worthwhile indulgences. He denied suggestions that his plans were 'opportunistic'. 'We are', his paper concluded, 'perfectly ready to sell our students degrees on the basis that they will secure their owners permanent employment in this world. Why not market theology products which promise to ensure their purchaser eternal happiness in the next?'

Brand consolidation

In what she described as 'a further development of the university's commitment to brand consolidation, the Head of our ever expanding Human Resources Department, Janet Fluellen has announced that all new academic appointments will take account of what she called 'subject symmetry'. This meant that although academic expertise would still play a part in the selection of the successful candidate, additional weight would now be given to those applicants whose general appearance and demeanour was consonant with their subject area. Ms Fluellen stressed that there were no hard and fast rules, but when pressed for examples, admitted that 'on the whole' preference would be given to applicants for physics posts who sported half moon spectacles, wild curly hair, and large boots, while extra weighting would go to those applicants in the humanities who displayed leather patches on their tweed sports coats, uncreased trousers, and the slightly twisted lower lip which indicated a personal history of pipe smoking.

She envisaged that such changes would not only improve students' ability to recognise staff members of their faculty, but were also very much in line with the university's recent appointment of a vice-chancellor who was in all respects indistinguishable from a hedge fund manager.

New degree proposal

Poppleton University will shortly unveil a new undergraduate degree in Jobs. Announcing the development, our Head of Curriculum Development, Janet

Fluellen pointed out that there were already several ongoing degrees at Poppleton which included an element of work experience. However, research among prospective students had revealed that they were only interested in taking a degree of any sort because of the employment it might ensure after graduation. In these circumstances it made sound commercial sense to offer a BA in Jobs in which work experience would take up the entire three years of the course. She believed that this development would do much to reduce complaints from students about their degree lacking relevance to their future employment intentions. 'No-one' she asserted, 'can accuse this new degree of lacking relevance to the workplace when it takes place entirely within that setting'.

Degree recall

Our thrusting Director of Corporate Affairs, Jamie Targett, has responded forcefully to demands the university should recall some of its recently issued degrees. Speaking to a hastily arranged press conference he said that the claims by some graduates that their degrees has been shown to be seriously faulty when examined by prospective employers was 'largely unwarranted'. He did, however, admit that a small number of degrees in Philosophy and Medieval Studies suffered from design faults which made them unsuitable for the rough terrain of the contemporary workplace. Owners of these degrees had now been invited to return them to the university workshop so that they could be fitted with what he described as 'additional commercial features'.

Index